A New Era in Computation

A New Era in Computation

edited by N. Metropolis and Gian-Carlo Rota

The MIT Press
Cambridge, Massachusetts
London, England

First MIT Press edition, 1993

Printed and bound in the United States of America.

Library of Congress Cataloging-in-Publication Data

A New era in computation / edited by N. Metropolis, Gian-Carlo Rota. — 1st MIT Press ed.
  p. cm.
"Articles originally appeared in the winter 1992 issue of Dædalus, volume 121, number 1"—T.p. verso.
Includes bibliographical references.
ISBN 0-262-63154-7
1. Parallel processing (Electronic computers) I. Metropolis, N. (Nicholas), 1915–   . II. Rota, Gian-Carlo, 1932–
QA76.58.N48   1993
303.48′34—dc20   93-8200
                                                              CIP

Dedicated to Jaqui Safra

Contents

VIII   *Contents*

Preface

COMPUTER SCIENCE IS STILL THE YOUNGEST and most en-
terprising branch of engineering. For the last forty-odd
years (since it was properly named, that is) it has held the
role of *Heldensoprano* of progress, singing the imminent redemption of mankind by the computer. Her bastard children, artificial
intelligence, information science, robotics, cellular automata theory, and complexity, are now claiming equal redemption time
with their mother. The secret of life, as well as the liberation from
human suffering, was supposed to flow like a corollary from basic
research in computer science, funded for many years by the federal
government with a largesse never before matched—and, dare we
say, never again to be matched—in support of any program. In
all fairness, it must be added that lately such bombastic claims
have been slightly toned down; artificial intelligence, for example,
is supposed to be undergoing a "winter."

The development of computer science is perhaps the dreariest
instance to date of factual fragmentation. In no other field of
science, engineering, or the humanities has a more detailed record
been kept of times, people, places, and events, going all the way
back to the primeval beginnings in the 1950s. Anyone interested
in the res gestae of computer hackers has full access to the records,
easily available in inexpensive diskettes.

And yet, it is hard to make history out of computer science. To
be sure, in the field of computer design, successive advances have
been inflexibly guided by the rigorous demands of algorithmic
betterment. One invention in design has followed another in a
predictable sequence broken only by the unforeseeable, but profitable, intrusions of materials science, where the most revolutionary discoveries are being made. A dialectician could parade the
history of computer design as a rare example of Hegel's philosophy of history.

It is therefore no surprise that innovations in industrial computation are by and large being reliably predicted. The speed of

computers available five years from now can be estimated with comfortable accuracy. The recently discovered world of parallel processing, coupled with mastodonic increases in storage facilities, will soon break through the three-dimensional barrier. No one has the slightest doubt that this latest triumph will yield immediate and immense economic benefits. The ever more radical computer revolutions, succeeding each other at a dizzying pace, are indeed worthy of the name, despite the distasteful fanfare of hype and public relations by which they are invariably heralded.

The story of inventions in software design is more capricious. It is as rich in melodrama as it is in marketable products. Today, more than ever, the demands for software offer limitless opportunities to the imagination, and the most adventurous and creative young minds are irresistibly drawn to software design. A successful software designer is nowadays granted the accolade of a Hollywood actor, though his or her professional career is likely to be shorter than that of a football player. It must be said to this country's credit that, to this day, American dominance of this field remains unchallenged.

The most amusing chapter in the history of computation will be the account (if it is ever written) of the predictions of social, political, and economic effects of the various computer revolutions. In making such predictions, the professional soothsayers have been strikingly wide of the mark. For example:

1. When the first word processors became commercially available, it was widely predicted that paper consumption would dramatically decrease. The opposite happened: paper consumption has almost doubled.

2. It was once a tenet of computer economics that as the manufacture of computers became a more arduous enterprise, a few large computer corporations would eventually gain control of the market for computers large and small. The opposite has happened: the larger computer firms find themselves outclassed by lissome, adaptable companies, ever reborn from their ashes like the Arabian phoenix, constantly changing their courses toward the flickering crest of an elusive wave.

3. Only a few years ago, it was assumed that most computer talent would be driven by peer pressure and by the lure of money into joining a few gigantic centers, leaving the rest of the country (and of the world) a computational wasteland. The opposite is happening: the most complex and most efficient computer assemblages of tomorrow are likely to be mosaics made out of smaller components located far and wide from one another, in MIT labs as likely as in someone's garage in Nebraska or Mississippi.

4. The advent of instant and inexpensive communication through computer networks to the four corners of the world is not turning out to be a leveler of cultures (Heidegger's foreboding *Einebnung*), nor even an obliteration of distances. The opposite is happening: people of like interests are being newly bound together in homogeneous cliques that cut across cultures and frontiers, by computer bulletin boards and by the cozy intimacy of fax and electronic mail. A new provincialism of preference is replacing the old barriers of nationality and ethnic origins.

5. The spread of illiteracy that was deplored as an effect of excessive television watching is no longer going to be the problem that it was predicted to be. Thanks to the new literacy of the word processor, children's vacant stares before the television set are giving way to the craftiness and ingeniousness that are being encouraged by their obsession with computer games.

6. Thanks to such novel modes of literacy, rationality, once the privilege of the happy few, may soon become so widespread as to be taken for granted. The day may not be far when rational behavior will be expected of any child as a matter of course, on a par with toilet training.

7. If that day ever comes, then the education of the young may hark back to those ideals that have been given short shrift since the Age of Enlightenment. Such might be (we would like to believe):

a. a richer interest in music, poetry, conversation, writing and the arts generally;

b. a more intense and rigorous religious life;

c. systematic training of the emotions side by side with the mind;

d. higher standards of authenticity in relationships among human beings.

Such silver linings may well lie behind the chaotic clouds that are now obstructing our right view of the future.

The present volume, drawn in part from an issue of *Dædalus*, offers a broad survey of the present state of computing, right after the advent of parallel programming. The broad coverage of the papers included here reflects the disparate tendencies that are now clamoring to be heard under the aegis of the computer.

Thanks are due to Global Pursuits, Inc., whose Advisory Board Members are W. Daniel Hillis, Daniel Kleitman, N. Metropolis, Gian-Carlo Rota, Jaqui Safra, Robert Sokolowski, Michael Waterman, and Karl-Heinz Winkler. Each contributed in the planning of this issue, and Global Pursuits provided the funding that was essential to it. We would note also the great contribution made by James Bailey, an author, who agreed to serve in an unofficial editorial capacity. The volume was collaborative in any number of ways, and needs to be read as such.

N. Metropolis and Gian-Carlo Rota

Confiamos
En que no será verdad
Nada de lo que pensamos.

Antonio Machado

A New Era in Computation

W. Daniel Hillis

What Is Massively Parallel Computing, and Why Is It Important?

W HY SHOULD THERE BE A VOLUME devoted to computation? Because there is a significant technology transition that is taking place in computers, and since it radically changes the cost and capabilities of information processing, it is likely to change our lives. The new technology is called *massively parallel* computing. On one hand, it is just a set of engineering ideas: a way of reorganizing the structure of the computer so that it can do many things at once. These ideas are simple and, in retrospect, obvious. On the other hand, the implication of these ideas is that the computer revolution has not yet begun to reach its limits. By the end of this article I will be writing about strange and unlikely sounding things, like home robots and virtual worlds. These things sound unlikely because significant technical advances—such as the automobile, television, the computer—generally have surprising consequences. It is always easiest to believe in a future that is a minor extrapolation of current-day trends. Such an extrapolated present is unlikely to happen in a time of rapid technological change. To help make this point and to set the ground for explaining the technology of parallel processing, I will begin with a story of how some simple ideas about reorganizing the flow of processing had a profound effect on our present-day lives.

In the 1790s, just before Thomas Jefferson was elected president the United States was in danger of getting into a war with the French. At that time, most of the rifles used by the US militia were made in France. In hopes of encouraging the development of an American

W. Daniel Hillis is Chief Scientist at Thinking Machines Corporation.

arms industry, Congress allocated funds for the purchase of twenty thousand domestically manufactured rifles. In those days rifles were made by hand, one at a time. Each rifle was slightly different, with its own individually crafted parts. The largest manufacturers were able to build only a few hundred rifles per year.

A gentleman in New England claimed that he could build and deliver ten thousand of the highest quality rifles, although he had never built a rifle in his life. He was Eli Whitney, the inventor of the cotton gin. Whitney planned to build the rifles out of interchangeable parts manufactured with the aid of water-powered machinery. Instead of building the rifles one at a time, parts would be produced from standard templates in batches of hundreds. By organizing his "manufactory" to take advantage of the economies of scale, Whitney believed that he could produce rifles at a rate and quality never before imagined.

Whitney's competition was understandably skeptical, but Thomas Jefferson, who was familiar with the latest innovations in French arms manufacture, was able to see the potential benefits of the scheme. Whitney was awarded a large federal contract and advanced much of the necessary capital. His methods worked and the arms that he eventually delivered were widely acknowledged as the highest quality rifles made in America.[1]

The methods that Whitney pioneered were later called *mass production*. Today they are applied to the manufacture of most high-volume products. Whitney's methods now seem obvious. It is hard to imagine that almost all manufactured goods at the time, from wagons and clocks to Whitney's own cotton gin, were not mass produced; yet they were not.[2] It is difficult for us to imagine how such seemingly simple ideas, like the use of interchangeable parts or the specialization of workers in different stages of assembly, could have had such a profound effect on our society. Yet mass production was important. It was important because it created an *economy of scale* in the processing of material goods, which in turn caused fundamental changes in the manufacturing sector of our economy and in the type of products it produced.

We are now seeing the emergence of a technology which will change the economics of information processing in much the same way that mass production changed the economies of manufacturing. This new technology is massively parallel computing. Mass computing is analogous in many ways to mass production. They are each a collection of techniques for organizing processing to take advantage of economies of scale. In the case of mass production, it is physical material that is processed; in the case of computing, it is information. Because both mass production and mass computation create economies of scale, they change the economics of production and encourage the centralization of certain functions; this in turn leads to changes in the types of products manufactured and the methods of distribution utilized. In both cases the range of applicability turned out to be much wider than initially expected.[3] Most important, both technologies have created the possibility and economic practicality of fundamentally new types of services and products.

The other critical thing about massively parallel computers is that they are *scalable:* it is always possible to build a more powerful machine by simply adding more processors. This means that there is no obvious upper limit on the computational power of the machines that we can build. This opens some possibilities.

Before speculating on what some of these new possibilities are likely to be, I'd like to first describe some of the methods of massively parallel computing. I will use the analogy to manufacturing because each of the principle methods of mass information processing has an analogy in mass production. In both a computer and a factory the basic method of achieving high throughput is to do more than one thing at once. There are basically three different techniques of organizing concurrent processing: pipelining, functional parallelism, and data parallelism. Each of these have their counterparts in a factory and in a computer.

One of the simplest methods of coordinating parallel activities is *pipelining*. It is exemplified by the sequence of operation on an assembly line. In an automobile factory, for example, the wheels of a car are attached at one stage of the assembly line, while the windshield is inserted at the next. The operations are scheduled sequentially and balanced in such a way that each takes approximately the same amount of time. A large number of vehicles advance through different stages of the sequence simultaneously.

The technique of pipelining is applied in most modern computers. For example, one stage of the pipeline may be preparing the data, while another is performing an addition, while another is storing the previous result. Some computers have dozens of operations "in the pipe" simultaneously. So-called vector computers work according to this principle.

Another technique of parallelism that can be used in conjunction with pipelining is *functional parallelism.* In an automobile factory the engine is assembled on one assembly line while the frame and body are assembled on another. The two lines proceed independently until the engine is placed into the body. Functional parallelism is also used in computers. For example, many modern computers have separate addition and multiplication units which can operate concurrently. Even single chip microprocessors can incorporate this type of parallelism.

Pipelining and functional parallelism are both useful techniques, but they are limited in the degree of parallelism they can achieve. They are not scalable. In an operation that has only ten steps, not more than ten things can be done simultaneously. In both the factory and the computer, there is far more to be gained from performing the same operation to many things concurrently than in doing many different operations at once. When performing the same operation on many items at once, the potential for parallelism increases with the amount of material being processed, rather than with the number of steps in the processing.

In computers, performing similar operations on many elements at the same time is called *data parallelism,* because it exploits parallelism in proportion to the quantity of data. This has the potential of improving processing rates not by just factors of ten, but by factors of ten thousand. The material counterpart of data parallelism can be found in high volume manufacturing. A machine that molds plastic forks forms hundreds at a time. A printing press draws all the letters on a page in a single operation. The millions of transistors on the microchip are fabricated and wired simultaneously. This type of coordinated parallel processing leads to the dramatic cost reductions of high-volume manufacturing.

Data parallelism is also the greatest source of economy of scale in computing. For example, a massively parallel computer may have sixty-four thousand processors that can add together sixty-four thousand numbers in one step. Like the letters on a printed page, not all the numbers need to be identical as long as the operations being performed are similar. If the operations to be performed are different on each element then sequences of *masking* steps may be used. This is like printing a page with some letters in red and some in black, using one step for each color of ink. Similar techniques are used to process data within a parallel computer.

The beautiful thing about data parallelism is that the opportunity for doing more than one thing at once increases with the amount of data being processed. The power of the solution scales with the size of the problem. A conventional computer takes twice as much time to process twice as much data. A massively parallel computer can often process twice as much data in the same amount of time by applying twice as many processors.

One of the most important design principles of mass production is the integration of storage and processing. In the workshop of an individual craftsman, the storage of materials is usually physically separated from the area of manufacture. The worker moves to the storage area to pick up a piece of wood or metal and takes it to the bench or the machine to work it into shape. As long as the operations that are being performed on the individual pieces are relatively time consuming, the time spent traveling to fetch the materials is not a limiting factor. If by some magic the operations of fabrication were sped up by a thousandfold, then the time traveling to fetch the material would become the limiting factor in the speed of processing. This is exactly what has happened in computers.

A conventional nonparallel computer can be divided into two parts, a *memory* for holding the data and a *processor* for transforming it. During normal operation of a computer, data is repeatedly moved from memory to processors, and the results are returned to memory. All this moving of data back and forth between memory and processor creates a significant bottleneck for the operation of a conventional computer, putting an upper limit on the speed at which it can process data.

The solution adopted in a massively parallel computer is the same as that in a modern factory: integrate the facilities for storage and processing. Instead of physically separating memory and processor (store room and workbench), bring the material that is to be operated upon near to where it is processed. A modern factory accomplishes this through a system of conveyer belts and locally distributed bins of parts. Large quantities of materials are moved at a time and held locally while being processed. A parallel computer accomplishes a similar effect by distributing the memory physically throughout the computer near the places where the data is being processed. In computer parlance, this is called a *distributed memory*. A massively parallel computer contains tens of thousands of simple processors, each with its own local memory.

Distributing the data to individual processors means that parallel computers must implement one significant function that has no real counterpart in mass production: communication. When large numbers of data elements are processed they usually cannot be processed independently; the computations interact. For example, in calculating the flow of air over an airplane wing, the calculations describing the flow of the air in one part of the wing must interact with others because one part of the wing affects another. To model the interactions between various parts of the wing the processors must communicate.

Communication is the most difficult part of parallel computation, and much of the initial skepticism about the applicability of the technology was based on concerns that many patterns of data interaction would force sequential processing of the data. As it turned out, the worry proved unfounded. Most patterns of interaction that occur in practice can be done in parallel. Still, the part of a massively parallel computer responsible for communication is the most expensive and complex part of the machine.

Most of the engineering in a massively parallel computer is not in the processors but in the switching system that allows them to communicate. In a Connection Machine, for example, a five-foot cube contains 65,536 processors and associated memory. Each silicon chip contains sixteen tiny processors and the memory associated with the chip is sitting in the same board a few centimeters away. Since 65,536 different memory locations can be accessed simultaneously, the processor to memory bottleneck is eliminated. The cube also contains a communication system that is the equivalent of a telephone system with sixty-five thousand subscribers, each of whom places thousands of calls per second. Miniature switching stations in the same chips as the processors steer messages through a web of hundreds of thousands of wires connecting various parts of the machine.[4] Massively parallel computers of the future will require even greater network capacity.

What impact will massively parallel technology have on our lives? Like mass production, mass computation dramatically changes the economics of large-scale processing. Mass production changed the world; so will mass information processing. The changes brought about by the adoption of mass production took place over a long period of time. After Whitney and others proved the success of mass production methods on rifles, it was more than fifty years before these methods were applied to the manufacture of sewing machines and bicycles. It took even longer for the methods to be applied to the production of loaves of bread and residential housing. Centralizing the production of these goods required the reorganization of systems of marketing and distribution, changes in the product being produced, and sometimes even in the taste of consumers. For example, it must have been "obvious" in 1790 that the methods of mass production would never be applied to the decentralized activity of baking bread. Doing so required significant changes in our methods of food distribution, the development of methods of packaging and food preservatives, and considerable change in the tastes and habits of the bread-eating public. Such changes require decades.

Mass production also enabled the creation of entirely new types of products such as telephones and automobiles, and brought luxury products such as clocks and windup toys into common use. The changes with the greatest impact took the longest time, because they required the most radical adaptations of society. Centralizing productions required the development of transportation capable of bringing the raw materials to the factory and the finished goods to the consumers, as well as the development of methods of mass advertising to ensure that large numbers of people would be willing to buy the same product. These changes required a long period of time and the potential of mass production required their development. The future of mass information processing is likely to be very much the same.

The first changes will take place in areas where large quantities of information are already being processed in one place. Examples include large-scale scientific and engineering processing and the management of large industrial and government databases. In many such applications massively parallel processing can be "dropped in" to an existing system with very little ancillary change. A typical example of a present-day application of massively parallel processing is its use by oil companies to process seismic data. These companies look for oil underground by creating acoustic shocks at the surface and measuring their underground reflections. These signals are converted to numbers that are analyzed to create a picture of the geological structures underground. Hundreds of millions of numbers are required to represent the measurement and, using conventional computers, the calculations can take days or even weeks. By taking advantage of the speed of a massively parallel computer they can be reduced to a few hours. This reduced processing time can be used to reduce costs but, more often, is used to improve the quality of the output, either by asking more questions of the data, or by using more sophisticated algorithms that provide a more accurate picture.

Several major oil companies are already using massively parallel machines for seismic processing modeling. Since finding new petroleum deposits is very valuable, the cost of purchasing and programming a massively parallel computer is easily justified. The primary limitation on its adoption in an application of this type is the availability of trained personnel. There is not yet a large base of existing applications software for parallel machines, so most users today run internally developed software. Parallel computers are inherently no more difficult to program than sequential computers, but present-day programmers are trained on sequential machines. When Eli Whitney built his first rifle factory, he deliberately set it up in a location where the available workers had no experience in existing methods of arms manufacture in order to avoid having to untrain workers of bad habits.[5] A similar trend seems to be taking place in parallel computers. High school students find concepts of parallel programming easy to learn, but programmers with years of experience sometimes find parallel programming counterintuitive. Although the problem will eventually disappear, it is the greatest near-term limitation on the utilization of massively parallel technology.

In some cases the use of parallel machines can actually reduce the need for programming. For example, the US Census Bureau recently experimented with a Connection Machine for use in classifying long-form census applications. The problem involved classifying respondents according to occupation and industry category. The census had 28 million natural language responses with which to classify individuals to one of 232 industry and 504 occupational categories. In the study the Census Bureau evaluated two different methods of classifying with the aid of computers. The first method, using conventional computers, required sixteen programmer-years to develop an expert system that was able to process about half of the forms automatically. The second method took advantage of a massively parallel computer to classify returns by comparing them to an existing database of a hundred thousand previously classified examples. This "memory-based reasoning" program required less than one-twentieth of the programming effort to implement, and yet it was able to accurately classify a larger proportion of the returns. This method of automatically learning from a large database requires so much computation that it would not be practical without a massively parallel computer.[6]

Other current applications of massively parallel computers include the design of aircraft, the prediction of weather, the production of animated special effects for films and commercials, the simulation of physical phenomena ranging from the subatomic structure of particles to the large-scale structure of the universe, modeling of mechanical structures such as crashing cars, breaking secret codes, and searching for information in large databases of documents. What these applications all have in common is the large amount of data being processed together in the same place. It is relatively straightforward to apply massive parallelism to problems of this type. But most of the potential beneficial applications of massively parallel technology do not already have the data in one place, because, at the moment, information processing is generally distributed whenever possible. The current trend is that most information processing is moving away from the central mainframe computer and toward the workstation or PC on the desktop. This is currently the case because of the diseconomies of scale in conventional nonparallel computers. In conventional computers, the machines with the highest performance are the least cost effective. For example, a large mainframe capable of executing 40 million instructions per second may cost $10 million, whereas a workstation capable of executing 4 million instructions per second may cost only $100,000. The performance differential is 10 to 1, but the cost differs by a factor of 100.

In recent years, this diseconomy of scale in conventional computers has forced a trend toward decentralization. Since workstations and personal computers provide more cost-effective computation than a sequential mainframe computer, as much of the load as possible is shifted away from the central mainframe. The computer system in a state-of-the-art computer facility is organized around a network that connects large numbers of independent workstations. Central databases are still kept on large machines, called *servers*. They are accessible by the workstations via the network. Large computations are still executed on the large machines, but such centralized computing is avoided whenever possible because of its high cost.

Most experts assume that the trend toward decentralization will continue, and that a larger and larger portion of the computing power will end up on the desktop. I believe they are wrong. For one thing, massively parallel computing does not exhibit the diseconomy of scale that caused decentralization in the first place. With a massively parallel computer performing a calculation, a large-scale computer can actually have lower cost per calculation than a number of distributed individual computers. This reverses the economic impetus for decentralization. Also, the workstation on the desk makes the centralization of computation and data storage more practical since it provides a user friendly interface into the central computer. In the future, I believe most desktop workstations will specialize in that portion of the computation directly associated with user interface, such as graphics and audio processing, while most computations and data storage will be handled centrally on parallel machines.

In this future, the workstation becomes the user's window into the network. Since the time required for the computers to communicate is imperceptible to humans, the interaction between the workstation and the parallel machine will be invisible. As far as the user is concerned, the machine on the desktop will behave as if it has the power and the data of the central parallel machine. For better or worse, this will make us even more interdependent than we are today.

If you find this image of centralization hard to accept, consider that a similar economy of scale has determined the organization of the electrical utility system. While it would be possible, in principle, for each home to have its own electric generator, it turns out to be more convenient and economical for large numbers of homes to share a common resource. By sharing the electric utility we are able to spread the capital cost of high peak capacity among many users. The result is that everyone connected to the electrical network gets access to as much electricity as they need. This level of service would be too expensive to provide in a distributed system.

The same principle of load sharing is applicable to computations on parallel machines. Unlike conventional computers, they can be scaled cost-effectively. If a user occasionally asks a very difficult question of the computer, then it is far more economical to draw on the power and data of a central system, than to provide that power and data locally. Imagine, for example, an engineer designing a bridge. Most of the engineer's time is probably spent drawing individual pieces, writing specifications, or interacting with other humans. Occasionally the bridge needs to be simulated to see if it can carry the required load or survive an earthquake. These computations are difficult. Putting a machine on the engineer's desk with the ability to perform the simulation quickly is not the best way to solve this problem, because the full capacity of the machine would rarely be used. Since such calculations require a large amount of data and a large amount of communication between various parts of the computation, they are most efficiently done in a centralized parallel machine where these resources can be shared.

Discussion of centralized systems raises issues of privacy, security, and individual control. These are very real concerns, but there is no fundamental technical reason why they cannot be addressed in the context of a centralized system. Private data and messages can be kept and transmitted in encrypted form, protected by a secret code from unauthorized access. (It is possible to make codes that even the fastest parallel computer cannot break.) Rules to limit access and protect data integrity are probably easier to implement in a central database than in a distributed one. Since the central mechanisms are shared, they can be more elaborate. This is why banks are safer than mattresses. Some users with special reasons to distrust the system will keep their data in isolated small computers, just as some people today keep their money outside of the central banking system. But the dominant mode of information storage and large-scale processing will be centralized. The result will be that the typical computer user of tomorrow will be no more limited by lack of computational power than the appliance user of today is limited by lack of electrical power.

High-bandwidth optical fibers will spread throughout the city of the future, linking every office and home into the network. The "net" will provide almost instantaneous access to the large massively parallel computers that are the repositories of data and the engines of processing. Every individual will have access to the most powerful computers in the world for business or recreation. The possibilities that this will create for new products and services are so wide ranging that they are difficult to imagine. I will discuss only two examples: the home robot and virtual worlds.

One of the new products made possible by everyday access to mass computers will be the home robot. By home robot I mean the mechanical domestic servant capable of mopping, dusting, ironing, straightening up the kid's room, clearing the dirty dishes off the table and washing them, doing the laundry, guarding the house from burglars, hooking up the VCR, tuning the piano, and walking the dog.

The mechanical and sensory aspects of this hypothetical marvel are well within the reach of current technology, and in sufficient volume they could be produced at prices comparable to that of a family automobile. The real problem is computation. Rudimentary versions of the necessary software for vision, motor control, recognition, and planning are being developed in laboratories today. But even the fastest computers available are far too slow to accomplish the tasks described above. In addition to the extensive software, such a computer would require access to a large database of commonsense knowledge: knowledge of clothing, video recorders, pets, and pianos. With any foreseeable technology such a processing system and database would be far too expensive to have in the home. It would also be wasted almost all of the time.

Access to a centralized computing utility would make the home robot economically feasible. Fortunately, difficult decisions, like "What task should I do next?" or "Do I throw away this piece of paper?" occur only rarely. A home robot would spend most of its time moving from one position to the next, or doing nothing at all. Simple tasks such as audio and video signal processing and motor control could be performed very nicely by a few microprocessors on board the robot. Whenever a real decision needed to be made, the robot would ask the centralized massively parallel computer. This machine could be shared by hundreds of thousands of homes. It would store a single copy of the database containing the accumulated wisdom of a hundred thousand robots. For example, if you spoke to the robot, a compressed form of your speech would be sent to the central machine for analysis, and instructions for how the robot should behave would be returned to the robot in a fraction of a second. The utility company would send you a bill at the end of the month.

This tale of home robots may sound fanciful. Yet, a century ago, a description of today's electrical network of megawatt utilities powering factories, refrigerators, television sets, and electric toothbrushes, would have seemed just as unlikely. I believe that the changes caused by these new developments in computing will be even more fundamental. At the risk of straining my credibility further, I will speculate about an even deeper change: the emergence of *virtual worlds.*

By virtual worlds, I mean places that people play, work, and interact that exist only within the computer. Only hints of such worlds exist today so it will be hard to imagine what I'm talking about, but I will begin by drawing attention to some of these existing hints. One of the most common applications of present day parallel computers is simulating reality. For example, an aerospace engineer may build a "model" of a airplane inside the computer and see how it "flies." In this case, the model is an abstract object, something like a three-dimensional drawing of an airplane, and the flight is a mathematical calculation of the physics of the lift and airflow. The result is a moving picture on a screen that looks very much like a wind tunnel simulation in which the engineer can watch the behavior of the "air" curling over the "wing" and measure the "pressure" that it generates on the airplane. In this case, the engineer is using the virtual world that is a simulation meant to mimic the real world in which the real airplane will eventually fly.

A very different hint of a virtual world is the stock exchange. When I first met my wife, she was immersed in trading options. Her office was in the top of a skyscraper in Boston, and yet, in a very real sense, when she was at work she was in a world that could not be identified with any single physical location. Sitting at a computer screen, she lived in a world that consisted of offers and trades, a world in which she knew friends and enemies, safe and stormy weather. For a large portion of each day, that world was more real to her than her physical surroundings.

If you doubt the seeming reality of a virtual world, talk to any twelve-year-old who plays a video game like Nintendo. Have you ever "been" to the dungeons in level three of Super Mario Brothers? Have you "touched" the life-giving magic fairy at the fountain in Zelda or "worn" a magic power ring? If you have not traveled to these places then you have missed part of the shared experience of the modern middle-class American childhood. You may have even seen pictures of a virtual world without knowing it. If you watched a recent film or commercial that includes special effects, you may have been looking at realistic renderings of moving three-dimensional objects that never existed outside the memory of a computer. These images are so detailed that they are indistinguishable from photographs of actual objects.

The examples I've given so far have been limited in the richness of their action by the fact that they take place on a television screen, but we already have technology available for deeper sensory immersion. For example, most commercial airline pilots train regularly on aircraft simulators which have not only the look and sound but the actual "feel" of flying a real airplane; they can feel the bump when they land. Experimental virtual reality simulators use head-mounted binocular displays to give the wearer a convincing illusion of moving around in a world that exists only within the computer. Two such users can "meet" within such a world and see the movements of each other's imagined bodies, even though their physical bodies may be half a world apart.

Try to imagine the virtual worlds that will be made possible by the power of a shared parallel computer. Imagine a world that has the complexity and subtlety of the aircraft simulation, the accessibility of the video game, the economic importance of the stock market, and the sensory richness of the flight simulator, all of this with the vividness of computer-generated Hollywood special effects. This may be the kind of world in which your children spend their time, meet their friends and earn their living. Perhaps your son or daughter will be an "architect" that designs public gathering spaces in virtual worlds, or a "doctor" that specializes in repairing virtual bodies, or a lawyer that specializes in laws of some particular virtual world.[7]

Whatever you imagine virtual worlds will be like, or whatever I imagine, is likely to be wrong. Profound change is inherently hard to think about. What is almost certainly true is that the future is not just a simple extrapolation of what we know today. Massively parallel computing transforms both the economies and the absolute capabilities of information processing. All that can be said for certain is that this is bound to cause changes and that change is difficult to think about. I am confident that once again reality will go beyond our imagination.

ENDNOTES

[1]This account of the rise of mass production is based on the events described in Denison Olmsted, *Memoir of Eli Whitney, Esq.* (New York: Ayer, 1972, reprint

of 1846 edition); and Jeannette Mirsky and Allan Nevins, *The World of Eli Whitney* (New York: Collier, 1952).

[2]A good history of the development and adoption of mass production can be found in David Hounshell, *From the American System to Mass Production, 1800–1932: The Development of Manufacturing Technology in the United States* (Baltimore: Johns Hopkins University Press, 1984).

[3]It is also interesting that both massive parallelism and mass production received their initial impetus for commercial development from the military. In both cases the existing manufacturers were skeptical but they were developed primarily by individuals starting new enterprises rather than the existing manufacturers. In both cases the federal government played a critical role in the development of the technology.

[4]A more complete description of the Connection Machine can be found in W. Daniel Hillis, *The Connection Machine* (Cambridge: MIT Press, 1985).

[5]Whitney was also interested in avoiding competition for labor and raw materials. An 1802 letter of his which mentions the value of starting with untrained workers is quoted in Mirsky and Nevins, 214.

[6]The census project and memory-based reasoning are described in R. H. Creecy, B. M. Masand, S. J. Smith, and D. L. Waltz, *Trading MIPS and Memory for Knowledge Engineering: Automatic Classification of Census Returns on a Massively Parallel Supercomputer*, Thinking Machines Corporation Technical Report (Cambridge: Thinking Machines Corporation, 1991).

[7]For some ideas about what virtual worlds may be like, the best source is science fiction. I recommend the work of William Gibson, or a story called "True Names" by Vernor Vinge.

John H. Holland

Complex Adaptive Systems

O
NE OF THE MOST IMPORTANT ROLES a computer can play is to act as a simulator of physical processes. When a computer mimics the behavior of a system, such as the flow of air over an airplane wing, it provides us with a unique way of studying the factors that control that behavior. The key, of course, is for the computer to offer an accurate rendition of the system being studied. In the past fifty years, computers have scored some major successes in this regard. Designers of airplanes, bridges, and America's Cup yachts all use computers routinely to analyze their designs before they commit them to metal. For such artifacts, we know how to mimic the behavior quite exactly, using equations discovered over a century ago.

However, there are systems of crucial interest to humankind that have so far defied accurate simulation by computer. Economies, ecologies, immune systems, developing embryos, and the brain all exhibit complexities that block broadly based attempts at comprehension. For example, the equation-based methods that work well for airplanes have a much more limited scope for economies. A finance minister cannot expect the same accuracy in asking the computer to play out the impact of a policy change as an engineer can expect in asking the computer to play out the implications of tilting an airplane wing.

Despite the disparities and the difficulties, we are entering a new era in our ability to understand and foster such systems. The grounds for optimism come from two recent advances. First, scientists have begun to extract a common kernel from these systems: each of the

John H. Holland is Professor of Psychology and Professor of Computer Science and Engineering at the University of Michigan and Maxwell Professor at the Santa Fe Institute.

systems involves a similar "evolving structure." That is, these systems change and reorganize their component parts to adapt themselves to the problems posed by their surroundings. This is the main reason the systems are difficult to understand and control—they constitute a "moving target." We are learning, however, that the mechanisms that mediate these systems are much more alike than surface observations would suggest. These mechanisms and the deeper similarities are important enough that the systems are now grouped under a common name, *complex adaptive systems.*

The second relevant advance is the new era in computation that is the theme of this issue of *Dædalus.* This advance will allow experts who are not computer savvy to "flight-test" models of particular complex adaptive systems. For example, a policy maker can directly examine a model for its "reality," without knowing the underlying code. That same policy maker can then formulate and try out different policies on the model, again without becoming involved in the underlying coding, thereby developing an informed intuition about future effects of the policies.

It is the thesis of this article that these new computation-based models, when constructed around the common structural kernel of complex adaptive systems, offer a much-needed opportunity: They enable the formulation of new and useful policies vis-à-vis major problems ranging from trade balances and sustainability to AIDS.

COMPLEX ADAPTIVE SYSTEMS

To arrive at a deeper understanding of complex adaptive systems—to understand what makes them complex and what makes them adaptive—it is useful to look at a particular system. Consider the immune system. It consists of large numbers of highly mobile units, called *antibodies,* that continually repel or destroy an ever-changing cast of invaders (bacteria and biochemicals), called *antigens.* Because the invaders come in an almost infinite variety of forms, the immune system cannot simply develop a list of all possible invaders. Even if it could take the time to do so, there is simply not room enough to store all that information. Instead, the immune system must change or adapt ("fit to") its antibodies as new invaders appear. It is this ability to adapt that has made these systems so hard to simulate.

The immune system faces the additional complication that it must distinguish self from other; the system must distinguish the legitimate parts of its owner from the ever-changing cast of invaders. This is a herculean task because the owner's cells and their biochemical constituents number in the tens of thousands of kinds. Mistakes in identification do occur in some individuals, giving rise to the usually fatal autoimmune diseases, but they are rare. The immune system is so good at self-identification that, at present, it provides our best scientific means of defining individuality. An immune system will not even confuse its own cells with those in a skin graft from a sibling, for example.

How does the immune system manage the ongoing process of adaptation that enables it to achieve such remarkable levels of identification? We do not really know, though there are interesting conjectures with varying degrees of evidence. Models of this complex adaptive system are hard to formulate. It is particularly difficult to provide experts in the area with models that allow "thought experiments," models that enable the expert to develop intuition about different mechanisms and organizations.

We face similar problems when dealing with the other complex adaptive systems.[1] All of them involve great numbers of parts undergoing a kaleidoscopic array of simultaneous interactions. They all seem to share three characteristics: *evolution, aggregate behavior,* and *anticipation.*

As time goes on, the parts evolve in Darwinian fashion, attempting to improve the ability of their kind to survive in their interactions with the surrounding parts. This ability of the parts to adapt or learn is the pivotal characteristic of complex adaptive systems. Some adaptive systems are quite simple: a thermostat adapts by turning the furnace on or off in an attempt to keep its surroundings at a constant temperature. However, the adaptive processes of interest here are complex because they involve many parts and widely varying individual criteria (analogous to the constant temperature sought by the thermostat) for what a "good outcome" would be.

Complex adaptive systems also exhibit an aggregate behavior that is not simply derived from the actions of the parts. For the immune system this aggregate behavior is its ability to distinguish self from other. For an economy, it can range from the GNP to the overall network of supply and demand; for an ecology, it is usually taken to be the overall food web or the patterns of flow of energy and materials; for an embryo, it is the overall structure of the developing individual; for the brain, it is the overt behavior it evokes and controls. Generally, it is this aggregate behavior that we would like to understand and modify. To do so, we must understand how the aggregate behavior *emerges* from the interactions of the parts.

As if this were not complex enough, there is a further feature that makes these systems still more complex—they anticipate. In seeking to adapt to changing circumstance, the parts can be thought of as developing rules that anticipate the consequences of certain responses. At the simplest level, this is not much different from Pavlovian conditioning: "If the bell rings, then food will appear." However, even for simple conditioning, the effects are quite complex when large numbers of parts are being conditioned in different ways. This is particularly the case when the various conditionings depend upon the interactions between parts. Moreover, the resulting anticipation can cause major changes in aggregate behavior, even when they do not come true. The anticipation of an oil shortage, even if it never comes to pass, can cause a sharp rise in oil prices, and a sharp increase in attempts to find alternative energy sources. This emergent ability to anticipate is one of the features we least understand about complex adaptive systems, yet it is one of the most important.

There is one final, more technical point, that needs emphasis. Because the individual parts of a complex adaptive system are continually revising their ("conditioned") rules for interaction, each part is embedded in perpetually novel surroundings (the changing behavior of the other parts). As a result, the aggregate behavior of the system is usually far from optimal, if indeed optimality can even be defined for the system as a whole. For this reason, standard theories in physics, economics, and elsewhere, are of little help because they concentrate on optimal end-points, whereas complex adaptive systems "never get there." They continue to evolve, and they steadily exhibit new forms of emergent behavior. History and context play a critical role, further complicating the task for theory and experiment. Though some parts of the system may settle down temporarily at a local optimum, they are usually "dead" or uninteresting if they remain at that equilibrium for an extended period. It is the process of becoming, rather than the never-reached end points, that we must study if we are to gain insight.

MASSIVELY PARALLEL COMPUTERS

The introduction of the digital programmed computer profoundly changed our view of what could be accomplished with computation. Massively parallel computers—computers made up of hundreds of thousands of interconnected microcomputers—will produce changes that are equally profound. It is not just a matter of speed, though that is important. Because a massively parallel computer can handle large numbers of actions simultaneously, it offers new ways of displaying and interacting with data. It provides ways of studying complex adaptive systems as far beyond the reach of a current workstation as that workstation's capacities are beyond the reach of an adding machine or a slide rule. Indeed, massively parallel computers should produce a revolution in the investigation of complex adaptive systems comparable to revolution produced by the introduction of the microscope in biology.[2]

The longer-range effects of massive parallelism are not easy to predict at this early stage, but a little hindsight offers some clues. At the beginning of the computer era, in the 1940s and early 1950s, most computer scientists foresaw increasing speed and storage, along with an ever-increasing ability to tackle scientific and business problems. But the magnitude of those increases as they unfolded, coupled with precipitous decreases in price, amazed us. They made possible widespread word processing, electronic mail, the personal work station, and related sets of activities, such as personal video games and simulations. This has produced new major sectors of the economy and has altered both the work and play of large numbers of people. This process of headlong increases in speed and storage, accompanied by decreasing prices, is already underway for massively parallel machines. The new "microscope" will soon be as pervasive as the personal workstation is today.

MODELS OF COMPLEX ADAPTIVE SYSTEMS

A complex adaptive system has no single governing equation, or rule, that controls the system. Instead, it has many distributed, interacting parts, with little or nothing in the way of a central control. Each of the parts is governed by its own rules. Each of these rules may participate in influencing an outcome, and each may influence the actions of other parts. The resulting rule-based structure becomes grist for the evolutionary procedures that enable the system to adapt to its surroundings.[3] We can develop a better understanding of these evolutionary procedures if we first take a closer look at this idea of a distributed, rule-based structure.

Most rules can be parsed into simple *condition/action* rules: If [condition true], then execute [action]. The simplest rules in this form look much like specifications for psychological reflexes: If [the surface feels hot], then execute [a backward jerk of the hand]; if [there is a rapidly moving object in peripheral vision], then execute [a movement of the eyes until the object is in the center of the visual field]. More complicated rules act on messages sent by other rules, in turn sending out their own messages: If [there is a message X], then execute [transmission of message Y]. Quite complicated activities can be carried out by combinations of such rules; in fact, any computation that can be specified in a computer language can be carried out by an appropriate combination of condition/action rules.

This distributed, many-ruled organization places strong requirements on computer simulation of complex adaptive systems. The most direct approach is to provide a simulation in which many rules are active simultaneously—a "natural" for massively parallel computation.

When many rules can be active simultaneously, a distributed, rule-based system can handle perpetual novelty. On encountering a novel situation, such as "red car by the side of the road with a flat tire," the system activates several relevant rules, such as those for "red," "car," "flat tire," and so on. It builds a "picture" of the situation from parts rather than treating it as a monolithic whole never before encountered. The advantage is similar to that obtained when one describes a face in terms of component parts, rather than treating it as an indecomposable whole. Select, say, 8 components for the face—hair, forehead, eyebrows, eyes, cheekbones, nose, mouth, and chin. Allow 10 variants for each component part—different hair colors and textures, different forehead shapes, and so on. Then $10^8 = 100,000,000$ faces can be described by combining these components in different ways. This at the cost of storing only $8 \times 10 = 80$ "building block" components. Moreover, when a building block is useful in one combination, it is at least plausible that it will prove useful in other, similar combinations. Building blocks thus give the system a capacity for transferring previous experience to new situations.

Massive parallelism is clearly an advantage in simulating a complex adaptive system conceived of in terms of simultaneously acting rules. An individual processor can be allocated to each rule, while the connections between the processors provide for rule interactions. The resulting model is both natural and rapidly processed.

To provide for adaptation, the system must have ways of changing its rules. Such procedures give the system its characteristic "evolving structure." There are two kinds of computational procedures that are relevant: *credit assignment* procedures and *rule discovery* procedures.

Credit assignment is necessary because one wants the system, and its rules, to evolve *toward* something. Credit assignment first requires a sense of what "good" performance is, then it requires a way to pick out and "reward" those parts of the system that seem to be causing good performance. A system that rewards good performance may never become optimal, but it can get better and better.

Credit assignment is a traditional problem in artificial intelligence research. In a rule-based system, the object is to assign credit to individual rules in proportion to their contribution to the system's overall (aggregate) performance. We can think of this credit as a *strength* assigned to the rule: The more a rule contributes to good performance, the stronger it becomes, and vice versa.[4] By "stronger" we mean that the rule, based on its past successes, is given a stronger voice in future decisions. As successive situations are encountered, the relevant rules compete to control behavior, the stronger rules being the likely winners. That is, if a rule has produced a good outcome in some situation in the past, then it is more likely to be used in similar situations in the future.

Credit assignment can enable a system to select the best from the rules it has, but it cannot supply the system with new rules. If it is to evolve to deal with new situations, the system will have to create new rules. For this the system requires some kind of rule discovery procedure. Rule discovery is a subtle process, because it is important that the discovery process generate *plausible* rules, rules that are not obviously wrong on the basis of past experience. The philosopher C. S. Pierce is quite informative on this matter.[5] To apply Pierce's reasoning to this model, it is convenient to think of rules as made up of smaller pieces, or building blocks. My own version of Pierce's commentary, then, is that the discovery and recombination of building blocks is an important step toward assuring the plausibility of newly invented rules.[6]

To approach rule discovery in terms of building blocks, it is useful to think of "breeding" strong rules. That is, strong rules are selected as "parents," and new offspring rules are produced by *crossing* the parents. The assumption is that strong rules have valuable building blocks inside them that should be incorporated into new rules. This process mimics the process whereby a breeder crosses horses or a farmer produces new varieties of hybrid corn. Here the object is to produce offspring rules that amount to plausible new hypotheses. Rule discovery procedures of this kind are called *genetic algorithms.*[7] A genetic algorithm "learns" automatically by biasing future generations of rules toward combinations of above-average building blocks (as, in genetics, coadapted sets of genes appear ever more frequently in successive generations). It can be proved that genetic algorithms find and recombine useful building blocks. They have counterparts in each of the known complex adaptive systems. Of course, many of the new rules generated by this process are nonsense, but nonsense rules do not promote "good" behavior and are systematically weeded out.

This rule discovery procedure, once again, lends itself to massively parallel computation. Crossing strong parents is a simple operation that imposes low processing requirements on the computer. Because the whole set of rules can be treated as a population, with mating going on simultaneously throughout the population, parallelism is easily exploited.

INTERNAL MODELS: THE FUNDAMENTAL ATTRIBUTE OF
COMPLEX ADAPTIVE SYSTEMS

There is still one property of complex adaptive systems that we have to examine more closely. Complex adaptive systems form and use internal models to *anticipate* the future, basing current actions on expected outcomes.[8] It is this attribute that distinguishes complex adaptive systems from other kinds of complex systems; it is also this attribute that makes the emergent behavior of complex adaptive systems intricate and difficult to understand.

It is interesting to note that we rarely think of anticipation, or prediction, as a characteristic of organisms in general, though we readily ascribe it to humans. Still, a bacterium moves in the direction of a chemical gradient, implicitly predicting that food lies in that direction. The butterfly that mimics the foul-tasting Monarch butterfly survives because it implicitly forecasts that a certain wing pattern discourages predators. A wolf bases its actions on anticipations generated by a mental map that incorporates landmarks and scents. The science of computer simulations itself represents man's attempt to make predictions ranging from the flight characteristics of yet untried aircraft to future GNP, but we have only recently been able to endow programs themselves with model-building capabilities. It is important that we understand the way in which complex adaptive systems build and use internal models, because so much of their behavior stems from anticipations based on these internal models.

An internal model allows a system to look ahead to the future consequences of current actions, without actually committing itself to those actions. In particular, the system can avoid acts that would set it irretrievably down some road to future disaster ("stepping off a cliff"). Less dramatically, but equally important, the model enables the agent to make current "stage-setting" moves that set up later moves that are obviously advantageous. The very essence of attaining a competitive advantage, whether it be in chess or economics, is the discovery and execution of stage-setting moves.

An internal model may, of course, be incorrect in some or many ways. But then hindsight can be used to improve the model; the model is modified whenever its predictions fail to match subsequent outcome (credit assignment again). The system can thus make improvements without overt rewards or detailed information about errors. This is a tremendous advantage in most real-world situations, where rewards or corrective information occur only at the end of long sequences of action. Whether one is playing a game of chess or making a long-term investment, the rewards for current action are usually much delayed. Internal models enable improvement in the interim.

AN INTERIM SUMMARY

Here's a condensed view of the description of complex adaptive systems presented so far. The systems' basic components are treated as sets of rules. The systems rely on three key mechanisms: *parallelism, competition,* and *recombination.* Parallelism permits the system to use individual rules as building blocks, activating sets of rules to describe and act upon the changing situations. Competition allows the system to marshal its rules as the situation demands, providing flexibility and transfer of experience. This is vital in realistic environments, where the agent receives a torrent of information, most of it irrelevant to current decisions. The procedures for adaptation—credit assignment and rule discovery—extract useful, repeatable events from this torrent, incorporating them as new building blocks. Recombination plays a key role in the discovery process, generating plausible new rules from parts of tested rules. It implements the heuristic that building blocks useful in the past will prove useful in new, similar contexts.

Overall, these mechanisms allow a complex adaptive system to adapt, while using extant capabilities to respond, instant by instant, to its environment. In so doing the system balances exploration (acquisition of new information and capabilities) with exploitation (the efficient use of information and capabilities already available). The system that results is well founded in computational terms, and it does indeed get better at attaining goals in a perpetually novel environment.

ACCESS TO SIMULATIONS OF COMPLEX ADAPTIVE SYSTEMS

Simulations of complex adaptive systems, executed on computers, produce floods of data. The result is reminiscent of the early days of "batch processing" on computers: When the output appears as interminable pages of printout and numerical tables, it is difficult to uncover significant or surprising interactions, much less react to them. The user can be reduced to observing, rather than experimenting and controlling. This need not be.

If we are to make parallel simulations of complex adaptive systems accessible, two criteria must be satisfied. First, the parallel simulation must directly mimic the ongoing parallel interactions of the complex adaptive system.[9] Second, there must be a visual, game-like user interface that provides natural controls for experts not used to exploring systems via computers. For example, a policy maker should be able to try out an economic model in much the way that a pilot tries out a flight simulator. Actions and decisions should be made in the usual way, without requiring any cognizance of the underlying computations. It should also be easy to see if the model behaves in realistic ways in well-known situations. This has the additional value of allowing experts to feed back "reality checks" to the simulation designers. Research initiatives at the Santa Fe Institute, in cooperation with a commercial firm, SimLabs, lead us to believe that powerful interfaces of this kind are possible for complex adaptive systems.

CURRENT SIMULATIONS OF COMPLEX ADAPTIVE SYSTEMS

We are only in the earliest stages of developing simulations of the kind just discussed, but there are some suggestive results. The work of Marimon, McGrattan, and Sargent on the evolution of money provides an early example. It was initiated in 1989 as part of the economics program at the Santa Fe Institute.[10] This study uses a combination of theory and simulation to study the effect of adaptive, rule-based agents in a classical trading model from economics, Wicksell's triangle. It shows that even when the artificial agents start with randomly generated rules, they soon decide upon a medium of exchange and reach close-to-optimal trading patterns. Among other studies, there is a new approach to understanding the immune system using a massively parallel computer,[11] and an actual policy study using data from the office of management and budget in Milan, Italy.[12] The latter is directly concerned with increasing the efficiency of decision making in the 730 offices scattered throughout the Lombardy region. The study's major objective, which it attained, was to discover which factors, from a very large number, were relevant to the various decisions made by the local offices. By using this information, the director structured decision procedures that would lead to increased efficiency in the local offices.

These early results are really only accessible to the computer savvy, but they point the way. In all three of the models cited, the study of the mechanisms providing evolutionary changes in the system's structure will encourage more realistic, more accessible models. We can then expect current exploratory research to expand into substantial advances available to a wide range of users.

MATHEMATICS AND THEORY

Complex adaptive systems are so intricate that there is little hope of a coherent theory without the controlled experiments that a massively parallel computer makes possible. At the same time, in an area this complex, experiments unguided by an appropriate theoretical framework usually amount to little more than "watching the pot boil." Sustained progress outside the guidelines of a theory is as unlikely as attempting modern experimental physics outside the framework of theoretical physics. After all, no system currently under investigation in physics is as complex as a full-fledged complex adaptive system. We need experiments to inform theory, but without theory all is lost.

Fortunately, there are several points at which we can bring mathematics to bear on the approach outlined above. We can show that, under certain conditions, appropriate credit assignment procedures do indeed strengthen the relevant stage-setting rules. We can also show that recombination, mediated by a genetic algorithm, does progressively bias the population of rules toward the use of above-average building blocks.[13] There are also formal frameworks that apply to the process of generating internal models, with accompanying proofs that establish some of their elementary properties.[14] On a broader perspective, there are relevant pieces of mathematics from mathematical economics and mathematical ecology that can be generalized to apply to all complex adaptive systems.[15]

The challenge is to weld these disparate pieces into a theory, a theory that explains the pervasiveness of the evolutionary processes forming the common kernel of all complex adaptive systems. The theory should elucidate the mechanisms that assure the emergence of internal models. Coordinated computer simulations should provide critical tests of the unfolding theory. The simulations should also suggest well-informed conjectures that offer new directions for theory. The broadest hope is that the theoretician, by testing deductions and inductions against the simulations, can reincarnate the cycle of theory and experiment so fruitful in physics.

To my knowledge there is only one organization, the Santa Fe Institute, that has taken the general mathematical study of complex adaptive systems as its central mission.[16] The institute has drawn to its campus a unique range of experts in physics, economics, and related mathematical disciplines. It has formed a working alliance with the University of Michigan to take advantage of that university's particular strengths in psychology, sociology, and business administration. Even though the institute is only five years old, these interactions have already produced substantial changes in the study of complex adaptive systems.

SUMMARY

Complex adaptive systems represent the kernel of some of our most difficult problems, ranging from trade balances to control of the AIDS epidemic. They can be simulated on massively parallel computers by defining a network of interacting rule-based components. By providing natural "flight-simulator-like" interfaces for such simulations, we can open these systems to exploration by policy makers and other experts who do not have the time to become computer savvy. This has the double value of giving the designers "reality checks," while allowing policy makers to explore the differences effected by different policies. By looking for pervasive phenomena in such experiments, we can implement the classic hypothesize-test-revise cycle for the study of complex adaptive systems. The experimental part of this cycle is particularly important, because such systems typically operate far from equilibrium, continually undergoing revisions and improvements. They do *not* yield to classic, equilibrium-based mathematical approaches that rely on linearity, attractors, fixed points, and the like. A new kind of mathematical framework is required, one that emphasizes continuing adaptation through recombination of building blocks.

Without such a framework, the computer-based experiments will be little more than uncoordinated forays into an endlessly complex domain. With such a framework, we can greatly expand our understanding of these important, difficult questions.

ACKNOWLEDGEMENTS

Research by the author, relevant to this article, was supported in part by the National Science Foundation, under grant IRI-8904203, and by the Santa Fe Institute. I would like to thank James Bailey of Thinking Machines Corporation for many helpful suggestions after a careful reading of the manuscript.

ENDNOTES

[1] See D. L. Stein, ed., *Lectures in the Sciences of Complexity* (Reading, Mass.: Addison-Wesley, 1989); and P. W. Anderson, K. A. Arrow, and D. Pines, eds., *The Economy as an Evolving Complex System* (Reading, Mass.: Addison-Wesley, 1988).

[2] J. H. Holland, "A Universal Computer Capable of Executing an Arbitrary Number of Sub-Programs Simultaneously," *Proc. 1959, Eastern Joint Computer Conference* (New York: Institute of Electrical and Electronic Engineering, 1959), 108–13; and W. D. Hillis, *The Connection Machine* (Cambridge: MIT Press, 1985).

[3] See J. H. Holland, K. J. Holyoak, R. E. Nisbett, and P. R. Thagard, *Induction: Processes of Inference, Learning, and Discovery* (Cambridge: MIT Press, 1989).

[4] Ibid., 70–75.

[5] C. S. Pierce, *Collected Papers, Science and Philosophy,* vol. 7, ed. A. W. Burks (Cambridge: Harvard University Press, 1958).

[6] J. H. Holland, *Adaptation in Natural and Artificial Systems* (Ann Arbor: University of Michigan Press, 1975).

[7] Ibid., 89–140.

[8] J. H. Holland, "Emergent Models," in A. Scott, ed., *Frontiers in Science* (Cambridge: Blackwell, 1990).

[9] S. Forrest, "Emergent Computation," in S. Forret, ed., *Emergent Computation* (Amsterdam: Elsevier [North-Holland], 1990).

[10] R. Marimon, E. McGrattan, and T. J. Sargent, *Money as a Medium of Exchange in an Economy with Artificially Intelligent Agents,* Santa Fe Working Paper 89–004 (Santa Fe: Santa Fe Institute, 1989).

[11] S. Forrest and A. Perelson "Genetic Algorithms and the Immune System," in H. Schwefel and R. Maenner, eds., *Parallel Problem Solving from Nature* (Berlin: Springer Verlag, 1991), 320–25.

[12] N. H. Packard, "Genetic Learning Algorithm for the Analysis of Complex Data" *Complex Systems* 4 (1990): 543–72.

[13] Holland, *Adaptation in Natural and Artificial Systems,* chap. 7.

[14] Holland, Holyoak, Nisbett, and Thagard, *Induction,* appendices 2A and 2B.

[15] Anderson, Arrow, and Pines, eds., *The Economy as an Evolving Complex System,* 75–97, 205–41.

[16] D. Pines, ed., *Emerging Syntheses in Science* (Reading, Mass.: Addison-Wesley, 1987).

Yuefan Deng, James Glimm, and David H. Sharp

Perspectives on Parallel Computing

J UST AS MACHINERY HAS LIFTED THE DEADENING weight of manual labor from our backs, the computer is removing the weight of repetitive mental tasks from our minds. At the same time, it increases enormously the number and complexity of mental tasks that it is feasible to undertake. Computers enable us to use technology, information, and knowledge to accomplish goals which would be impossible without them. The computer is a critical technology for the competitive position of major industries. It is critical for our national security. It is also an increasingly important factor in medical and biological understanding, diagnosis and treatment.

WHY COMPUTE FASTER?

It is the increasing speed of today's computers which defines their tremendous value to society. Table 1 illustrates the times required for solving representative medium-sized and grand challenge[1] scientific problems on typical computers.[2] For example, a grand challenge problem which would require fifteen hundred years to solve on a low-end scientific workstation could be solved on a Connection Machine (CM-2 with sixty-four thousand processors) in just one year! On a teraflop machine—currently under development, with delivery tentatively expected by 1995—the same problem could be solved in ten hours.[3] The basis for comparison is an estimate of sustained performance.

Yuefan Deng is Assistant Professor in the Department of Applied Mathematics and Statistics at the State University of New York at Stony Brook.

James Glimm is Distinguished Leading Professor and Chair of the Department of Applied Mathematics and Statistics at the State University of New York at Stony Brook.

David H. Sharp is a Fellow in the Theoretical Division at Los Alamos National Laboratory.

Machines	Moderate Problems	Grand Challenge Problems
TFlop Machine	2 seconds	10 hours
CM-2 64K	30 minutes	1 year
CRAY Y-MP/8	4 hours	10 years
Alliant FX/80	5 days	250 years
SUN 4/60	1 month	1.5K years
VAX 11/780	9 months	14K years
IBM PC/8087	9 years	170K years
Apple Mac	23 years	450K years

TABLE I. Typical times for solving medium-size scientific problems and representative grand challenge problems on various computers. A *K year* (kilo year) is a thousand years.

System performance refers to the computational problem sizes which can be handled within acceptable time and cost limitations. Performance can be divided roughly into three aspects, which may have differing importance in distinct applications. The first is the raw computation speed (arithmetic operations per second). The second is memory, or the amount of input data, program instructional data, and intermediate computational results (scratch paper) which can be stored at any one time. The third important performance attribute is I/O (input/output), or the rate at which data can be entered into and retrieved from the machine.

Computational performance is measured by human as well as system criteria. The human criteria are the knowledge of computational algorithms, or ways of translating ideas and formulas into computer language, and the problem-based understanding, or science, put into the problem.

Parallel computing is a method to improve system performance dramatically. The distinction between parallel computing and its opposite, serial computing, lies in the order of events. In serial computation, all operations proceed in a definite, well-defined sequential order. With parallel computation, many operations are performed at the same time. The biological model for parallel computation is the brain, which contains many (approximately 10^{10}) computational elements (neurons), many of which are active and are occupied with numerous unrelated tasks at the same time (breathing, thinking, drinking coffee, and so on). As with the brain, parallel computation achieves its performance through the replication of a large number of relatively simple units.

Society and Science in the Computer Age

The tasks accomplished with the aid of computers involve not only words and numbers, but the control of machines themselves. Indeed, these tasks extend to the organization of society itself, which can attain goals undreamed of without computers. Thus the computer completes the Industrial Revolution, begun with the invention of the steam engine, and ushers in its own era. This new age, in contrast to the Industrial Revolution, is characterized by the primacy of information rather than machinery. It could therefore be called the Information Age. Its onset, which we are currently experiencing, is the Information Revolution.

The organization of a large multinational corporation would not be possible without the use of computers for the communication, transfer, processing, and assessing of information, for the processing of data and the keeping of records. Universities also require computers devoted to organizational tasks, for the same reason. Computers are used for financial planning, analysis of economic data, and processing of bank checks. They drive fax machines and copiers. Smart telephones with redial and memory capabilities are only the beginning of what is possible in this direction.

The telephone switching network is a massive, parallel, and distributed computing network. Decisions on the routing of messages are made instantaneously, in response to network capability and traffic loads. It is for this reason that telephone companies have been among the pioneers of computer development. The operation of a modern telephone system would be impossible without computers.

Airline reservations, as we know them today, would likewise be impossible without a computer-accessible database. These reservations also provide valuable projections to the airlines, which monitor their own future reservations to project traffic patterns. Scheduling is also done by computer, so that the correct size plane is available at the correct airport at the correct time. These schedules are adjusted seasonally to account for shifts in traffic patterns, but they must often be adjusted more rapidly—daily, for example—as in response to weather-induced disruptions of the schedule. For such problems, the value of a rapid answer is very much larger than that of a delayed answer. If scheduling problems could be solved in a matter of minutes, with faster computers of the future, decisions as to whether to delay a given aircraft to meet incoming connections could be based on the effects such decisions would have on the schedules and connections for the remainder of the day. This example is illustrative of a much broader class of discrete optimization problems, which arise in a variety of contexts, including transportation, inventories, layout, packing, and route planning for robots.

Bar code readers and cash registers are computer terminals, in the sense that they are often connected to a central computer, which tallies totals and change for each sale, keeps records, and determines the day's receipts. A large organization could potentially use this system as a massive distributed parallel computing system, which could monitor sales and inventory on an hourly or daily basis, with breakdown by product, product category, or region.

Computing is the foundation for the engineering management of major industries. Perhaps more important, excellence in engineering computation, such as computer-aided design and computer-aided manufacturing (CAD/CAM), is an important aspect of competitive viability. The design of automobiles is heavily dependent upon computers. Their manufacture uses computer-controlled machine tools and automation, computer-assisted inventory control, simulation studies in factory layout, and the routing and scheduling of work in progress. Distribution and marketing utilize computer-based optimization studies. Throughout industry, computers are widely used to control manufacturing processes, from the control of temperature and pressure in a chemical vat or the inflow of chemical feed stocks, to the control of metal processing and machining equipment, to control of temperature and pressure for the growth of crystals for semiconductor fabrication. Computers are also making their way into consumer products—the "smart" (electronically controlled) carburetor is an example.

The best tools currently available for understanding the solutions of the equations of quantum physics—both at the atomic and the subatomic level—are computational. Theories of supernova depend on computational solution of the equations of continuum, atomic, and subatomic physics, and have received striking confirmation by the supernova event of 1987.

The above discussion describes the past and short-term projections into the future. Some currently solved or partially solved problems will be solved more rapidly and more reliably, with better accuracy and fewer assumptions. Moreover, the answers will be put to wider use. Such projections are likely to err by being too timid. Massive and cost-effective increases in computing capability will have long-range and qualitative changes which are more difficult to predict, but may be more profound. The most important consequences of a massive increase in computing power could very well be ones not foreseen here.

Dramatic scientific success is envisioned in a number of currently intractable areas. Examples where such a breakthrough might occur are not difficult to imagine. Genetic diseases may be cured in the future, with the assistance of computer-supported pattern recognition to extract information from the genetic code. The origins of the universe can be explored through computer modeling of proposed physical processes and physical laws. The scientific relation between the microphysics of atoms and quantum mechanics and such macrophysics as material properties (strength, hardness, texture, durability) may be determined in a routine and quantitative fashion. These connections are known in principle, but are very difficult to trace quantitatively today. Massive increases in computing power, and the decisive role of computation in the solution of such problems, will result in computation becoming a senior partner in the scientific enterprise.

New intellectual disciplines will come to the fore. Pattern recognition and machine intelligence are likely examples. Predictions of these capabilities were associated with the optimism which prevailed concerning artificial intelligence (AI) in the 1950s. The predictions did not come to pass and have fallen into some disrepute.

We believe that the predictions will, in the main, turn out to be correct. However, it is clear that the time scales and difficulties were grossly underestimated. In particular, the need for fundamental science, relevant to the area of application, was greatly underestimated. Computing capabilities alone will not be sufficient. Also underestimated was the gradual nature of scientific progress; science more often progresses incrementally and only occasionally in large breakthroughs. The time for progress in the relatively more tractable areas of physical science was also underestimated. John von Neumann's predictions in the 1950s concerning weather forecasting are only today coming true.[4] The AI projections of speech and handwriting recognition, language, vision, and robotic capability are all likely to occur. Massive increases in computing power are absolutely necessary, but, as noted, it would be unrealistic to think that computation alone will suffice. In addition to increased computational power, entirely new theories of knowledge and speech may well be needed.

Computer-assisted decision making will become commonplace, so that the doctor, lawyer, nurse, or engineer will have access to a large computerized data base in which information can be searched by reference to key words. Beyond the reference material, the computer will offer assistance in decision making. Simple professional tasks, such as the preparation of routine legal documents, will not require professional assistance. The library of the future—with computer-based storage, retrieval, and data search, of which we have heard more than we have seen—is still a valid concept. Publishing will be revolutionized as well, and communication in general will be transformed. More records will be stored in computer-readable form, and large-scale data analysis will be common.

The quality of large-scale econometric, sociometric, and political surveys will increase and a quantitative formulation of the sciences of human behavior may become possible. For example, large-scale epidemiological studies with many controlled variables will, in the authors' judgment, provide new examples of such a science; the tobacco and asbestos connections to cancer were established primarily on the basis of statistical analysis. Patterns of automobile injuries are also subject to statistical analysis. Present evidence for the possibility of such a science of human behavior also includes the significant increase in the length of economic expansions and the decrease in length and severity of recessions (as charted since 1750), presumably due in part to the successful use of computer-assisted econometric models. A company's consumer products can be rapidly and accurately distributed to those specific geographic areas where particular models are most desired. Market promotions can be targeted to selected ZIP codes, census tracts, or population segments.

Work at home—telecommuting—will become more common. Advantages of telecommuting include savings in time and energy, decreased traffic and air pollution, and increased parental supervision of children. The automobile will acquire fail-safe collision avoidance intelligence. Medical prosthetic devices will become smarter. Art will be generated by computer graphics, but will still be created by a human artist who will control the computer by talking to it. The world champion chess player will be a computer. We propose, with perhaps a touch of whimsy, that this champion computer will be programmed by a collaboration between a computer scientist and a (human) chess player.

Impact on Science

The computer has given rise to a new mode of scientific practice, and scientific computation today stands beside theory and experiment as a fundamental methodology of science. Scientific computation is on a rising growth curve, and we believe that we are still near the beginning—or, at most, the middle—of this growth. That we are not near the end of the growth period can be seen from the large number of near-term prospects for dramatic progress from the points of view of hardware, software, and applications.

To understand why we want to compute faster, we first look at how high-speed computation has transformed fluid dynamics and other branches of continuum physics in the past thirty-five years. In most areas of fluid dynamics, the computer is the primary experimental tool. Laboratory experiments serve to validate computational codes and usually serve to validate the final result of a computational investigation. However, a very large part of the scientific exploration between these two steps is done exclusively by computer. Writing in the early 1950s, von Neumann observed that "fluid dynamics is stagnant across a broad front."[5] Such a statement could not be made today. Accurate five-day weather forecasts, the computation of flow fields around airplane wings and the design of transonic aircraft, stress loading in complex structures, multidimensional shock wave interactions, and the beginnings of reliable turbulence computations are a reality today. The implications for science, technology, and industry have only partially been realized, and because the improvement in capabilities in both hardware and algorithms have occurred so rapidly, even today's computing capabilities have considerable unexplored consequences.

In this context it is natural to ask, Why not coast for a while and let science and technology catch up rather than push at the frontiers of computational feasibility? The answer is that, for every problem which can be solved by today's computing technology, there are scores which are clearly inaccessible today. Consider which of these types of problems are the more important. The problems with the most dramatic consequences typically require solutions which are out of reach today. Their solutions require large increases in computational power, in addition to other scientific input.

Let us dream (but not too implausibly), and ask what could be done with an improvement in computing power by a factor of 10^6. This is precisely the improvement which occurred in the period from 1955 to 1990. We suppose that the increase in speed is achieved within today's costs, so that the new computational power will be affordable, and we suppose that the increase in computational power occurs across the entire range of computers, so that PCs and scientific workstations become correspondingly more powerful at their present price. These assumptions apply to the previous thirty-five years and do not appear excessive as a projection for the future.

First, we list problems which are being solved but not well or not well enough. Actually almost all of the problems mentioned above are not being solved well enough. To understand the difficulties, consider the example of weather forecasting. The most important feature of atmospheric flow is the jet stream. Its dimensions are about two hundred by three thousand miles as it crosses the United States. Large-scale storm systems may measure about three hundred miles in diameter, while individual clouds and thunderstorms may have lengths under one mile. The wind currents in a thunder storm will change significantly over fifty feet, and the size of a hail stone or rain drop is measured in fractions of an inch. Put more succinctly, weather forecasting has important features which interact with one another and which occur on multiple length scales. We call this the problem of multiple length scales; this is a very common problem in science and technology. Important phenomena often occur on very different length scales—but still interact—so that a correct computation would have to include very small length scales as well as large ones, those natural to the problem as a whole. In the modeling of fluid flow in oil reservoirs, for example, it is not uncommon to use elementary computational units (grid blocks) of a size which include several oil wells, perhaps a thousand feet apart. However, there are important fluid events at the length scale of one foot or even smaller, where the elementary mixing of reservoir fluids occurs. All intermediate length scales display reservoir heterogeneity in the rock properties as well, so that an increase in computational resolution by a factor of 10^3 would clearly be of use here. However, this increase must be applied in both horizontal directions, with some slightly smaller factor in the vertical direction, and with smaller computational time steps as well, so that improved computational requirements of 10^{11} would be justified, if available.

It is easy to show that a wide range of important problems will require a factor of 10^{12} or more in increased computing power for their solution. The correct computation of small and large length scales leads to these requirements. If the large object (jet stream) has a size ratio of a thousand to one to the small structure (thunderstorm), these computational requirements arise.

Assuming that only half of this improvement comes from hardware and the other half from improved algorithms—so that brute force computation of intractable problems is not attempted—we see that a factor of 10^6 in raw computing power is just about right. The proposed high-resolution computation would require a comparable increase in data. Where will the data come from? Emerging techniques of cross-well seismic data could be the answer for the petroleum reservoir simulation problems. The analysis of this data is another computationally intensive problem, which, to be effective at this level of detail, could require a 10^6 increase in speed.

The problem of oil reservoir modeling is typical. The computational glass is only half full. In the design of aircraft, turbulence adjacent to the wing is underresolved and for this reason the location of the point of turbulent flow separation and parameters of stall are not reliably determined by computation. Because of the very large number of active length scales present in turbulence, the computational requirements for this problem are similar. Typically, numerical resolution omits at least three orders of magnitude of fine-scale turbulent structure. Because the problems involve three space dimensions as well as time, this fact translates into computational requirements on the order of 10^{12} which, if half of the improvement is to come from better algorithms and modeling, leads to a requirement of 10^6 in improved hardware capabilities.

Multiple length scales are only one of the reasons for requiring increased computational power. Complex physical and chemical processes are another. In each case, detailed computational cost estimates can be projected. The analysis of combustion in an automobile engine and the design of fuel-efficient and environmentally safe engines are others. Virtually every important problem solved today could be solved better, with dramatic implications for science and technology. The proposed factor of 10^6 in improved computational performance is not excessive.

The requirements for massive increases in computational power are not confined to the physical sciences. There are presently about a thousand human genes for which the DNA sequence is known. Comparison between DNA sequences and pattern recognition among sequences is a standard tool for extracting biological meaning from this data base. The comparison and pattern recognition algorithms require greatly increased computational effort as the size of the data base increases. These searches strain existing computer capabilities. Moreover, there are about 10^5 genes in the human genome. Plans to sequence the full genome will create the need to be able to test similarity of genes across the entire data base, and will require improved computer power in the range of 10^{13} at a minimum, to be achieved by some mixture of hardware and algorithm improvement. An important reason for studying genes is to study the proteins they encode. Biological activity is determined, to a large extent, by the three-dimensional shape of the protein made by transcription of the gene. This type of problem creates the need for comparable computational power.

THE WAVE OF THE FUTURE

Parallel computing is faster and cheaper than serial computing. It is the *only* route to faster computing presently envisaged. Serial and parallel computing are following different trend lines. Parallel computing started more slowly, but it is on a more rapidly growing trend line. The lines have crossed recently, so that parallel computing is now somewhat faster and about a factor of ten cheaper than serial processing. These differences, now small, will become dramatic in the near future. They provide an imperative for a significant change in scientific culture.

Intrinsic Advantages

Parallel computers use many slower processors to achieve the effect of a fast computation. In doing so they use well-developed and robust technology in the design and manufacture of their components. That is, they use component technology which is also usable in large markets. The component technology, and often the components themselves, are off-the-shelf, as compared to the expensive and highly specialized technology used in high-performance serial supercomputers. For this reason, the cost of design, manufacturing facilities, software, and the like is reduced and can be amortized and shared over a large number of users. Economies of scale in procurement of components or component technology go far beyond those available in serial supercomputers. This leads to a lower cost per unit element. In terms of absolute capabilities, today's parallel computers are about comparable to the fastest serial computers, while their memory and I/O capabilities are about a factor of ten better. In terms of future trends, the difference is even clearer—the trends decisively favor parallel computing. To justify these statements, Figure 1 illustrates performance versus cost for a number of current computers. The performance is measured in computational speed in units of mega-flops. We see that low-end serial computers and high-end parallel computers lie on one cost line, while high-end serial computers share a less favorable cost line.[6]

Figure 2 displays performance capabilities versus time, and we see two trend lines; these also strongly favor parallel computers over serial computers. The performance is again measured in computational speed but in units of million instructions per second (MIPS).

Constraints

There are essentially four factors that limit the scale of parallelism: financial, hardware, and software constraints, and the limits imposed by an architectural design learning curve. Computer architecture involves the choice of design principles and major design decisions. The learning curve recognizes that the details of designing a usable computer are quite complex, requiring the balance of many components and the solution of many problems. The design learning curve does not represent an absolute limit, but only states that parallel computational power can, in a practical sense, be increased only at a certain rate. The constraint imposed by the learning curve results from a decision to follow the bottom up principle of design, whereby components and connection technology are improved incrementally, the results are tested in collaboration with the user community, and only then is the next improvement considered. The financial limits are time dependent and, at current prices, would allow an increase in performance by a factor of at least ten for a machine with general purpose capabilities. Allowing for economies of scale, improved cost/performance of individual nodes and perhaps peak utilization, near-term factors of 10^3 in performance seem very likely from the point of view of financial feasibility.

Hardware limits have not yet been approached by current parallel computers. Stated differently, hardware is not the constraint which sets the size of today's parallel computers. The Connection Machine has sixty-four thousand processors. It has relatively weak processor nodes and could be strengthened by adding more processors or stronger nodes, either of which seems to be practical. The new Intel Hypercube—iPSC/860—has 128 relatively powerful processors, and a more powerful machine could be derived from it, again either by adding more processors or by using more powerful ones. Both of these improvements are currently in the planning stage. The goal of the joint DARPA-Intel Touchstone project is to produce a machine by 1995 with two thousand processors and capable of teraflops.[7] Similar upgrades are planned for the nCUBE.

Software constraints refer to programmability, serial bottlenecks, load balancing, and Amdahl's law. Amdahl's law states, in qualitative terms, that there are effective limits on the amount of usable parallelism, in the sense that sooner or later some of the processors will be waiting for others to complete their tasks before they can continue with their own. Serial bottlenecks are an extreme form of this situation in which one processor works and all the others wait. Load balancing refers to the fact that the division of labor may not be perfect—some of the processors may finish early and wait for some results to come from the more heavily loaded processors, while the others continue. Software constraints also refer to program complexity issues and debugging, which are more difficult in the parallel case.

Software constraints are the principal current limitation on the effective scale of parallelism. The problem can be formulated as two questions: Can the difficulties be overcome, as a matter of principle? Are they worth solving; that is, are they solvable at a cost which makes parallel computing viable? The title for this section reflects the authors' belief that both questions have a positive answer. The value of the solution is, in effect, the value of the answer to the computa-

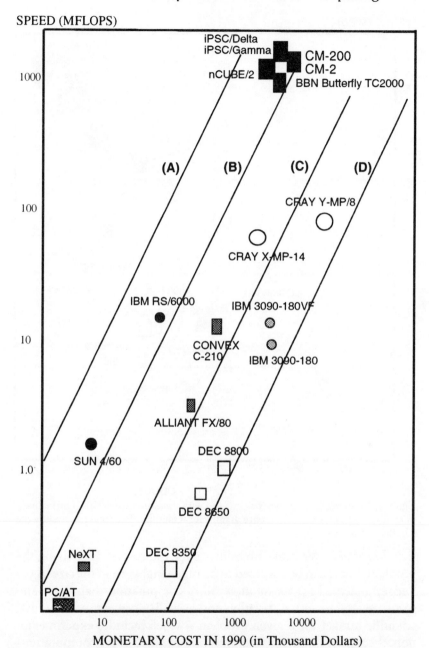

Figure 1. Computational power versus cost. The lines labeled (A), (B), (C), and (D) divide the cost-effectiveness ratio into five regions. The ratios on these lines are 1, 0.1, 0.01, and 0.001, respectively, in units of megaflops per $1,000. The solid squares are the parallel computers.

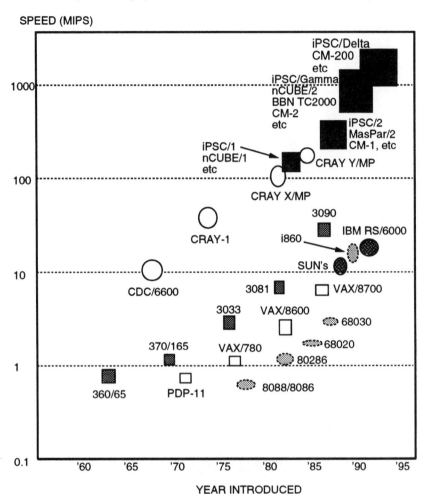

Figure 2. Computational power has evolved with time since the 1950s. Distinctively shaped symbols represent distinctive architectural families. The solid squares are the parallel computers.

tional problem. We make no estimate for the cost of *not* solving the problem, but it can be assumed to be much higher than the size of the budget allocated for its solution. Since computation (hardware and software combined) is usually not even 10 percent of the total scientific budget for a given problem—which includes experimentation, theory development, and the labor involved in the computations of a scientific inquiry—cost considerations for the solution of the programmability problem do not seem likely to be a limiting factor.

Similarly, program maintenance and development costs are likely to be approximately equal to hardware costs. Thus, if parallelism can reduce hardware costs by a factor of ten at present and by significantly more in the future, increases in cost for parallel programming difficulties do not appear to be a limiting factor.

Programmability

Programmability of parallel computers is their major current limitation and the major scientific question on the horizon concerning their use. Why do we believe that the programmability problem can be overcome? First of all, progress which has occurred so far provides justification for optimism (see figure 3). Second, the intrinsic nature of the problem leads to the scientific judgment that the problem is solvable.

Important components of the problem—such as linear algebra packages and differential equation solvers—have been parallelized. A few application problems have been solved, including certain aspects of global climate modeling, aerodynamic simulation, and petroleum reservoir modeling.

There are two classes of solutions to the programmability problem. Either the programmer works harder or the machine designer works harder. Either the programmer is innovative and manages to use a machine which designers can build, or the designer is innovative and manages to build a machine which the programmer can use. No doubt both programmers and designers will be innovative. We discuss the solutions to the programmability problem primarily from the programmer's perspective.

The difficulties are communication, memory management, synchronization, and load balancing. The communication problem has two aspects. The first is the need to have the right data at the right place (that is, the processor where it is needed) at the right time. This is required for successful memory management—the process of specifying where each bit of data is located, and where it is to be moved. Memory management is partly a programming complexity issue. In this sense it is an irritation, and, ultimately, an economic cost to be borne. It will be solved only if there is a strong motivation, as is provided by the faster and cheaper hardware. The second aspect of communication is the efficiency with which data is moved from one processor to another.

Some segments of a computation can be performed in any order. Others must, due to logical necessity, be performed only after some other operation takes place. For example, the addition of two numbers cannot take place until each has been read from memory. The sum of the two numbers must be obtained before it can be recorded. We use the term *synchronization* for the process of placing computations in their correct order, to the extent that this is necessary. It is desirable to have long blocks of instructions for which synchronization is not important. Such questions either did not arise for serial machines or were dealt with by a compiler. A compiler translates human-generated computer instructions, written at a high level, into a very detailed and specific set of computer instructions. In other words, it is the part of the process of generating computer instructions which is totally automatic and solved by the computer itself without the intervention of the user.

The hardware advantages of parallelism (cost and speed) must be sufficient to overcome the software disadvantages. Many different programmability issues must be dealt with when designing software for parallel machines. These programming difficulties raise questions of scientific principle; they provide the basis for the statement that parallel computation will require a large-scale effort to discover new computational algorithms. There have been several proposals to deal with these problems. The proposals are very general and the difficulty is either to apply them to special cases, or to figure out what to do when they do not apply.

Two approaches to solving the communication problem are *decomposition* and *scheduling*. In the decomposition strategy, the problem is broken down into a large number of small, relatively isolated subtasks, with little intercommunication. For example, the task might be to solve a partial differential equation in a given region of space. The communication would then take place across the boundaries of the subregions. The number of processors equals the number of tasks. The programmer assigns a task to each processor, which stores its own data and communicates boundary information. When using the scheduling strategy, the number of tasks should be much larger than the number of processors. Each processor selects a task from the queue. In this case, the entire data of the task must be communicated.

Communication costs, measured in units of time—clock cycles, for example—specify the delay to move data from one location (on one

SPEED (MFLOPS)

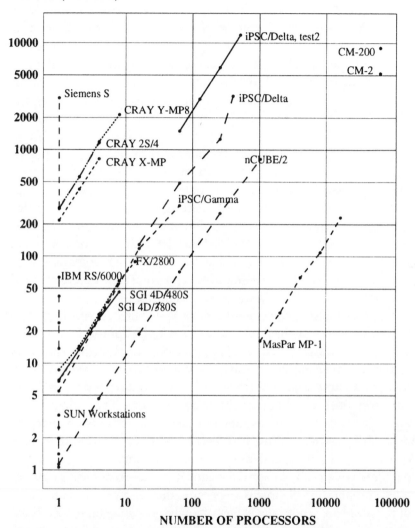

NUMBER OF PROCESSORS

Figure 3. Tests of parallel computers show an increase in speed approximately proportional to the number of processors. The tests shown here are based on the parallel machine benchmark called SLALOM. Three types of single-processor machines—IBM, Siemens, and SUN—are included for comparison.

processor) to a new location (on another processor). These costs are minimized in a problem-dependent fashion. In the case of decomposition, one picks tasks which are relatively independent. The data and communications required for a given task must be large in proportion to the interdependencies, for which intertask communication is required. In the case of scheduling, one wants all data for a given task located in one or a small number of processor memories. In both cases, one should be able to proceed from the beginning to the end of a task without additional outside data (or with very few data communication steps). The total amount of data to be communicated is less critical than the number of individual communication steps needed, or the degree to which it is dispersed over many processors and must be assembled. This is true because the main cost of a message is in its set up or initiation; only a smaller part of the cost is due to its length. Presently available commercial parallel computers have very high communication costs. Moreover, there is a start-up cost associated with any communication step, so that short messages are penalized severely; messages must be bundled into large chunks and communicated as a unit. It seems likely that the current high communication costs will be greatly reduced. Improved computer architecture will thus substantially provide the solution to this problem.

There are also problems—such as distributed control, pattern recognition, or visualization—where a parallel approach is intrinsically more natural than a serial approach. Examples where this may be the case arise in the analysis of seismic data, which are characterized by multiple sensors (each sensor is a recording device similar to a microphone) resulting in multiple data streams. The biology of the eye suggests that vision has similar aspects. There are many independent data streams, and the first level of analysis of each data stream is a local operation, and thus is more conveniently considered in parallel than serially. In both cases, the initial levels of analysis are the most computationally intensive because they apply to the entire data of the problem, while later stages of analysis operate on reduced data of much smaller volume. Similar considerations apply to speech processing, for which there is only a single data stream. This stream can be split into pieces. The initial—and most computationally intense—stages of processing will be local and can be done naturally in parallel. As with visualization, the input may consist of overlaid data streams from distinct time steps or regions of space, and the output can be regarded as having multiple data streams, one to each pixel in the display device.

A USER'S PERSPECTIVE ON PARALLEL ARCHITECTURE

The primary options in the design of a parallel computer include the system memory access scheme, instruction concurrency, and the degree of parallel granularity. Shared and distributed memory are the two most conventional memory access schemes. Based on the instruction concurrency, machines are divided into four categories of which multiple instruction multiple data (MIMD) streams and single instruction multiple data (SIMD) streams are the most popular. The fourth category—multiple instruction single data (MISD)—is not relevant to our topic. Single instruction single data (SISD) streams are the type used in traditional serial computers.

Every piece of data input to a computation, as well as the data for intermediate and output steps, must be stored. In a shared memory architecture there is a common memory shared by all processors, and all processors have equal access to it, as long as no space and time collisions occur. In other words, different processors can access one location at different times or different locations at the same time. Shared memory, in this sense, is limited to a small number of processors and does not allow the potential of parallel computing to be fulfilled. Shared memory is very desirable from a user's point of view. The alternative is distributed memory, in which each processor has its own local memory. If one processor needs data from the memory of another, the data must be transmitted in a communication step. Intermediate arrangements, in which memories are shared among clusters of processors, are also possible. Beyond the sharing of memory in hardware, that is, in terms of its physical location in the computer, a further possibility exists for the apparent sharing of data as perceived by the user. This arrangement, called virtual shared memory, means that each processor has an address space for the memory of all (other) processors, and requests or stores data without specifying its processor explicitly. In order for virtual shared memory to succeed, two conditions must hold. The problem and its description by the programmer must make only modest demands for cross-processor memory requests. Also, communication speeds must be rapid, so that high levels of communication optimization are not critical.

There are two ways in which virtual shared memory has been achieved in practice. In the case of the Bolt, Beranek and Newman Butterfly, high-quality communications were part of the design, and the result was higher system cost—about twice the cost of the individual nodes. In other words, communications were, in total, about equal to the processor costs. In the Connection Machine, a large number of relatively slow processors were used, so that communication speed (which must be measured as a ratio with respect to processor speed) was easier to attain. The Intel and nCUBE designs have relatively slow communication (due to their use of faster nodes), with the result that virtual shared memory is not practical to support and the total system cost is very close to the cost of the individual processors. That is, the communication aspect of the system is not apparent in the price. We see at present a three-way trade-off to be made concerning shared memory, namely expensive communications, slow processors, or no support for virtual shared memory.

We next compare SIMD and MIMD architectures. In the single instruction (SIMD) process, synchronization occurs at every clock tick. Each elementary instruction on each processor is identical for each machine cycle. This is the architecture of the Connection Machine and MasPar, while the Intel iPSC families, nCUBE, and BBN Butterfly TC1000/TC2000 computers follow the MIMD choice. One can think of SIMD as a super vector machine. In a vector machine, all registers proceed in lock step and perform the same operation on each clock cycle. The operations in a SIMD machine are fully general and are not limited to simple arithmetic operations such as addition and multiplication.

MIMD is a more flexible approach because it does not require a lock step synchronization of programming instructions at every clock tick. There should ideally be as little synchronization as possible in a MIMD calculation. For example, in a time-dependent or iterative computation, synchronization should occur only once or a small, fixed number of times per time step or iteration. Additional flexibility is the main advantage of MIMD. On this basis it is a serious contender as a replacement for the present generation of general purpose supercomputers. In contrast, SIMD is proposed either as a special purpose processor or as a subunit of a general purpose processor.

The final architectural choice we consider is the degree of parallel granularity, or the numbers and relative strength of the processors employed. The Connection Machine uses fine-grained parallelism with a large number of weak processors, while later models of the iPSC series and the nCUBE family use moderate numbers of relatively powerful processors. In terms of computing power, the two classes of machines are in the same range and are equally cost effective. The fundamental reason for this is that their basic building blocks—PCs or workstations—have a constant cost effectiveness ratio of megaflops per dollar, that is, unit speed per unit cost.

CONCLUSION

The central problem of parallel computing is to produce a (relatively) inexpensive, powerful, and usable machine. This has not yet been fully achieved, but the progress toward this goal is highly encouraging. Even the partial solution presently achieved has considerable significance in its own right. It is the belief of the authors that parallel computing will fulfill its promise—it will result in a dramatic increase in computational power with profound consequences for the conduct of science and the organization of society.

ACKNOWLEDGMENTS

Y. Deng and J. Glimm are supported by the Applied Mathematics Subprogram of the US Department of Energy DE-FG02–90ER25084, the National Science Foundation, grant DMS-89018844, and the ARO, grant DAAL03–89-K-0017, and by the US ARO through the Mathematical Sciences Institute of Cornell University under subcontract to SUNY Stony Brook, ARO contract number DAAL03–91-C-0027. D. H. Sharp is supported by the US Department of Energy and the same ARO center.

ENDNOTES

[1] A *grand challenge* is a fundamental problem in science or engineering with a broad application, whose solution would be enabled by the application of the high-performance computing resources that could become available in the near future.

[2] These figures were accumulated by experience, and have not yet been precisely determined for the newer computers. For more established results, the numbers

were obtained from published sources, based on careful benchmarks and studies. See J. J. Dongarra, "Performance of Various Computers Using Standard Linear Equations Software," *Supercomputing Review* (July 1990): 49–56; J. Gustafson, et al., "SLALOM," *Supercomputing Review* (July 1991): 52–59; and T. H. Dunigan, "Performance of the INTEL iPSC/860 Hypercube," ORNL preprint ORNL/TM-11491, June 1990.

[3] 1 teraflop = 10^{12} (1 trillion) floating-point operations per second; 1 gigaflop = 10^9 (1 billion) floating-point operations per second; 1 megaflop = 10^6 (1 million) floating-point operations per second.

[4] J. von Neumann, "The NORC and Problems in High-Speed Computing" in John von Neumann, *Collected Works*, vol. 5, ed. A. H. Taub (New York: Pergamon, 1963), 238–47.

[5] Ibid.

[6] See Dangarra and Dunigan.

[7] In November 1990 Intel announced the shipment of its Delta System—an advancement of the iPSC/860 with 528 processors and a peak speed of thirty-two gigaflops—to the Concurrent Supercomputing Consortium (CSC).

Brosl Hasslacher

Parallel Billiards and Monster Systems

T HE COMPUTER PLAYS A CONTROVERSIAL ROLE in today's science. In some areas the impact of large-scale computation is so dramatic that it has become indispensable—coequal with analytic methods and experiment. For large areas of science, however, massive computation is stigmatized as a tool of last resort—having the odor of inferior understanding attached to it—as though the researcher was not clever enough to avoid it.

If the new era of parallel computation only serves the art of making large programs run faster, it is unlikely to affect this situation. It will certainly be embraced by current computation specialists. In engineering parallel processing makes possible large simulations and the processing of large amounts of information and is an inevitable evolutionary step in the ability to compute. It will change the technology of the world in unforeseen ways, but it will only capture the attention of research scientists in general if it can be turned into a new and useful instrument of thought for their problems.

Parallel computing will be especially interesting to research scientists if it becomes a powerful tool for dealing with nasty problems: quite complex systems whose behavior and foundations are not deeply understood. By itself, parallel computation cannot do that—one has to place it in a more sophisticated framework, of which being parallel is a natural property but not the sole one.

This informal essay will introduce one such framework, a new family of computational tools called *lattice gas automata* that are naturally parallel. I will make suggestions for the use of these tools by a larger scientific community. These tools may be thought of as new sorts of computational eyes.

Brosl Hasslacher is a Physicist in the Theoretical Division at the Los Alamos National Laboratory.

The standard picture of computation is based on the metaphor of a single number theorist with unlimited memory. Calculating serially, the number theorist has exact instructions on how to proceed, called *algorithms*. These algorithms form a program, which control the course of the computation. Where the computational task is to simulate a physical phenomenon, the program has traditionally been built around a partial differential equation. Over the last several centuries scientists discovered partial differential equations that were able to encode the behavior of many important physical systems. For example, Maxwell's equations describe the behavior of electrical and magnetic systems; the Navier-Stokes equation describes the behavior of fluids.

Although the equations themselves are quite complex, it is known that they can be solved with an extremely simple sequential computing apparatus. This simple device was proposed by Alan Turing in the 1930s and is known today as a Turing machine. His machine is central to the study of problems in the theory of computation. No more powerful computational model has yet been found in the sense that every other computational scheme can be simulated by a Turing machine, so Turing's model is the standard tool for thinking about computation.

We will now describe a completely different computational archetype. It is based on a physicist's way of seeing the world rather than a number theorist's and on methods that physicists have found especially powerful in the study of systems made of many simple locally interacting parts. There are two central concepts. First, algorithms are replaced with the idea of imposing constraints on an otherwise free system. Computation proceeds by the propagation of constraints rather than by the execution of an algorithm. Second, the single agent of computation (the algorithm) is replaced by many independent agents called cellular automata. Each automaton operates freely and independently but within the imposed constraints. Anything can happen that does not violate a small set of rules.

This computational strategy is no more powerful than Turing's model, but it approaches the problem of simulating large and nonlinear systems from a more natural outlook. It is more natural in the sense that nature does not solve partial differential equations to figure out what happens next. Particles of matter collide and interact under the constraints of physical law and successive states of the system emerge from rather simple dynamics.

This approach gains its computational efficiency from the fact that the rules involved are simple and therefore inexpensive to carry out. The complex behavior we are interested in emerges from the way these simple systems evolve on a large scale. I will illustrate such a system with an imaginary and very primitive blind insect. Although it is blind, it has complete control over its own inner world. Because it is blind, it lacks the idea of motion—it has no conception of the continuous and smooth movement that we take as obvious. But because it has an active imagination, it can conjure up its own image of the world and that image will be simpler in structure than we would normally consider reasonable.

Now, by observing only what it imagines, can this primitive insect learn some of the same things about fluids that we do by observing them directly? Its internal image is a large symmetric square grid like a chessboard. On the intersections of this grid it imagines colored dots. Each dot can have one of four colors, depending on the direction it was moving in when it arrived at that intersection, or node. Thus, the color of the light is a memory—it remembers what happened earlier.

Since the insect does not use the idea of continuous motion, all that can happen is dots disappear from a node and reappear at another adjacent node; they appear to hop. But the insect has a magical power; it can reach into this lattice of lights and command that certain properties of hopping apply to every node in its world. These properties are the constraints of the computational system. One constraint is that all the lights hop in parallel. The insect controls hopping in the gas with the ticks of a clock; all the lights hop to another node at the tick. Thus, the world of this insect hops through time as well as space.

The lights live on a grid which we said is square, but does not need to be so. On a square grid there are four different directions from each node and we give the lights four different colors. Now the insect imposes another constraint: barring collisions, every light keeps hopping in the same direction as it was hopping. If, for example, the insect imagines an initial condition of lights all along the bottom of its grid, all lit with an "up" color, then they would hop up the grid, one step per clock tick, and disappear off the top, all at the same time.

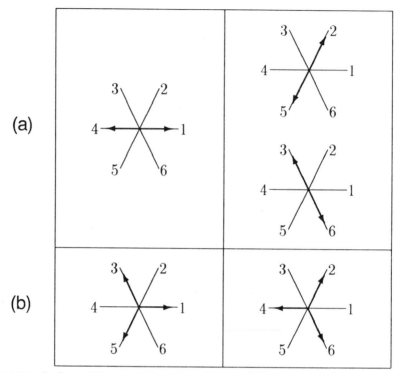

(a) Two bodies collide at a single node and move off along one set of diagonals. (b) Three bodies collide at a single node and move off along corresponding diagonal paths (in the right-hand diagram).

Such a world would be quite boring. To make it more interesting it imagines lights of differing colors (directions) scattered on the lattice at random. In this more complex world, it is inevitable that multiple lights will end up at the same node at the same time step, a situation known as a collision. But the insect imposes another constraint: two lights of the same color cannot land on the same node at the same time step. So, the worst that can ever happen is that four lights hop onto the same node at the same time step.

If two or more lights collide where do they go next? The insect adds a set of *collision rules* that dictate the outcome of each possible collision (see diagram).

The insect now sits back and watches the pattern of lights flickering in its imagination. Is it able to draw correct conclusions about the behavior of real-world fluids? With this arrangement, the answer is no. There is a subtlety: the symmetry of the square grid.

This deceptively irrelevant degree of freedom in the model held up the discovery of the simplest model of ideal fluids for a decade. Looking down on our insect's world, we would say that since it has all the basic conservation laws of the molecular models of fluids it should evolve the collective behavior characteristic of fluids in the large, but it doesn't. It develops correct sound waves, but the square symmetry of the lattice eventually shines through to the macroscopic scale and the resulting descriptive equations have nonlinearities that are not present in fluids. At this point one would say that this world was too simple after all, and the insect cannot connect to the concept of fluids.

However, by looking carefully at the implications to behavior in the large of the symmetry of the underlying world, a model with a hexagonal lattice instead of the square one and with suitably enlarged interaction rules was discovered that repaired all these problems. The new model was intended to be the simplest, totally discrete parallel world that would recover the full dynamics of an ideal fluid over a small range of fluid parameters. Within this parameter range standard tools from statistical mechanics show that such simple dynamics recover the Navier-Stokes equation for an ideal fluid as the equation describing its large-scale behavior.

There should have been no surprise when the usual zoo of complex fluid behavior (instabilities, vortex phenomena, turbulence, and so on) came out of computer simulations of the new model, but scientists were surprised. It seems to be a part of our learned heritage, our prejudices toward the way the world works, to instinctively feel that phenomena as complex as fluid behavior cannot come from such a simple model. But it is exactly in this element of surprise that the potentially great impact of the idea resides. As mentioned in the introduction, parallel computation will only capture the attention of research scientists if it can be made into a new instrument of thought for their problems. Here, clearly, is a new (and controversial) instrument of thought. If it survives the scientific scrutiny that any new idea demands, its impact could be great.

A vivid memory stays with me about the fluid model, and I expect similar events with automaton models in other fields. My colleagues and I stayed up most of one weekend to get our first hexagonal model experiment running on a high-resolution color display and set it up so that, in addition to the underlying lattice gas, it also displayed the velocity flow produced around a simple obstacle. After a thousand time steps, quite clear and beautiful velocity patterns characteristic of flow past a flat plate appeared on the screen. We froze the simulation, left the display on, and went home. The next morning I found a group of physicists, many of them fluid experts, standing in the doorway of my office staring silently at the screen in total shock, disbelief, and awe; my office was quite crowded that day. It is not so easy to shed the conditioning of a lifetime.

Let's return to the insect's world and look at it from the viewpoint of computation. Imagine now that we made a film of the internal world of the blind magical insect—with one frame of the film corresponding to one time step of the insect's imagination—and projected it on a screen. Remember that the insect does not know how to count; it has no concept of number. Can the picture on the screen be the same as what we would call looking at the same phenomenon? Or more to the point, imagine we also had a computer simulate—by algorithm and number representations—some physical phenomenon. Then we took the output of such a machine, converted it to graphics in the standard way, and made a film of it. Could we by any test tell the two movies—one based on the insect's imagination and the other based on an algorithm—apart? The answer is that, for a wide class of physical phenomena, there are rules and grids such that there would be no way of distinguishing between the film from the blind insect and the film from a standard algorithmic machine.

If you are not a physicist, you might say that this can't be. The insect's world is so primitive that not much can happen. The insect isn't "computing" anything. It has no notion of algorithm or computation. It has no concept of number. The only outcome of this setup is a mass of blinking colored lights, which is not a very faithful view of the world. But we have shown how the idea of algorithm is not needed and that this hypersimple insect does, for many systems, evolve all the phenomena we would describe by more traditional means. This insect sees.

Those who are familiar with some physics will recognize that the insect's world is statistical mechanics in an especially stark form, operating in a highly constrained world where every variable is discrete and interactions are local. This is what I meant by a physicist's eyes. Computation is done by constraints rather than algorithms. Phenomena normally described by certain partial differential equations emerge from the gas as large pieces behaving as a unit, which we call *collective modes*. This means roughly that we can assign descriptive variables to large sections of the gas as though they were not made up of many individual pieces; these have new dynamics along large length and time scales.

Statistical mechanics is not a simple idea. It took a considerable part of the last century for physicists to accept it as a valid description of the world; many phenomena must happen in concert if a statistical mechanical picture of the world is going to work. The elegant part is that the necessary and sufficient conditions for this to happen are very few. The insect was designed to have them all. Notice that I never mentioned probability, for the insect's world is also alarmingly deterministic and reversible. This insect is truly remarkable—it is the computational counterpart to the physical Maxwell's demon. But the insect demon can not only separate hot from cold, it can also simulate very complex systems in a naturally parallel and local way. Its world is called a *lattice gas automaton*.

Now you might say that the description I have given is just a series of mental pictures rather than formal mathematical relations. Underlying the pictures is an extensive mathematical formalism, which the pictures were designed to encode. The step from the pictures to formal description is a small one. Most of us can imagine pictures, but the mathematics and physics behind them are equipment I do not assume many readers will have. The descriptions of the lattice gas automaton that I gave are not whimsical. Lattice gases were discovered using just such images. But now I point out that the original problem need not have been physics; it could have come from economics or cell biology or many other disciplines. I chose physics for the insect example because here I am dealing with the idea of a fluid and all the phenomena that can happen in a fluid—the statistical mechanics of a fluid can be made very simple. Later in this article we will see that the insect's images define the architecture of a new and powerful family of massively parallel machines, requiring only electronic glue to realize. They also give us new viewpoints on systems made of many simple elements interacting in a local way. For many complex systems, these hyperdiscrete worlds are new tools of thought.

In a sense we have been describing a contrast between two different ways of producing a movie on a screen. One method starts with partial differential equations and produces, typically through the medium of a sequential computer, a series of movie frames. The other starts with a lattice and a simple set of collision rules and produces, typically through the medium of a parallel computer, the same series of movie frames. Are they really the same? The answer to this question, case by case, is a necessary step in the validation process of any new algorithm. This process has just begun within the scientific community, but for certain specific cases it is true. How can this be, and, even if it is true, why would one prefer the latter? After all, the sequential method starts with the solidity of the partial differential equation. The lattice method starts with absurdly simple—and perhaps inadequate—collision rules.

The answer to this question requires a closer look at the two actual processes. The traditional process indeed starts with a partial differential equation that basically encodes simple conservation laws in an elegant and compact form; one can write such a description in a few lines. Unfortunately, if the system is highly nonlinear, one can spend a long time finding approximate solutions to it, and the analytic tools that were designed for linear systems are most likely going to fail. Nonlinear systems are very complicated and our ability to extract analytic information from them beyond one space dimension is quite limited. The evolution of such systems appears as a stack of disjointed pictures, good in various regimes of some tunable parameter. But the analytic pictures do not fit together too well at the edges and the pictures are incomplete. So one resorts to simulating the equations on an algorithm-based computer—parallel or not does not matter.

What happens now is an inelegant disassembly of our beautiful and compact, continuous and smooth description of the system through the partial differential equation. First, the equation under study must be put into discrete form because a computer only recognizes bit streams. This means making an arbitrary web-like description of the system, using straight lines and points, finite difference schemes, and so on. These grids are designed to approach continuity and smoothness when the number of approximating elements gets large. Next, we put all this in an algorithmic form written in some high-level language. Inside the computer, high-level languages are converted by translation automata, called compilers, into machine instructions. These are switches that control the dynamic wiring path through the hardware of the machine, which only manipulates binary bits. Here lies the paradox. By the time the algorithm has been reduced (inside the computer) to a form that can be worked on, the original idea of number has been taken away. What is left is, in fact, a gas of zeros and ones.

The internal machine representation of our problem is even further complicated by the arbitrary architecture of real machines. These machines have components and interconnections which are basically fixed by current electronics technology, constraints on the economics of construction, and a designer's idea of the class of problems for which the machine will mostly compute.

In short, the inputs and outputs of this methodology, namely the partial differential equation and the movie coming out, are elegant and attractive, but the process in between—the process that actually happens inside the computer—is a tangle whose relationship to those inputs and outputs has been stretched severely to get it to work. Constraints on the construction of algorithmic machines in effect induce an arbitrary bit gas representation of our problem in the machine. The process starts out as elegant but elegance disappears very quickly.

The reason is that the whole procedure comes down on the problem from above, starting from a continuum description and encoding it using algorithmic methods. It is not evolving the solution to the original equation by using collective modes in this peculiar gas. It is executing an algorithmic description of a rather arbitrary discretization procedure. From the viewpoint of statistical physics, we have built an inefficient gas of lights (zeros and ones) that is simulating the problem in a unnatural space—the space of the algorithmic number theorist who has no interest in how the world operates at the microscale.

The automata method has the opposite characteristics. It starts out as a rough world but the process inside the computer refines it into elegance. The simple blind insect builds up a skeletal microworld from below. With such simple tools it cannot hope to simulate phenomena directly, but it also knows that it does not need to do so. It constructs the simplest possible discrete light gas with deterministic local interaction rules for lights hopping on the hexagonal grid. Statistical mechanics guarantees that, for certain grids and rules, the solution to the partial differential equations of a fluid will emerge in short order as collective modes in the gas. The gas will also generate them without the error inevitably connected with the representation of number in any machine, because the lights are exactly conserved and treated equally. So, this gas description is also exactly reversible.

Remember that the insect's world does not include the concept of number. The idea of number in the setup of the gas is an artificial external concept, just as numbers do not come naturally out of a flowing stream—measurements must be made to extract them. One must take an image of the insect's world and postprocess it—essentially performing experiments on it, such as averaging over regions of the gas to get numerical velocity and vorticity fields. The more accurate the number required, the larger the averaging region and density of lights needed. It is clear that numbers generated from such a world are expensive; extracting numbers consumes large amounts of external computational resources. It has been done for fluids and related transport models, but if one wants very high accuracy it is better to forget about the insect's world and use more conventional techniques.

EXPLORING MONSTER SYSTEMS

It is inevitable that the constraint-based approach has been applied first to applications—such as fluids simulation—that have already been addressed using existing methods. New techniques are invariably applied first to older, well-understood problems. But the real future of the methodology lies in applications where traditional methods have not been successful at all: phenomena for which no fundamental partial differential equations have been discovered, only patchwork descriptions. Many of these exist in disciplines now considered soft sciences. I have in mind large-scale economic models, sociological schemes, molecular cell dynamics, and the like.

In these systems complexity is usually both emergent and Byzantine. This means that organized extended structures evolve and dominate a system, and the structures themselves are so complex that, when first seen, they produce a sense of beauty followed by a deep feeling of unease. One instinctively realizes that the analytic tools that worked so well in the past are going to be of little use. We will call such large nonlinear systems with emergent and Byzantine behavior *monster systems*.

The typical future applications for lattice gas/cellular automaton formalisms and machines will be in the search for workable models of important systems for which no such models are currently known. Their role in the standard engineering disciplines as described in the above section on fluids will remain, in my view, rather special, because these disciplines already have workable algorithmic models.

The strength of the lattice gas/cellular automata methods is that they do show the qualitative behavior of complex systems with astonishing fidelity and so are natural for studying monster systems. In particular, they can aid the search for useful models. Many different sets of natural constraints can be chosen and simply tried out to see if they generate the behavior being sought.

The nice feature of this approach is that, in most cases, complex emergent structures depend only on a very few features of the underlying microscopic world. One can reduce the number of variables in a problem enormously. This is already a large step toward testing hypotheses and finding which are the fundamental concepts for a problem. Short of divine inspiration, which is a scarce event, this is the next most powerful tool. I believe these tools are sufficiently developed that they should find wide use in research areas that are presently filled with intractable models whose bases are quite subjective. Here, for the first time, we have tools that can usefully guide thinking about monsters.

Not everyone likes this view of how to explore conceptual space. It is too far from logical deduction and the so-called scientific method. Pattern has replaced number as a prime concept and this makes some uneasy. But when faced with a monster system— especially in a field where experiments are impractical and the data you do have are accidental, as in economics or sociology—one is in a very delicate regime; any active research scientist will recognize that immediately. The crucial part of the work is to find rich questions to ask, the right concepts that form the key to the lock. One can create a range of possible worlds inside a machine to test hypotheses. This does not mean exhaustive search, but rather informed hunting. Using such parallel strategies, especially with the coming of astronomically fast parallel machines, one can evolve a virtual universe quickly. This is a totally new tool, and it would be foolish not to use it as a new set of computational eyes.

CELLULAR AUTOMATA MACHINES AND QUANTUM NANODEVICES

Clearly, among the problems defined above as "monsters" there are many that are important to society. There is a real need to be able to simulate economies in the same way that we simulate fluids today. There is a real possibility that the combination of these new constraint-based approaches and parallel computers will be able to make meaningful progress in these notoriously thorny fields.

There is also the possibility that today's computers, even parallel ones, will not be powerful enough to do the job. However, this possibility is actually a reason to pursue these new methods even more aggressively; it may be practical to build constraint-based computing systems inordinately more powerful than anything we have today. Constraint-based computing fits very naturally inside a computer. It is hard to discover the right constraints, but once one does, it is easy to glue together the electronics to carry them out.

In contrast, when one thinks about the very large-scale integrated circuit chips that are used today to build conventional computers, an alarming thought occurs. These devices, for all their apparent compactness, are using not single or few electrons to process information but electron gases moving in a statistical way through wires. Their fundamental storage and computing elements operate by statistical mechanics—that is, using large ensembles of electrons. Compared to the atomic scale, the switches and wires on these chips are huge. And yet, the economics of the semiconductor industry demands that the density of active devices on a chip increase at a high rate if the industry is to survive. Everything on a chip must get smaller, both the devices and the wires connecting them. To the device physicist, this is called the *downscaling problem,* and it is forcing researchers to think about new ways to compute with devices on the scale of about a hundred nanometers and below—nanodevices. In the simplest terms, present architectures imply large separations between devices—this means long wires. Paradoxically, wires cannot be shrunk at the same rate as devices. But, potentially, the whole problem of long wires can be bypassed if the computer is used to carry out lattice gas/cellular automata computations instead of traditional algorithmic ones. This is because the efficient operation of cellular automata uses interactions with nearby devices rather than being isolated from them.

One can imagine using the natural embedding of lattice gas automata into the quantum domain to build compact and astronomically fast lattice gas automata simulators. The resulting nanochips would be resistant to disturbance by noise and could heal themselves around defects. There would be no hard-wired path for signals; the computation would be done by a gas. As device physics learns to control structures near atomic scales, as we are already doing with scanning tunneling manipulators, we can eventually grow atomic computers, a possibility first seriously analyzed by Richard Feynman in the 1950s in a paper which now seems uncannily prophetic.

SUMMARY

The parallel computing age inherits a body of algorithms from the sequential computing age of the past fifty years. These algorithms, largely based on partial differential equations, are in active computational use in many engineering disciplines. These users are now shifting to parallel machines in numbers sufficient to ensure the success of parallel computing.

But, as I have attempted to show in this paper, parallel computers have the potential to do much more than that. To be specific, they have the ability to bring a new form of constraint-based computing methods to the fore. These in turn have the potential to bring the benefits of accurate computer simulation to the class of monster systems where traditional methods have not been successful. These approaches have the potential to stimulate a new form of computer hardware, incomparably more compact and powerful than anything available today. If so, they will capture the attention of research scientists outside the present domain of computation. They will do so by indeed becoming a new instrument of thought.

James Bailey

First We Reshape Our Computers, Then Our Computers Reshape Us: The Broader Intellectual Impact of Parallelism

TODAY WE MARVEL AT THE INGENUITY OF ENGINEERS who, in the 1930s and 1940s, created a new and seemingly unprecedented wonder: the computer. In the decades which followed, new versions of these computers have become ever faster and less expensive. Amidst the marveling, however, we often overlook a curious point; the fact that it took no time at all for these supposedly unprecedented marvels to be filled up with useful work. Immediately as the first electronic computers were put together, trusted algorithms were waiting to be fed into them. It was almost as if computers had existed and been used all along.

They had, and they were, although prior to 1940 all computers were people. A creative partnership between scientist and computer had already existed for centuries. The role of these human computers is relevant today precisely because of the ease with which they were annihilated by their electronic substitutes. The first electronic computers of the 1940s succeeded so quickly because they copied the sequential architecture of human computers. In so doing, they inherited all the sequential ways of expressing and formulating science that had developed over twenty-five hundred years, a period in which computers shaped science far more than science shaped computers. In effect, the architects of the 1940s packaged their wonderfully speedy electronic circuits in anthropomorphic forms to meet an existing market. They left essentially unchanged the computational partnership that scientists were, in the words of John von Neumann, "uniformly used to since the days of Gauss."

James Bailey is Director of Marketing at Thinking Machines Corporation.

It is only today, for the first time in history, that we are genuinely *reshaping* our computers. We are making them parallel. A parallel computer operates on thousands of pieces of data at once and can keep track of extremely complex interactions among them all. Parallel computers are organized much more directly around what electronic circuits are good at than they are around what people are good at. As such, they are adept at carrying out computations that no human computer in their right mind would ever attempt.

Viewed in this light, the stakes are wonderfully high this time around. Parallel computers threaten to reshape thinking that has gone unchallenged since the time of Newton, Descartes, and even Aristotle. What shape will this new thinking take? The first step in answering this question is to become more familiar with the old world of sequential computing, and to see what is now open to change. The second step is to look at some new forms of computation, ones that are just emerging today. With their emphasis on "changing all of the data all the time" these algorithms are very different from anything that has come before. It is a very exciting time. As we finish reshaping our computers, they are already beginning to reshape us. Since the influence of computation on thought is considerable, anyone interested in the overall history of ideas should be paying attention to computing right now.

COMPUTER SCIENCE AS ARCHAEOLOGY

Looking back into the human computing era is not easy. The formal field of study called *computer science* and its vocabulary originated in the 1950s when the human computer era was on its way to oblivion. As a result, no sixteenth-century text describes computers as "having about seven scratch pad registers" or a book of sines and cosines as "storing a little over a megabyte." In fact, sixteenth-century texts rarely mention computers at all. Computers found no audience for their memoirs; they are not buried in Westminster Abbey. When they pretended to the status of scientists or mathematicians, they were rudely put down. As John Napier's biographer notes scornfully, "Many a man passes for a great mathematician [just] because he is a huge computer."[1] The partnership between science and computation was real, but it was not a partnership of equals. Then, as now, a computer was something a scientist wanted to employ, not be.

In this sense, an Elizabethan computer is analogous to an Elizabethan actor: individually obscure but collectively very influential on what a play could or could not be. Only occasionally does a Shakespeare stop to note that he was writing his plays so as to be performed by human actors—but he was. And his success was absolutely dependent on writing plays that took into account the strengths and weaknesses of these actors. We can see the tradeoffs at work whenever a playwright strains against them, as in the use of soliloquy or deus ex machina, or even the use of a professional gymnast in a contemporary production of *Peter Pan*. Consider the analogous dilemma of the Renaissance scientist:

> His [Flamsted, the Royal Astronomer at the time of Newton] salary was only £100 a year, and he was allowed nothing from Government, either to provide or repair instruments, or to pay the expenses of a computer for reducing his observations. He was, therefore, obliged to purchase, or to construct with his own hands, the instruments which he used, and to pay the expenses of a servant capable of making the calculations which he required.[2]

What kind of science would he choose to do, knowing that the ensuing computations would have to be carried out by himself, or someone just like himself architecturally? What kind of algorithmic mind-set would he bring to his job? And what fruitful avenues of scientific investigation would he never pursue at all, for want of the appropriate computational resource? In short, how much would his computer shape him?

Both sides of the scientist-computer partnership offer clues to the answer. On the computer's side, there are a few rare cases where one actually wrote about his craft.[3] Also helpful are the cases where scientists explicitly reflected on their computational resource. From these sources emerges a model of what a human computer actually was. On the scientist's side, there are the main currents of the science itself, and whether they closely and explicitly mirror the strengths and weaknesses of those computers. A final source of insight is provided by cases where scientists proposed algorithms incomputable by humans. Did good ideas get lost simply because they were not sequential?

FOR THE "RELIEF OF MEMORY"

Given the comparative speediness of today's computers, it is natural to assume that computation rate was the controlling architectural issue in the human computing era. Such was not necessarily the case. Memory architecture was the most-noted frustration. For example, Pierre Duhem, writing at the turn of the century, comments on the way human memory weakness affects the expression of science. "He [the physicist] will choose a certain formula because it is simpler than the others; the weakness of our minds constrains us to attach great importance to considerations of this sort."[4] Formulae are programs. A memorable formula is in fact preferable to an efficient one. A computer that reckons slowly will still get the answer eventually, but a computer that forgets its program is doomed. John Napier is just one example of those who put Duhem's premise into action.

> Those versant in spherical trigonometry know that sixteen cases in spherical rectangular triangles may be proposed, and of these there are ten or twelve so difficult that authors who have written on the subject have been oblidged [*sic*] to construct a table to consult for the relief of memory; Napier's rule reduces all these cases to a single rule, composed of two parts, whose elegant form is particularly apt to impress itself profoundly on the memory.[5]

The memory being referred to by both Duhem and Napier is long-term, or program memory. It has been realized for at least a hundred years that computing involves two kinds of memory. The second, which registers intermediate results, is even more limited.

> As regards the second direction in which memory is active, it may be noted that, according to Bidder, the key to mental calculation lies in registering only one fact at a time, the strain in calculation being due to this work of registration. Thus, in a complex multiplication he goes through a series of operations, the last result in each operation being alone registered by the memory, all the previous results being consecutively obliterated until a total product is obtained.[6]

None of this is true any more. Current computer memories are both capacious and cheap. If an algorithm is twice as bulky but gets the answer twice as fast, that is a wonderfully good trade-off. The essential characteristic of a parallel computer is that it keeps thousands of intermediate results active at once. So the approaches of Duhem, Napier, and Bidder no longer have computational advantage. In particular, algorithms that operate on all the data values at once are now very plausible.

Aristotle, in his analysis of human memory, focuses on an aspect of memory architecture that goes even deeper. Using the term *change* to refer to a piece of data stored in memory, he observes that human memory is designed to read out data sequentially, not randomly.

> And thus whenever someone wishes to recollect, he will do the following. He will seek to get a starting-point for a change after which will be the change in question. And this is why recollections occur quickest and best from a starting point. For as the things are related to each other in succession, so also are the changes. And whatever has some order, as things in mathematics do, is easily remembered. Other things are remembered badly and with difficulty.[7]

Indeed. How awkward it would have been if human memory architecture were *not* aligned with the structure of scientific and mathematical algorithms. But Aristotle's observation raises a far more unsettling question. Why exactly is it that mathematics "has some order?" How much of the reason is independent of the historical accident that mathematics was invented at a time when all the computers available to carry it out were sequential? Perhaps whole new forms of reckoning exist, forms that only make sense in parallel. If they do, and our reshaped parallel computers lead us to discover them, will we even call them *mathematics?*

PRESUPPOSING AN ORDER AMONG OBJECTS WHICH DO NOT FOLLOW ONE ANOTHER NATURALLY

The assertion that mathematics "has some order" embeds a telling ambiguity. *Order* is as much a synonym for comprehensibility as it is for sequentiality. Putting information *in order* implies making an improvement to it, not just a rearrangement. In his *Discourse On Method,* René Descartes elevates this sequentialism to be one of his four laws of correct thinking:

> Conducting one's thoughts in order, by beginning with the simplest objects, easiest to know, in order to rise gradually, step by step, so to

speak, to the knowledge of the more composite ones, and even presupposing an order among those objects which do not follow one another naturally.[8]

The interaction between thought pattern and world view could not be clearer. Descartes felt that his own mental processes were more efficient when he put them into order. So, he did. But then, and this is the decisive step—or misstep—he goes on to *impose* the notion of sequentiality on objects in the physical world, whether they are inherently sequential or not. Aristotle introduces the same potential distortion when he suggests that "we think of the stars as mere bodies and as units with a serial order indeed but entirely inanimate."[9] In both cases, of course, the imposition of sequentiality made good practical sense. It allowed scientific investigation to get started. As Kuhn notes, "Seen on a clear night, the skies speak first to the poetic, not to the scientific imagination," and that "systematic study requires the ability to select stars for repeated study wherever in the heavens they appear."[10] Without ordering, there is no opportunity for selection, or even for enumeration.

One way to achieve order is to limit one's scientific focus to phenomena which already exhibit it intrinsically. Newton's celestial mechanics, the most celebrated science of the human computing era, is a prime example. The movement of a planet through space is inherently sequential. In Newton's case, it is known that he kept the limitations of human computers explicitly in mind. As de Gemaches noted in 1740, "His work did not bear on any subjects except those that could be treated by means of the calculations he knew how to make."[11]

Planetary orbits were among the grand challenges of seventeenth-century computation. It is also the case that these methods had major impact on the design of the first electronic computers in the 1940s. A planet's position at any moment in time is integrated from its previous position and momentum. Because a planet has only one position, the equations of its motion around the sun keep only a few intermediate results active at each step in the computation. The formulae themselves are brief and easily impressed upon the memory. Generations of computers found both their training and their careers in these computations and the related ones of navigation. Newton's laws and human computers were made for each other, perhaps literally.

It was via the science of ballistics that Newton's work came to impact the design of the electronic computers in the 1940s. Ballistics, like celestial mechanics, epitomizes sequential computing. The goal is to compute the trajectory of an artillery shell, given its initial velocity. Many of the great minds of western science, including Galileo, Lagrange, Laplace, and Euler, worked on the subject; it has always enjoyed lavish government funding. Significant progress was made in the twentieth century when astronomical techniques were employed. As Bliss notes, "The method adopted in this country [America] was one of approximate numerical integration which was remodeled for ballistics from earlier uses in astronomy by Professor F. R. Moulton and his associates."[12] The methods of Moulton provide a charming glimpse of what computing was like sixty years ago.

> The first few steps in the computation of a trajectory should be made with relatively short time intervals, since there are so few differences to guide the estimates at that stage. The sizes of the intervals should be adjusted at all stages so that improved values of the variables are not too far from estimated ones. A typical example is a trajectory which has been used as a model by Jackson. The computation has intervals of 1/4 second each from $t = 0$ to $t = 1$, 1/2 second each from $t = 1$ to $t = 2$, 1 second each from $t = 2$ to $t = 12$, and 2 seconds each from $t = 12$ to $t = 48$. The time of flight is very close to 48 seconds. . . .
>
> A novice at computing will possibly find the computation of a trajectory confusing at first. But it is interesting to see how rapidly the work proceeds after some practice, and especially when two or three computers collaborate in using the tables or a computing machine, and in recording the results.[13]

It is important to underscore the practical nature of ballistics calculations. These are not abstract descriptions of theoretical calculations. Ballistics computations were actually carried out and carried out in volume. For example, America's Aberdeen Ballistics Research Laboratory employed almost two hundred computers during World War II. They computed the range tables without which artillery officers could not level their guns. The same point applies to celestial mechanics. Planetary orbit computations were actually performed, to the point where the existence of Neptune was worked out computationally before it was seen telescopically. Thus the authority of the field of mechanics was doubly established: first by the reputation of its scientists all the way back to Newton, and second by the practical success of its computational algorithms. The artillery shells landed and the eclipses happened where the computers said they would.

BUT IMAGINE . . .

Obviously, celestial mechanics and ballistics both align strongly with Descartes's desire to "conduct one's thoughts in order." The computations involved are an ideal fit to the strengths and weaknesses of human computers. The programs are short and easy to remember, and the number of active data elements remains small throughout the computation. The tightness of the fit can be seen even more clearly when it is contrasted to some examples of science that did *not* follow the sequentialist mold.

Galileo's *Two New Sciences,* published in the same decade as the *Discourse,* provides a counterpoint to Descartes's sequentialist prescription. Written in the form of a dialogue, it deals with both principles of motion and also the resistance of solid bodies to fracture. Most of it is given over to theorems of a geometric form. There is a particularly clever theorem among the proofs about the relationship in time of two balls descending different inclined planes.[14]

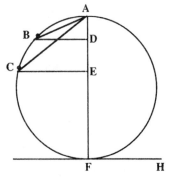

THEOREM 6.6. *If from the highest or lowest point in a vertical circle there be drawn any inclined planes meeting the circumference the times of descent along these chords are equal to each other.*

At this point in the dialogue, the speaker asks, apologetically, for his companion to "Please allow me to interrupt the lecture for a moment in order that I may clear up an idea which just occurs to me." He then goes on to imagine (but not prove) the parallel implications of Theorem 6.6.[15]

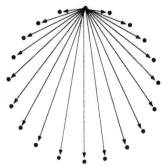

But imagine a vertical plane from the highest point of which are drawn lines inclined at every angle and extending indefinitely; imagine also that heavy particles descend along these lines with a naturally accelerated motion and each with a speed appropriate to the inclination of its line.If these moving particles are always visible, what will be the locus of their position at any instant?

The answer, of course, is an ever-expanding circle, the same shape that is obtained by sending the balls outward from a central point. But this answer is a *parallel* answer, not a sequential one. It depends upon all of the objects being changed at once. If one rolls, or computes, the balls sequentially, "in order," the circular shape never emerges at all. The answer is also an inherently *visual* answer, as Galileo makes clear when he says, "If these moving balls are always visible." No single number can really capture or communicate it. For whatever reason, Galileo does not actually supply pictures. The visual representations above do not appear in the original.

The fruitfulness of this parallel way of thinking becomes patent when Galileo takes it to three dimensions and notes that "an infinite number of spheres are produced about a single point, or rather a single sphere which expands in size without limit." He then concludes:[16]

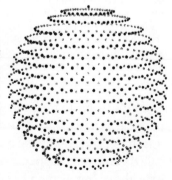

The fact that one can take the origin of motion either at the inmost center or at the very top of the sphere leads one to think that there may be some great mystery hidden in these true and wonderful results, a mystery related to the creation of the universe (which is said to be spherical in shape), and related also to the seat of the first cause [*prima causa*].

This is as far as he sees fit to take it. A very early and very beautiful theory of an expanding universe ("a single sphere which expands in size") and a first cause is left to die undeveloped. There is no attempt to compute rates of expansion or the size of the initial mass or anything along those lines. Galileo's brief foray into cosmology—and parallel science—achieved none of the visibility and influence that Newton's subsequent work on single planet behavior enjoyed.

Joseph Fourier provides a nineteenth-century example of parallel science that is somewhat more sophisticated. His *Analytical Theory of Heat* focuses on the flow of heat in solid objects. Most of the analysis deals with the objects as single blocks and analyzes heat flux between pairs of points in the continuum of matter. But he, like Galileo, pauses at one point for a side excursion into a parallel view of the problem. He notes that the flow of heat through a bar may also be analyzed successfully by breaking the bar into a number of discrete pieces and thinking of heat as being "communicated" between the pieces. He chooses to put these pieces into a ring, because that simplifies the problem.[17]

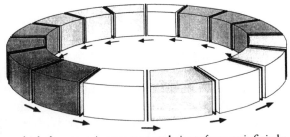

Suppose *n* equal prismatic masses to be placed at equal distances on the circumference of a circle. All these bodies, enjoying perfect conductibility, have known temperatures, different for each of them; they do not permit any part of the heat which they contain to escape at their surface; an infinitely thin layer is separated from the first mass to be united to the second, which is situated towards the right; at the same time a parallel layer is separated from the second mass, carried from left to right, and joined to the third; the same is the case with all the other masses, from each of which an infinitely thin layer is separated at the same instant, and joined to the following mass. Lastly, the same layers return immediately afterwards, and are united to the bodies from which they had been detached.

Fourier's basic methodology is the one still used today to model physical behavior inside a computer. Known as *finite element analysis*, it depends on dicing an object into myriad small discrete pieces, called *elements*. Elements are linked to their neighbors, two in the case above but as many as eight or ten in the complex topologies of modern grids. And each element has a boundary condition, a rule specifying how it interacts with the outside world. Fourier specifies

"Dirichlet conditions," meaning that no heat escapes. Heat only moves between elements, via the communications links.

By substituting a different geometry, this same methodology is appropriate, for example, for predicting whether the nose cone of a space shuttle will burn up on reentry. Heat is applied to the elements that constitute the cone itself. As they heat up, they communicate some of that heat to their cooler neighbor elements further back along the fuselage. These in turn communicate it to their neighbors, or to the air around them. If the heat is dissipated quickly enough, the temperature of the nose elements stabilizes; if not, they burn up. Equations of heat transfer, together with knowledge of the heat dissipation characteristics of the materials involved, determine how much heat moves from element to element at each unit of time.

As with Galileo, Fourier uses parallelism as a critical simplifying assumption: "From each of which an infinitely thin layer is separated *at the same instant.*" But, also like Galileo, he treats the whole enterprise almost as an aside, and goes back to more conventional forms of analysis for the rest of his book. He never translates his parallel science into any form of parallel computation. Lewis Richardson, working in the 1920s, does make such a translation into parallel computation. Compared to Galileo's and Fourier's treatises, his *Weather Prediction by Numerical Process* is obscure, but it was well known to subsequent computer architects, such as von Neumann. In his book, Richardson boldly proposes to predict the global weather by a process of parallel computation. His algorithm was inspired by the fact that the weather stations of Europe could be fitted roughly into a checkerboard pattern. He established a computational equivalent of this checkerboard for which he borrowed the term *lattice* from crystallography. He then developed discrete versions of the fluid flow equations to be applied at each lattice point. His first attempt required six weeks of computing to advance the weather at one lattice point by three hours, but that did not deter him. By optimizing his computing sheets, Richardson brought the time down below a hundred hours, so that thirty-two human computers could keep up the pace at an individual lattice point. He calculated that he would need two thousand lattice points worldwide. With all this in mind, he architected his parallel computer.[18]

Sixty-four thousand computers would be needed to race the weather for the whole globe.... Imagine a large hall like a theatre, except that the circles and galleries go right round through the space usually occupied by the stage. The walls of this chamber are painted to form a map of the globe. The ceiling represents the north polar regions, England is in the gallery, the tropics in the upper circle,  Australia on the dress circle and the Antarctic in the pit. A myriad computers are at work upon the weather of the part of the map where each sits, but each computer attends only to one equation or part of an equation. The work of each region is coordinated by an official of higher rank. Numerous little "night signs" display the instantaneous values so that neighbouring computers can read them. Each number is thus displayed in three adjacent zones so as to maintain communication to North and South on the map. From the floor of the pit a tall pillar rises to half the height of the hall. It carries a large pulpit on its top. In this sits the man in charge of the whole theatre.

WHAT WE WERE "UNIFORMLY USED TO SINCE THE DAYS OF GAUSS"

Although these early examples of parallel science are exhilarating, they were outside the mainstream. So it should come as no surprise that, when the transition to electronic computing occurred in the 1940s, it was the tradition that we associate with Descartes, Newton, and Moulton that held sway. To be more accurate, it was the tradition of generations of anonymous computers which held the sway—it was precisely the carrying out of Moulton's algorithms that motivated the construction of von Neumann computers. H. H. Goldstine, von Neumann's collaborator in systems design both during and after World War II, states:

> The reason why we wish to discuss this recondite and perhaps uninteresting branch of mechanics [that is, ballistics] is because it was to have a vital impact on our subject. We shall see how the ballistical needs of the United States were to be a primary incentive for the development of the modern computer.[19]

As I have said, one of the main functions of the [Aberdeen] Ballistic Research Laboratory was the production of firing and bombing tables and related gun control data. It is worth saying a few words about such tables so that the reader will have some conception of what was being undertaken. The automation of this process was to be the *raison d'être* for the first electronic digital computer.[20]

This linkage cannot be emphasized too strongly. The raison d'être of the first electronic digital computer was the computation of algorithms that had been refined for centuries around the strengths and weaknesses of human computers. Goldstine personally managed Aberdeen's staff of 176 computers, whose job it was to compute range tables. They were not able to do the job quickly enough.

[A] typical firing table required perhaps 2,000–4,000 trajectories— assume 3,000. Thus, for example, the differential analyzer required perhaps 750 hours—30 days to do the trajectory calculations for the table.

The estimates reveal a situation that was unsupportable both because the volume of work was too large and perhaps more importantly, because the work had to be done very promptly to avoid delays in putting weapons into the hands of the troops in the field.[21]

Ballistics computations were not the only calculations being contemplated in that period. Von Neumann was very familiar with Richardson's work, and returned to it in later years. During the war he split his time between Aberdeen and Los Alamos; at Los Alamos he worked on hydrodynamics calculations. In an unpublished paper written during the war, von Neumann and Goldstine list continuum dynamics, classical electrodynamics, and hydrodynamics as other important influences.

But it was ballistics that held people's attention, because ballistics calculations were already being carried out. Von Neumann and Goldstine were *not* inventing the computer. They already knew what a computer was, what a computer did, and how long it took a computer to do it. In fact, they used ballistics trajectory calculations as the standard benchmark of electronic computer performance partly *because* it was so easy to compare to what had come before.

Such a typical problem is the determination of an average ballistic trajectory. A good analyzer will usually require 10 to 20 minutes to handle this to a precision of about five parts in 10,000. Trajectories have been run on the ENIAC and require 0.5 min. for complete solution including printing of needed data.

The computation of a ballistic trajectory considered above is a reasonably typical instance of a simple system of non-linear, total differential equations. As we saw, it involves about 750 multiplications.[22]

A final factor driving the architects to an inherently human computer architecture was the electronic memory technology of the period. The first von Neumann computers used mercury delay lines which could only read out data in a fixed "order," exactly as Aristotle describes the human memory as doing.

When contrasted with the parallel computational approaches of Galileo, Richardson, and Fourier, it is clear how little the von Neumann computers deviated from the uniform human computing tradition stretching back to Gauss and before. Even when they had become standard, von Neumann computers were still being described in anthropomorphic terms.

> And now we come to the concept of a stored program. . . . Suppose you wished to give your assistant a large number of instructions for manual computations all in advance. You could do this by supplying him with a prepared set of instructions, or you could dictate the instructions and have him write them down, perhaps at the top of the same sheet of paper on which he is later to perform the computations. Two different situations are here involved. . . . The second is becoming quite common in the newer machines and is the case usually meant when the term "stored program" is used.[23]

> The third or "high speed" store is quite small and holds only that information needed in the course of a calculation—the sort of thing that a clerk would hold in his head while working out the answer.[24]

THE SKIES SPEAK FIRST TO THE POETIC, NOT THE SCIENTIFIC IMAGINATION

At one level, the difference between the sequential and parallel algorithms is mechanical. Any computation that can be carried out by a parallel computer can also be carried out by a sequential computer—and, in fact, they are. It is one of the great ironies of computational history that the primary use of sequential (von Neumann) supercomputers in the 1980s was to carry out the inherently parallel n-body algorithms of Galileo, the finite element algorithms of Fourier, and the finite difference algorithms of Richardson. Now that parallel processors are available, they are allowing these algorithms to be carried out on much larger, more detailed data sets. For this reason alone, they are likely to become predominant in the marketplace.

But the opportunities for exploiting parallel computation are already moving beyond mere mechanical improvements. Today at least three new threads of development are becoming visible. The first is the shift from presenting results as numbers to presenting results as pictures. Known as *scientific visualization* and already underway in the sequential computing era, this shift is actually implicit in Galileo, Fourier, and Richardson. They all introduce their ideas by saying "Imagine . . . " since imagination was the medium of visual communications most available to them.

The shift to visual forms of answers is both important and inherently tied to parallelism. It is important because the mode in which something is communicated affects the contents of that communication. The influence of communication on the structure of science itself was one of the important contributions of Ernst Mach. It was his view that "the first real beginnings of science appear in society . . . when the necessity for the communication of experience arises."[25] How would a shift from a number-based form of communication to an image-based form of communication affect the content of that communication? The philosopher Suzanne Langer, writing in the 1930s, makes an instructive distinction, one which emphasizes the parallel nature of visual communication. She calls her first type of communication *discursive,* and typifies it by language, although the same points hold for numbers.[26]

But words have a linear, discrete, successive order; they are strung one after another like beads in a rosary; beyond the very limited meanings of inflections, which can indeed be incorporated in the words themselves, we cannot talk in simultaneous bunches of names.

The second she calls *presentational,* which she typifies by pictures.[27]

Visual forms—lines, colors, proportions, etc.—are just as capable of *articulation,* i.e., of complex combination, as words. But the laws that govern this sort of articulation are altogether different from the laws of syntax that govern language. The most radical difference is that *visual forms are not discursive.* They do not present their constituents successively, but simultaneously, so the relations determining a visual structure are grasped in one act of vision. . . . An idea that contains too many minute yet closely related parts, too many relations within relations, cannot be "projected" into discursive form.

In short, there are things one can say in the presentational (parallel) form that simply cannot be said in the discursive (sequential) form: "Too many relations within relations *cannot be projected into discursive form.*" A modern computational fluid dynamicist, studying the flow of air over the wing of a supersonic airplane, would say, "Too many vortices within vortices cannot be comprehended simply from a printout of numbers." Where the relevant science lies in the *relations* among elements, as it did in Galileo's multiple moving objects, words fail, and so do individual numbers.

In Galileo's time, artists communicated one set of truths in the parallel (presentational) mode; scientists communicated a different set of truths in the sequential (discursive) mode. When the skies spoke to the poetic imagination of Galileo, he had no computational place to go with his insights. Today's Galileos do, and that is becoming one of the significant impacts of parallelism. It is no accident that the fields of scientific visualization and parallel processing have emerged in the same decade. They are, in a sense, two sides of the same coin. A number is akin to a single pixel on a computer screen. Its expressive power is limited. Scientific visualization renders whole fields of data onto a computer screen at once, so relations within relations can be "grasped in one act of vision." Parallel processing is the most natural and logical way to generate and manipulate those fields of data.

Numerical algorithms have traditionally had a great advantage: they produce numerical results. But if results are no longer desired in numerical form, then the ability to produce numbers is no longer an advantage. In fact, the first generation of scientific visualization programs is made up of hybrids. The first part of the algorithm computes numerically; at the very end, a "graphics postprocessor" takes the numbers and translates them into the pixels that make up an image.

A radically new form of parallel computation is now growing up around the realization that numbers are not necessarily the best medium for building pictures. These new forms, generally called *lattice gas* or *cellular automata* algorithms, are the second of the three principal new developments. A cellular automata algorithm uses no numbers at all. Instead, it allows millions of simple-minded objects to interact on a playing field akin to a checkerboard. At every step in the computation, all the objects move to an adjacent cell. When two collide, they bounce off. Depending on the rules of movement used, one of a variety of patterns of behavior emerge. These patterns are directly projectable onto a computer screen since the field of objects is directly analogous to a field of pixels. Such algorithms exist, and the first of them are now functioning on parallel computers. They have been used to solve heat flow problems similar to Fourier's and to model fluid behavior. In the latter case they treat a fluid as millions of tiny independent particles each bumping and jostling each other in simple ways. Traditional methods view the same fluid as marching numerically to the beat of the Navier-Stokes equations.

Particle-based fluid simulation methods are quite natural, because a brook is in fact made up of myriad jostling water molecules. They are also an excellent match to what electronic circuits do best. Real numbers are quite ungainly from the point of view of an electronic circuit; blacks and whites, or zeros and ones are much more simpatico with the way an electronic circuit operates. But the method is totally inhuman. Efficient for circuits, it is incomputable by humans, who prefer numbers. Hence it is hard to build up trust on the part of those who work with these systems. Impressionistic forms of validation ("Looks like a fluid. Swirls like a fluid. Must be . . . ") are not satisfying. So these methods are slow to find acceptance. But these methods are coming nevertheless. Some of the most advanced work in this area is described in "Parallel Billiards and Monster Systems" by Brosl Hasslacher in this issue.

The third line of parallel development takes its inspiration from Darwin. If evolution may be thought of as computing a range of selected species, then the computation is clearly a parallel one. A parallel computer can be set up to allow the same kind of evolution to occur. Instead of a single all-knowing program, the computer is given myriad flawed programs called *agents*. Initially, all agents have equal voice in the way the overall computation proceeds. Results are then compared to what the answer should have been. When the computed results are close to the desired one, those agents who helped the most are rewarded with a larger voice next time. They become more dominant while the more feckless agents wither away.

Over time this porridge of competing agents can *improve* its behavior. The pot is continually stirred by mutating agents spontaneously and allowing them to mate. For example, the first half of one agent program might be mated to the last half of another, and a new agent is created. A description of a somewhat similar kind of system may be found in "Complex Adaptive Systems" by John Holland in this issue. The internal mechanics of these systems are complicated, but their potential uses are very straightforward. They hold great promise for modeling the behavior of systems that have defied analysis by traditional numerical techniques. The behavior of an economy is one such example. More radically, these techniques might some day make parallel computers self-programming. Rather than specify a program, the user would specify what they want the computer to do, and it would evolve its way there.[28]

FIRST WE RESHAPE OUR COMPUTERS, THEN OUR COMPUTERS RESHAPE US

Scientific visualization, lattice gas algorithms, and genetic algorithms: all are genuinely new ways of thinking about problem solving and computation. They underscore the difference between the current revolution in computing and the transition that occurred in the 1940s. As mentioned already, there was no delay in using the results that the first electronic computers produced. There was no anxiety about their validity, because the answers could be checked directly. The results from the electronic computer were compared to the results of the same calculation, using the same algorithm, from a human computer. The results of lattice gas and genetic computations enjoy no such cultural preacceptance, but their potential to change the way we think about the world is all the greater for their unorthodoxy. They are clearly a better, more efficient fit to the parallel electronic circuitry itself. Thus, fifty years after the first electronic computers were fabricated, their potential to reshape us may be taking hold at last.

It is not uncommon for the true impact of a new technology to remain veiled for a generation or two. Such was the case with the steam engine.[29] Early steam engines were often relegated to a downstream role by mill owners. Their job was simply to pump water back up into the mill pond after it had passed over the water wheel. It was a role dictated not by what they were inherently good at, but rather by a seasonal bug in the way mill streams work. Only decades later did this age-old culture recognize and reorganize itself around the unique capabilities of the engines themselves. Only then did the Industrial Revolution truly take hold.

The partnership between human scientist and human computer is even more ancient than the partnership between miller and mill stream. It is reasonable to assume that there will be a lag between the time when we reshape our computers and the time when they reshape us. Or maybe it is not reasonable at all. Maybe it only *sounds* reasonable because we are all still trained to believe that orderly, sequential processes (first this happens, then that happens) are more likely to be true. Maybe it will turn out to be more accurate to have said that "As we were reshaping our computers, so simultaneously were they reshaping us."[30] Maybe when things happen in this world, they actually happen in parallel.

ENDNOTES

[1] Mark Napier, *Memoirs of John Napier of Merchiston* (Edinburgh: William Blackwood, 1834), 501.

[2] Sir David Brewster, *Memoirs of the Life, Writings, and Discoveries of Isaac Newton* (Edinburgh: Thomas Constable, 1855), 162.

[3] In early times, computers were males. By World War II, computing had become a predominantly female profession.

[4] Pierre Duhem, *The Aim and Structure of Physical Theory* (New York: Athenaeum, 1962), 171.

[5] Napier, 505.

[6] W. G. Smith, "Notes on the Special Developments of the Computing Ability," in E. M. Harsburgh, *Modern Instruments and Methods of Calculation* (London: G. Bell and Sons, 1915), 63.

[7]Richard Sorabji, *Aristotle on Memory* (Providence: Brown University Press, 1972), 55.

[8]Duhem, 65.

[9]Aristotle, *On the Heavens II*, 11.292a1–19.

[10]T. Kuhn, *The Copernican Revolution* (Cambridge: Harvard University Press, 1957), 87.

[11]Duhem, 49.

[12]Gilbert Bliss, *Mathematics for Exterior Ballistics* (New York: John Wiley and Sons, 1944), 42.

[13]Ibid., 51–52.

[14]G. Galileo, *Dialogues Concerning Two New Sciences* (New York: Macmillan, 1914), 188–89.

[15]Ibid., 192.

[16]Ibid., 193.

[17]J. Fourier, *The Analytical Theory of Heat* (New York: Dover, 1962), 238.

[18]Lewis F. Richardson, *Weather Prediction by Numerical Process* (New York: Dover, 1965), 219. Illustration by Alf Lannerbaeck.

[19]H. H. Goldstine, *The Computer from Pascal to von Neumann* (Princeton: Princeton University Press, 1974), 72.

[20]Ibid., 136.

[21]H. H. Goldstine and J. von Neumann, "On the Principles of Large Scale Computing Machines," in *Collected Works of John von Neumann,* vol. 5 (New York: Pergamon, 1961–1963) 6.

[22]Ibid., 9.

[23]Samual, "Computing Bit by Bit," *Proceedings of the I.R.E.* (October 1953): 127.

[24]J. W. Cox, "Britain's First Municipal Computer," *The New Scientist,* 4 April 1957, 30.

[25]E. Mach, Popular Scientific Lectures, Chicago, Open Court, 1898, 191.

[26]S. Langer, *Philosophy in a New Key* (New York: New American Library, 1951), 76.

[27]Ibid., 86.

[28]M. Browne, "Lively Computer Creation Blurs Definition of Life," *New York Times,* 27 August 1991.

[29]R. J. Forbes, *The Conquest of Nature* (New York: Mentor, 1968), 46.

[30]M. Bailey, personal communication.

Robert Sokolowski

Parallelism in Conscious Experience

P ARALLEL PROCESSING HAS BEEN AN IMPORTANT THEME in computer science, where an architecture based on massively parallel systems has opened up new possibilities for more powerful computation. Parallel processing has also been invoked in the neural sciences, as parallelisms of different sorts have been found to occur in the brain and nervous system. Both these instances of parallel processing, in computers and in neural networks, have only recently been invented or discovered and both depend on advanced scientific knowledge. In my paper I wish to explore a kind of parallelism that is quite familiar to us and that requires very little scientific theory. Its familiarity may allow it to serve as a bridge between our ordinary experience and the more exotic instances of parallel processing found in computers and neural networks. This essay will examine the role of parallelism not in the computing machine but in its user.

I

The parallelism I wish to examine occurs in our normal conscious experience. Our experiencing is always dual. As we are aware of things in our surroundings, we are also always aware of things given in what we commonly call our internal mental imagery. We always live in a blend of perception and imagination. We are aware of the things we see, hear, touch, taste, and smell, but concomitantly we are imaginatively aware of someone's face, a walk down a street, or an absent fragrance, as these things show up in mental space. We could say that we always live in two worlds: the world that surrounds us at

Robert Sokolowski is Professor of Philosophy at The Catholic University of America.

any given moment and the world of our imagination. We could say this, but such a formulation can be misleading, because the imagined world is not coherent and systematic and stable enough to be called a *world* in the strict sense of the term; still, this way of stating it does point us in the right direction. We always live in a double manner, consciously processing what is around us but also processing things and contexts that are not around us. We always exist here and now, but also there and then, elsewhere and elsewhen. We live in experiential parallelism.[1]

Suppose I want to drive to a place to which I have already driven once or twice. I think I know the way but I am not sure. To fix the route in my mind, I imaginatively run through three or four of the crucial turns and moves I must make when I actually begin driving: yes, I exit the highway just after that bridge, later I turn right before the Exxon station and enter that divided road, I will also pass the high school on the right, I turn at the top of that hill. When I organize the drive in my mind, I do not simply recite these words or state these instructions to myself; I imagine myself making these turns and moves and stops. I rehearse these actions mentally. I do so, moreover, while I am seated at home thinking about the trip, surrounded by my desk, sofa, lamps, rugs, and pictures. The crucial turns and moves are lived through, even though I am at home and not driving while I live through them. I live in two dimensions, in two parallel tracks. I displace myself into a time and place different from those I bodily occupy.

The two tracks are very different in their consistency. The perceptual track is steady and stable. The desk remains there continuously and I can continuously look at or feel it. I can concentrate on it and narrow my focus onto particular parts of it. But the internal track is episodic, fleeting, gappy, indistinct, and sudden. Bits and pieces dart by, and it is hard for me to concentrate on aspects of the things that come to mind. I can bring up closer looks (for example, I can imagine the Exxon station from another angle; I can call up the view I had of it when I once bought gas there), but even this sort of focusing is erratic and sudden. Rather than continuously imagining the thing in question, rather than holding it there before me as I can hold a box up to my view, I seem to repeat over and over again various darting views of it. But this scrappy character of my internal rehearsals does not change the fact that my internal experiencing goes on in a dimension different from that of my external activity and experiencing. The fact that my internal "world" is not as steady and distinct as the surrounding world does not do away with the fact that the two domains run parallel to each other. It does not destroy the fact that formally I live in two dimensions.

The internal projection of myself driving my car is only one example of the experiential parallelism I wish to describe. Countless others could be given. When I wish to write a letter, I formulate phrases and sentences internally before I put pen to paper; sometimes I may have the gist of the whole letter composed before I begin to write. If I have gone through a difficult situation, an unpleasant argument, say, with someone else, I keep imaginatively running through what happened, experiencing it over and over, trying to let it settle down and take on some sense for me. The anticipated letter and the remembered argument are, like the projection of my driving, scrappy and episodic, but they do exist in a dimension different from that of my present surrounding world. The letter will be in the future and the argument was in the past, but I live in the letter already and I live in the argument still; they will take place or they have taken place somewhere and somewhen else, but I rehearse or repeat them here and now. It is the two dimensions—one here and now, the other there and then—that are important, not the precise identification of any particular item in them.

Sometimes we become almost totally absorbed in one or other of the two dimensions. Sometimes we become so lost in reverie or anticipation that we practically lose all contact with our surroundings, but the surroundings and our awareness of them still remain there on the margin. Sometimes we are so taken up by the event actually before us that we almost lose our internal life and practically erase any distance between ourselves and what is going on in those "other worlds"; but again the other dimension still remains on the margin. We always oscillate between the two dimensions, and if we were to lose completely either one or the other, we would lose something essential to our human life. Our human life rests on the interplay between the two dimensions.

Sometimes our internal imagining has to do with the future, as we rehearse some activity we intend to undertake (we buy a future on the margin), and sometimes the imagining has to do with the past, as we repeat, perhaps obsessively or perhaps with delight, what we lived through earlier. In still other cases, our imagining may be neither of the future nor of the past but located in no particular time at all, as we daydream about ourselves in some undetermined situation.[2] For the purposes of my paper, these temporal differences are secondary; the duality, the duplication of awareness is the thing I wish to stress, whether it projects us into the future, into the past, or into no particular time at all. The main point is the parallelism between the perceptual and the imagined. Indeed, sometimes we are not sure whether we are anticipating or remembering as we internally run through the action in question; as I rehearse making the turn before the Exxon station, am I simply repeating something I did in the past, or am I anticipating what I will do when I get to that point in the future? It does not matter. The important thing is that I am not just caught up in the things around me, but also alive to something somewhere and sometime else.

II

Straddling the perceptual and the imaginary makes it possible for us to deal with present and absent things, and also to have a more or less explicit awareness of presence and absence as such. The two tracks we live in are not merely psychological; they also have an effect on the way things are given to us. If I meet someone whom I long wanted to meet, he is given to me precisely *as present* in contrast to the many times I only imagined meeting him. If I have lost a friend, my remembered conversations with her—indistinct and fugitive as they may be—present her to me precisely *as absent,* as not there among the other people around me. The presence and the absence of things become highlighted as they are contrasted with one another, and our living in two parallel dimensions is what makes this recognition of presence and absence possible.

Negotiating the difference between presence and absence is of crucial importance for the human condition. It is not just one among many of the things we happen to do. It is central to our personal identity and it establishes both the emotions we undergo and the higher cognitive activities we carry out. What are attachment and loss, if not ways of dealing with presence and absence? What is grief but a response to the irretrievable absence of something good or the fixed presence of something hateful? What is joy but a response to assured presence, and what is anxiety but apprehension about something absent that threatens to become present? Only man of all the animals "is famished even by future hunger,"[3] and he suffers so because of the two dimensions of presence and absence that run parallel in the way he lives.

What sort of agents could we be if we did not enjoy this duplicated life? What sort of thinking and judging could we carry out without it? How could we deliberate about what we should do if we could not project ourselves imaginatively into situations we will have to face? How could we suffer regret if past actions did not reactivate themselves over and over again in our parallel experiencing? Mental disturbances arise when we cannot let the past be truly past or when we cannot be confident that we will remain ourselves and not be destroyed by what will arise in the future. Part of ego strength lies in the assurance that things remain what they are even when we let them go into absence, that letting them go is often the only way to continue "owning" them in a new and more appropriate way. A parent lets a child go at some point in life as the proper way and the only way to remain the parent of that child, to allow the child to remain an offspring in the way in which it should. The identity of the parent and the identity of the child are both preserved and enhanced by this new level of absence and presence. Thus we lead our human life by working through the present and the absent, and the parallelism between them occurs because we live in both the perceptual givenness of presence and the imaged givenness of absence.

We must be more precise about how the internal, imagined dimension occurs. There is a strategic error that we must take pains to avoid. We might be tempted to think that in our imagined awareness, we look at or hear internal images of things; that besides looking at this lamp and that staircase and hearing this music being played, I also turn inward and look at a replica of an Exxon station or hear a copy of the violin sonata I heard in concert last week. But this would be an incorrect description. In imagination we do not simply experience internal pictures. What occurs in imagination is that we experience ourselves doing something (driving the car, walking along the road) and experiencing something (seeing the Exxon station, hearing the sonata). We as agents and as experiencers become duplicated when we imagine. In imagination, we do not see an image of an Exxon station; rather, we imagine ourselves seeing the

Exxon station. We displace ourselves into a different context. In imagination, "I" become dual: I am both the imagining me and the imagined me. In remembrance, there are two of me: the remembering me and the remembered me.

When I imaginatively repeat something I experienced before, I do not only recall the things I saw and heard at the time. I also call back a sketch of my own body as it was a part of that experience then. I call myself back as I was then, experiencing whatever it was that occurred at that time. I do recover the thing that was given then (the Exxon station, the music), but I also recover myself as the one to whom that thing was given then. I relive an earlier part of my life, with the things that were given in it, and I do so here and now. I displace myself and live in parallel. If I am dealing with the future, I anticipate myself in this or that new context, and if I lapse into daydreams, I displace myself into no particular time or place, neither into the future nor into the past. But in all these cases it is not just what is given that runs parallel to my present experience; I run parallel to myself as well.

When I remember or anticipate or project myself in this way, it is always myself that I find. I could never find, to my surprise, someone else showing up in my memory as the one who was driving by the Exxon station, or showing up in my anticipation as the one who had to face my boss tomorrow. It would be an incoherence to think that anyone else could ever surface as the one into whom I could displace myself. In memory, anticipation, and projection I always find myself.

Furthermore, my personal identity is not that which is found simply in the here and now or simply in the there and then; my personal identity is not found in either one of the two parallel dimensions alone. Rather, my personal identity is constituted precisely in straddling the two dimensions of the perceptual and the imaged, the existent and the projected. I here and now and I there and then are two profiles, two perspectives on one and the same "me." "I" am the kind of thing that is built up precisely through the manifold displacements that occur through my life. I am formally the same one always, no matter how young or old I am, no matter where I am. This dual frame of parallel processing is always there, and I awaken into it as the same one again every time I come on the scene. Even my moments of disorientation are moments in which I am trying to find my balance within my form of presence and absence.

The interplay between two dimensions is also visible when we encounter other persons. It is what makes another person have depth. When we meet someone else, we know that they are not just what they are in their immediate bodily presence; the countless memories and anticipations that occur within that body make that person so deeply different from any other. We may perceive this especially when we meet an adult whom we knew, and last met, as a child: I last met Annie when she was six, and here she is now at forty. All those intervening years and everything that happened in them are there "in" her. That particular past, all those possible recollections, in which she will always only find herself as the formal center, are embodied in her. They are the particular blend of presences and absences that make her who she is now and enable her to anticipate her own future; but they also are played off against me as I talk with her and bring my own identity, the recollections and anticipations through which I am woven, into an exchange with hers. We might be able to share some memories, but each of us will always be a surprise to the other, because of the depths that are proper to each of us alone. As John Le Carré has one of his characters say of George Smiley, "I knew he had been distracted by some private memory among the thousands that made up his secret self."[4]

III

Certainly there is a physiological basis for the experienced parallelism that we have been describing. Certainly there is some sort of neural storage of earlier perceptions, and also some sort of retrieval or reentry that allows them to show up again and to be played off against the perceptions we currently have. As far back as the middle of the seventeenth century, Thomas Hobbes spoke of imagination as "decaying sense."[5] He explained it as a motion in the brain that continues after the stimulus that initiated it is removed, and he compared this motion in the brain to the ripples that continue in water after the stone that started them has come to rest. The neural sciences now have much more sophisticated ways of describing the "motions" that occur in the brain and of mapping the areas in which the motions take place, but Hobbes's colorful description still helps us to focus on the issue at hand.

Neural motions are different from simple mechanical motions, such as the ripples in a pond, because they can be reactivated and repeated. To extend the metaphor, it would be as though the pond were able to reenact a particular set of ripples that occurred last Thursday, and also as though a new stone thrown into the water could revive and reactivate the ripples engendered by a similar stone three weeks ago. The pond would have to store its earlier ripples, and by reactivating them it would be able to anticipate future ones. Moreover, the pond would not just have the ripples, whether immediately caused or reactivated. It would also have to present to itself the thrower of the stone, to recognize this thrower as the same or as different from someone who threw another stone the day before. It would also have to identify itself as the same pond that saw both throwers. Ponds do not do this sort of thing, but we do, and when we begin to talk about neural pathways and motions in the brain and nervous system, we must adjust our language appropriately. Neural processes are mechanical events, but they are not merely mechanical events.

What exactly is it that is stored in the brain? We might want to say that a representation is stored there. This is acceptable, but we have to specify what sort of representation it is and what it represents. Suppose I am leaving on a trip. I lock the door of my house, and I do so slowly and deliberately, so that I will not worry later whether or not I locked it. A half hour later, as I am driving away, I remember clearly that I did lock the door; I can reactivate my action and I can visualize the door there and then, I see myself turning the key, and I know that I did this action just as I was leaving home that morning. All this is stored somehow in my neural nodes; but what exactly is stored?

Several distinctions are necessary. First, there is a kind of storage even while I am not recalling the event. The relevant chemical adjustments distributed among the neurons of my nervous system are a kind of representation, but an inactive one. Another kind of representation occurs when the neural nodes are activated and the imaged experience of locking the door darts by. But even here we have to distinguish. It would not be accurate to say that this active recall brings about a copy or a picture of the door and the key. It would not be accurate to say that when I recall the event, I now, in addition to seeing cars and trees and the road, also see an inner picture of a door and a key turning in it. Such a description would not be faithful to the logic of remembering. Instead, what occurs is that I represent the actions and the experience of locking the door. What is represented is "myself turning the key in the door." I do not store the door and key, nor do I store a copy of the door and key, but I do store the earlier experience, which of course requires a visualized door and key as part of itself. My earlier self, and a sketch of my body at that time, are part of what I store, just as much as the visualized door and key. Moreover, I do not only store but also activate this earlier experience. I can activate it as many times as I want, and sometimes it gets activated apart from my wanting. Something I see or hear or smell may just bring it to mind. As time goes on, and if I am in the habit of always taking such care in locking my door, the various instances of doing so blend together and I am left with a generalized "myself locking the door" which is tied to no particular moment, but even then it is a complete experience that is stored, not a picture of a door and key. Even in that generalized, schematic representation, I am there as the one locking the door.

Neural nets thus permit me to relive earlier actions and experiences and to anticipate new ones. Neural nets also permit me to perceive things and to undergo situations in the present. Somehow, these neural networks and their interactions also permit the interplay between present perceptions and memorial or imaginative reactivations, along with the corresponding sense of self-identity that is constituted in this interplay. The mechanics of such neural activities are only beginning to be studied.

Clearly, it takes time for such neural networks to be established, both in the individual and in the species. The nets used for storage, the networks that have to be distributed over many cell groups, have to be formed through repeated experiences. The neural system of an infant, for example, takes time to build up a repertoire in reserve that can be reactivated and played off against incoming stimuli and thus serve as a recognition code or category for what is being perceived. In the case of the simpler animals, the brain and nervous system are less developed and hence allow lesser storage of earlier experience, but they do allow some; the more storage there is, the more sense of self the individuals of that species will have. Greater complexity in the neural system allows greater storage and more intense parallelism. The "visual" neurons and the nervous system of worms, for example, permit an elementary reaction to light and minimal storage, but they do allow some storage and hence some possibility of recognition and learning. Even the simple bacterium has a rudimentary sense of time, being able to discriminate between stimuli that come before and after others.[6] The sense of time is related to a sense of self, so as we move higher up the ladder of neural complexity, we find the possibility of greater parallelism, a more refined sense of time, and an increasing sense of self, until we come to the kind of self-identity and responsibility that is possible for man.

IV

In speaking about the parallelism we experience between perception and imagination, we have so far focused our attention on the "subjective" side of experience: we have described how the parallelism provides dimensions within which our own self-identity is established. But there is an "objective" side to this experience as well, and although we have only touched on it from time to time in our analysis so far, it deserves further exploration. In our experiential parallelism we not only establish our own identity but also bring to light the identity of the objects we encounter. How does this happen? How does experiential parallelism disclose the identity of the objects of experience?

Suppose I see a figurine in a store and take an interest in it. I think about buying it but leave the decision for later. After I leave the store, I think further about the figurine and imagine what it looks like, how it would look in this or that spot in my home, and the like. As we have said, imagining the figurine means imagining myself seeing it again and again. The figurine is imagined in its absence.

Suppose I go back to the store to look at the figurine again. When I see it again, I do not just perceive it; I now recognize it as the same one I saw before. What permits this recognition is the fact that a blend of imagination and perception takes place. The imagined seeing, which can take place when the figurine is absent, can also occur in the company of perception. It fuses with perception. It is this fusion that provides the dimensions within which the identity of the object is presented to me. Without the imagination, without the rerun of my earlier perceptions, the current perception would not allow me to recognize the figurine as the same again; without imagination, everything would be entirely new to me and nothing would be familiar. Thus, the two dimensions of perception and memory not only allow me to achieve self-identification; they also allow me to achieve the identification of objects.

Peter Strawson, drawing on the philosophy of Kant, has well formulated this blending of imagination and perception. He says that when we experience a familiar object, "the past perceptions are *alive* in the present perception. For it would not be just the perception it is but for them."[7] He says that the experience of objects as familiar to us "is, as it were, soaked with or animated by, or infused with . . . the thought of other past or possible perceptions of that same object." He says that "non-actual perceptions are in a sense represented in, alive in, the present perception." Strawson develops these ideas as an interpretation of Kant's remark that "imagination is a necessary ingredient of perception itself."[8]

Strawson also calls on Wittgenstein to describe how imagination works in perceptual recognition. Wittgenstein discusses the experience of *seeing* something *as* this or that: I see someone as my postman, as my barber, as happy, as sad; I see a triangular figure as a sketch of a mountain, as a wedge, as a directional sign pointing to the left. Such *seeing as,* such recognition of aspects, involves a blend of imagination and impression. One of the most vivid examples that Wittgenstein gives is the experience of suddenly recognizing someone as an old friend: "I meet someone whom I have not seen for years; I see him clearly, but fail to know him. Suddenly I know him, *I see the old face in the altered one.*"[9] Seeing the old face is the work of imagination, which blends with the perception of the new face and permits a recognition of identity. As Wittgenstein puts it, "It is as if an image came into contact, and for a time remained in contact, with the visual impression."[10] Sometimes we see an aspect suddenly, but normally the aspect is simply there continuously in the thing we perceive: Strawson distinguishes between cases in which visual experience is "suddenly irradiated" and cases in which it is "more or less steadily soaked" with the interpretation we bring to it.[11]

Such blends of imagination and perception occur on an elementary level of consciousness, even before concepts are formed. An infant who recognizes its mother need not be said to have a concept of its mother; it is enough that the present impression reactivates past experiences that fuse with the impression going on now and allow the object to be identified. When such identification occurs, moreover, the child also builds up its own self-identity; as it fits new things into the experiences it has had in the past, and as it expects things to cohere in the future with what it has had given to it earlier, it also fits itself into what it has been and what it expects to become. The affective aspect of such identification, the sense of things as either reliable and benevolent or erratic and threatening, is of crucial importance in this establishment of the self through time.

The blending of perception and imagination can occur on a preconceptual level, but it also gives rise to linguistic and conceptual possibilities. The presence of imagination in perception allows us to see aspects of the things we encounter, but then it becomes possible for us to find words to name those aspects, and other words to name the things whose aspects they are. This verbal achievement makes it possible for us to control our perceptions to some extent, to make ourselves and others see things in certain ways. We take advantage of the parallelism and the fusion of imagination and perception to slant perceptions as we want them to be taken. The verbal achievement also makes it possible for us to control our imagination to some extent; we become able to use words to call up certain things from the past or from our general stock of images. We do not only remember passively, we also recollect; we do not just undergo upsurges of association, we also use words to name what we want to imagine. When we do this, we also call up ourselves as experiencing those things imaginatively, and we as users of language become even more deeply identified as selves than we were through the more simple, spontaneous parallelisms of imagination and perception alone. We stand out more vividly as speakers who take responsibility for certain claims.

The introduction of language and other symbolic elements greatly increases our ability to deal with absence, and as a consequence it also intensifies what we experience as presence; the present is played off against much more varied kinds of absences than it is for creatures that do not have a linguistic power over absence. But no matter how powerful our linguistic and conceptual control over absence becomes, our whole cognitive life remains based on and draws its life from the parallelism and blending of impression and imagination.

The dependence of higher cognitive activities on the blend of perception and imagination is brought out dramatically in mental illness. Such illness usually involves an inability to integrate one's present self with the self of past experience and future expectation. Whether because of affective trauma or physiological imbalances or both, we now reject what we were before, and also find that we cannot distinguish ourselves sufficiently from it. The past experience is reactivated not as past but as present, people in my present life are made to be the targets of past experiences in their unresolved intensity, and I find I cannot distinguish myself now from myself then. It is insufficient to address such early conflicts in mere words, in purely cognitive exchanges; what is necessary is to reactivate the early conflict in an imaginative replay that truly fuses with a perception and yet distinguishes itself from it; such a synthesis and distinction occurs in transference.[12] Only then, only when imagination and perception become parallel and not fused, do the dimensions of then and now, my present and my past, and "you" and "them" become liberated from the confusion in which they were bound.

The word "consciousness" should be mentioned here.[13] Etymologically, the word stems from the Latin *conscius,* an adjective that means sharing knowledge, especially secret knowledge, with others, or being privy to a crime or plot. The related Latin noun, *conscientia,* also has as its primary meaning the holding of knowledge in common with others; it often means complicity in crime. A derived meaning of both words is that of being inwardly aware of one's own past deeds. Our contemporary sense of "consciousness" has shed the aspect of sharing knowledge with other people; it signifies primarily our private way of knowing or being aware of something. Still, it retains an overtone of shared knowledge, because it implies a kind of awareness of myself, and hence a kind of duality within myself. To be conscious is not just to know something, but to be aware that I am knowing it, to have some distance to myself as I know it. Such a duality and consciousness arises when my impressional self is played off against my imagined self. "Consciousness" means complicity with my past or future self, with my displaced self. Thus, what we call consciousness is possible only because of the parallelism between imagination and perception.

V

The blending of imagination and perception, and the recognition of objects that such blending permits, have been the subject of neurological investigation. To take one prominent example, Stephen Grossberg has developed a theory of adaptive resonance, in which he describes the storage, in both long- and short-term memory, of neural configurations that are formed as a result of experience. These neural nodes serve as stable recognition codes and categories for new stimuli.[14] On the basis of extensive experimental data, theory building, and thought experiments, Grossberg claims that cognitive activity involves not only a passive reception of data but also an active intervention of stored codes which both match the input and adapt to variations. Grossberg is interested both in clarifying the neural processes that underlie cognitive activities, and in discovering new architectures for intelligent machines that will be used in technological applications.[15]

The adaptive resonance described by Grossberg is a neural activity that can be associated with the "imagination" we have been discussing in the passages we have cited from Kant, Wittgenstein, and Strawson. And while it is one thing to ferret out the structures of adaptive resonance in the brain and nervous system, it is another, more philosophical thing to describe how these neural structures serve representations in perception and recognition. Clearly, the internal templates are not the same kind of sign as the words, symbols, and pictures we encounter normally. What kind of sign are they?

Let us approach this problem obliquely. When we perceive and recognize something, the stored codes and categories are activated and matched against the input given to us at the moment. We might think that this matching involves comparing the input with an internal image or map that we call up from storage: here the input, there the map, and between them the comparison. While such a comparison might occur in, say, a guidance system, it could not occur in the brain, because it would require that we stand at a distance from both the input and the template and compare them. Also, it would not be a single act. It would be made up of three elements—two acts of viewing plus a comparison—and would not be a single perception. Let us then say that the pattern we activate from storage is like a transparency that we hold between our eyes and the object. We look through the transparency, and the object shows up as either matching it or differing from it. This comparison is better because it blends the template and the object into one act of viewing, but it is still inadequate because the template remains a thing that we could look at by itself, even while we hold it up between ourselves and the thing we see through it. Let us move closer, then, and suppose that the activated template is located on the lenses of goggles that we wear, or perhaps on contact lenses. This is better, because now we do not see the lenses at all, but still in principle we could always take them off and look at them as objects in themselves. They still remain too distant to us. What we want is something that is more part of ourselves than the contact lenses are. Furthermore, neither the map nor the transparency nor the lenses have any sense of my own body built into them and, as we have seen, imagination involves a displacement of oneself into one's future or past self.

So we move from a transparency to contact lenses to something "inside" the brain. But the internal representation in the brain takes on a new mode of being, one quite different from the pictures and other representations we find the in the "external" world. For one thing, we cannot perceive our own internal representations when they are activated. We cannot see the neural nets that fire when we recognize the figurine. We could not see them even if we changed the direction of our focus (as we could with the transparencies and contact lenses). The activated neural nets are always "behind" our field of perception, always hidden. They allow us to see, but they cannot be seen by us while they carry out their work.

Another person—a neurologist, for example—could, in principle, view the activated neural nets and the parallelism in them, but for him they do not serve as internal representations. For him they are only electrical and chemical activations in the brain he is examining. He knows they are an internal representation only because we tell him what we see when these activations occur. The activated neural nodes are opaque to him, since he cannot see anything through them, but they are transparent to us, since we see something through them but cannot see them themselves. Brain signs, therefore, are radically different from worldly signs. A normal sign can always be taken by the same person in two ways, as a material thing in itself (a mark, a sound) or as representing something else. Brain signs can also be taken in two ways, as distributed neural activations and as re-presentations of something else, but they cannot be so taken by the same person; the two ways of being taken are correlated to two different people, the neurological observer and the subject whose brain is activated.[16] The neurological observer can know that this or that neural activation represents this or that object, but he knows it only because his subject tells him what he perceives or remembers when the activation occurs. The neurological observer must be able to enter into conversation with his subject if he is to know what his neurological observations signify. This tells us is that we can explore the nature of internal representation only if we pay attention to the status of the neurological observer. We cannot limit ourselves to the neural system alone. The problem of the scientific observer is as much an issue in neurology as it is in quantum physics.

The issue of parallelism opens new possibilities in the neural sciences and in computer hardware and programming; but it also raises philosophical questions about human consciousness and its interaction with both computing machines and the brain and nervous system.

ENDNOTES

[1]Everyone knows that we experience mental imagery, but not everyone has remarked upon the constant parallelism between the imagined and the perceived. Few philosophers have made this parallelism a theme for reflection. The issue has been extensively treated by Edmund Husserl, especially in connection with his studies on the experience of time. See Edmund Husserl, *On the Phenomenology of the Consciousness of Internal Time*, ed. Rudolf Boehm, trans. John Barnett Brough (Dordrecht: Kluwer, 1991). Some helpful comments about imagination are made by Gilbert Ryle in *The Concept of Mind* (London: Hutchinson, 1949), chap. 8, "Imagination."

[2]On the various ways in which we can be present to our imagined scenes, see the chapter entitled "The Meanings of 'Fantasy'," in C. S. Lewis, *An Experiment in Criticism* (Cambridge: Cambridge University Press, 1961), 50–56; see also Robert Sokolowski, "Picturing," *Review of Metaphysics* 31 (1977), 3–28. Although we will not, in this essay, discuss the phenomenon of dreaming, it is clear that in dreams the "internal reruns" of experience predominate over any input from current stimuli. The remark of Carl Jung is pertinent here: "Presumably we are dreaming all the time, although we are not aware of it by day because consciousness is much too clear. But at night, when there is that *abaissement du niveau mental*, the dreams can break through and become visible." From Carl Jung "The Tavistock Lectures, Third Lecture," in *The Symbolic Life*, trans. R. F. C. Hull, *Collected Works*, vol. 18, ed. Herbert Read, Michael Fordham, and Gerhard Adler (Princeton: Princeton University Press, 1976), 78–79. Samuel Beckett heard this lecture and was very much influenced by it; see Deirdre Bair, *Samuel Beckett* (New York: Summit Books, 1990), 208–9, 400–401, 639.

[3]Thomas Hobbes, "On Man," trans. Charles T. Wood, T. S. K. Scott-Craig, and Bernard Gert in *Man and Citizen,* ed. Bernard Gert (New York: Humanities Press, 1972), 40.

[4]John Le Carré, *The Secret Pilgrim* (New York: Knopf, 1991), 246.

[5]Thomas Hobbes, *Leviathan,* ed. Michael Oakeshott (Oxford: Blackwell, 1957), part 1, chap. 2, p. 9.

[6]"A bacterium detects a spatial gradient of attractant not by comparing the concentration at its head and tail, but by traveling through space and comparing its observations through time. . . . A bacterium decides whether or not to tumble by comparing the concentrations of attractants and repellents sensed in the past second with those encountered three seconds before." Lubert Stryer, *Biochemistry* (New York: Freeman, 1988), 1008, 1010.

[7]Peter Strawson, "Imagination and Perception," in *Freedom and Resentment* (London: Methuen, 1974), 53.

[8]Ibid. 43; Immanuel Kant, *Critique of Pure Reason,* trans. Norman Kemp Smith (New York: St. Martin's Press, 1965), A120, footnote.

[9]Cited and italicized by Strawson, 60, taken from Ludwig Wittgenstein, *Philosophical Investigations,* trans. G. E. M. Anscombe (Oxford: Basil Blackwell, 1958), 197.

[10]Wittgenstein, 207.

[11]Strawson, 58.

[12]The role of transference has been well described by Hans W. Loewald in his descriptions of the psychoanalytic situation and the relationship between analyst and patient. See the papers entitled "On the Therapeutic Action of Psychoanalysis" and "Psychoanalytic Theory and the Psychoanalytic Process," in *Papers on Psychoanalysis* (New Haven: Yale University Press, 1980).

[13]For the meanings of the following Latin words, see the relevant entries in the *Oxford Latin Dictionary.*

[14]See, for example, the essay by Stephen Grossberg, "How Does a Brain Build a Cognitive Code?" in Boston Studies in The Philosophy of Science, *Studies of Mind and Brain,* vol. 70 (Boston: Reidel, 1982), 2–52; and Gail A. Carpenter and Stephen Grossberg, "A Massively Parallel Architecture for a Self-Organizing Neural Pattern Recognition Machine," in Stephen Grossberg, ed., *Neural Networks and Natural Intelligence* (Cambridge: MIT Press, 1988), 251–315.

[15]See Grossberg, *Neural Networks,* viii.

[16]On the status of the neurological observer and the nature of the brain-sign, see Robert Sokolowski, "Knowledge and Its Representation in Writing, Computers, and the Brain," in Ottavio Barnabei, Alessandro Borromei, and Camillo Orlandi, eds., *The Brain and Intelligence, Natural and Artificial* (Bologna: Edizioni L'inchiostroblu, 1990), 197–207.

Felix E. Browder

Of Time, Intelligence, and Institutions

A CCORDING TO SOME CLASSICAL DEFINITIONS of humankind, man is the rational animal, man is the political animal, and man is the tool-making animal. There is a broad range of insights on human existence and human institutions that can be framed in terms of these definitions, especially if one allows them to interact. It is in this context that we place our discussion of massively parallel processing in connection with the institutions of American society.

In a technical sense, the term *massively parallel processing* refers to the ongoing development of high-speed digital computers involving many thousands or even millions of individual processors, each carrying out its own computations and interacting within a complex network. Though the idea of such systems goes back to the earliest days of modern digital computers at the end of the Second World War, their practical implementation as an important alternative to sequential computers using a single stream of computations (or vector processors using a small number) is a product of the last decade. It is only in the past year that there has been broad acceptance of the thesis that massively parallel computers can be developed within a very few years which can solve a broad class of problems a thousand times as fast as present-day supercomputers (which the more conventional supercomputers cannot be made to match).

How can one assess the significance of such a prospect? The answer has two essential elements: the consideration of the impact that the digital computer has had and will have on the scope and nature of what human beings can do, and the role within that impact

Felix E. Browder is University Professor at Rutgers University.

of the effective speed of computation and problem solving. Of all the tools that mankind has developed in its whole history, and especially in the past several decades in which science-based technology has multiplied many fold, the electronic digital computer has been the most flexible and the most universal in application. It has become the tool to create tools, the fundamental *enabling technology*. Its use in that role depends on the ease with which it can be used, which itself depends on the speed with which the computer can be effectively employed. The computer can be used to design tools and processes, to analyze their effects and modify their design accordingly, and even to create them in a concrete form.

The digital computer is the paradigm of the smart machine. Its active life depends on the streams of instructions which are its software. This software is an embodiment of man's rational capacity in a logicomathematical form. Whether it can replace this capacity even on its mathematical side is a subject of great controversy. What is not in controversy is the subsumption of the computer's running instructions within the framework of human rationality and the fact that, up to the present at least, intelligent human beings must create the software using their intelligence and their problem-solving experience.

Thus, one reaches two fundamental structures of human action deeply involved in the computer: time and intelligence. Under the aspect of eternity, as embodied in the timeless mathematical analysis of abstract computation with an unlimited number of steps, computer architectures are irrelevant and everything can be computed by the universal Turing machine. However, human action in its usual forms is not under the aspect of eternity. It is governed by time, and in a more subtle and complex form than the regularity of physical processes which we identify as physical time. Quite aside from the time structure of individual human existence which has its beginning and its end, consider the dramatic foreshortening of historical time in revolutionary periods as we have witnessed recently in Eastern Europe and in the Soviet Union. Consider, on the other hand, the consistent, rapidly accelerating pace of the scientific-technological revolution of the past two centuries.

For the world dominated by the use and development of the computer, to use the old expression, time is of the essence. So is intelligence, trained and active intelligence. The greatest capital good that any nation can possess today is the effective active skill of its citizens within a framework of social institutions and goals in which they have the opportunity and motivation to use their skills for socially fruitful ends.

For man as the political animal, and, in particular, for the United States in the new post–Cold War world dominated by a ferocious economic competition in goods generated by high technology, the concepts of time and intelligence are of equally decisive importance. Markets for products formed by high technology are ruled by a new law of increasing returns rather than the classical principle of diminishing returns. This new law, however, depends on the strategy of using new skills and innovative manufacturing capacities to move at a rapid pace from markets for goods with saturated consumer demand to new markets for new goods with new consumer demand. The Japanese have demonstrated the use of such strategies in a convincing way in such areas as electronics and automobiles.

Behind such an economic strategy there must be a scientific and technological infrastructure and the effective intelligence to use that infrastructure for the implementation of a realistic economic strategy. Strategy means planning a path in time by using step-by-step procedures. It means intensive realistic analysis of the environment in which the strategy is to be implemented, including the understanding of one's competitors and their competitive advantages or disadvantages. The United States in the past decade has exhibited several gross competitive disadvantages. Among them is a curious inability to formally recognize that real competitors exist for American firms outside the national boundaries and that, in the new scavenger or vulture capitalism of the 1980s (as some of the participants themselves have chosen to call it), planning by American companies beyond the next quarterly or annual report has become difficult if not totally impossible. In many industries, American companies have contracted rather than developed their corporate research efforts, almost always on the basis of the doubtful relevance of the research objectives to short-term profitability. Keynes once remarked, in response to the equally dubious economic strategy of waiting for the long-term equilibrium (if such long-term equilibria actually exist), that, in the long-term, we will all be dead. American companies are intensely involved in a communal effort to prove that, in the short-term, we shall all be dead as well.

There has been one reserved domain in American political and economic life where the iron law of total confusion has not been allowed to reign unchecked, and it is the exception that proves the rule. That exception, of course, is the domain of the military. Impelled by the confrontation with the Communist bloc in the Cold War and by the prospect (fortunately never achieved) of military confrontation resulting from the Cold War, the United States formed and implemented coherent plans for military research and development. In its most recent phase under the Reagan administration we have seen three-quarters of the national expenditure for research and development devoted to the military. For its own purposes, this effort succeeded. Though never applied in an actual Cold War military confrontation, it found a test exercise under ideal conditions in the Gulf War. A painless military triumph was achieved over Iraq by the use of smart weapons involving digital computers and electronics. In the meantime, the United States has won the Cold War; the Communist bloc has dissolved. What do we do next? The United States has achieved a unique position of military and political hegemony on a global basis, whose substantive function appears to be to keep the world safe for Japanese economic hegemony.

To paraphrase William James, for the purposes of national policy, we need a moral equivalent of the Cold War as well as an economic equivalent of the Cold War. It has been observed that, on occasion, nothing fails like success. Still, it would be highly ironic if, in demonstrating the bankruptcy of the Communists' feudal version of the command economy, the United States would incidentally demonstrate the ultimate failure of its own version of laissez-faire capitalism and its mindless worship of the market. From a political point of view, the public interest is defined to be the sum of private interests in their narrowest sense, weighted according to a scale of political leverage. This sort of political mechanism and psychology, which we might call the Pork Barrel State, fails often even to fulfill its most elementary purposes, as the many discussions of the prisoner's dilemma in rational choice theory bring out.

Though it would be impossible to justify the scale of past expenditures on military research and development either in terms of trickle down effects on basic knowledge in science and engineering or in terms of impact on national competitiveness in global markets, there are several areas of applied science, especially computers and materials, where the impact of defense mission-oriented research has played a decisive role. In particular, the initiatives of DARPA on high-performance computing and its application has been central to federal involvement in stimulating the development of this "enabling technology." More recently under the Bush administration, with the strong advocacy of members of Congress, particularly Senator Gore as well as the president's science advisor, funding has been added to the budgets of several federal research agencies to implement a new high-performance computing initiative. The objective of this new program—besides creating networks through which high-speed computations could be transmitted to all corners of the United States—is to implement the use of ever more effective computation on a variety of so-called grand challenge problems, many of which are obviously relevant to US economic competitiveness. Whether the federal agencies can get their act together in a timely and effective way remains to be seen, especially in view of their usually murky internal politics. However, in this direction at least, an effort is being made to create a national science and technology policy.

Since the Second World War, the United States has created the strongest and most vigorous science and engineering research establishment in the world by one or several orders of magnitude. This research structure has been based on two principal features which have turned out to be unprecedently fruitful. First, scientific and engineering research has been concentrated primarily in the universities, particularly in the so-called research universities which had pioneered the joint mission of research and teaching between the two world wars. A new concept of graduate education in the sciences and engineering was introduced in the United States which involved active participation in research and introduced a continual wave of new and highly active participants in the research process as graduate students and postdoctoral fellows in ongoing research programs. Young faculty members could begin research programs of their own and need not necessarily continue to the work of their elders. Second, new federal research agencies were created for the support of research in the sciences. These were the National Science Foundation and the National Institutes of Health. These agencies were founded with the explicit intention of managing their affairs by using the highest available standards of scientific evaluation. They have managed relatively well in avoiding the grip of the Pork Barrel State.

In the past forty years, the American research universities have become the home of scientific research, and science has transformed the universities, though not to universal satisfaction. On a world level, the American university is America's most successful nonde-structive institution, and its most prestigious parts are its science research and graduate programs. That is why many of the world's brightest youth now populate the science and engineering graduate programs of American research universities. The possibility of such recruitment is an enormous strength for the United States, as is the possibility of assimilating many of these young people into major roles in American life. This historical American pattern continues to be enormously attractive to talented young people throughout the world and, to some degree, makes up for the catastrophic state of the education of children in America's own precollegiate school systems.

The American universities, when they are adequately fulfilling their central function, are the forcing grounds of the *intelligence* of the country. When, either by compulsion or inclination, they focus their central energies on fund-raising, political manipulation, or defensive public relations, their central function is often diminished. Whatever attacks the elan of the American university system damages one of the central sources of the country's strength.

In conclusion, let us draw the moral that the future achievement of the United States in science and technology must, in a large part, derive from American universities and the talented young people they educate. Thus, in terms of our original focus on massive parallel processing, the full vigor of this development can only be achieved if it is fully interwoven with the main thrust of scientific and engineering research in the universities. Only then can the dynamic of the trained intelligence of the country be realized at its highest level.

Geoffrey C. Fox

Parallel Computing and Education

I N THIS ISSUE WE HAVE LEARNED THAT parallel architectures will lead to computers of dramatically greater performance and capability. How and why will this affect education? Will the impact be incremental, as happens when one discovers a new elementary particle, which appears as an extra chapter in a multi-volume book on introductory physics? Or will the impact be dramatic, as in biology where areas such as genetic and molecular biology have revolutionized the core knowledge taught in the field? I believe the latter is a better analogy, and that as educators adopt the use of parallel computers, these machines will lead to major changes, both in the way we teach, and in what we teach. Many agree with this assertion, and a few have started to implement its consequences.

This essay is constructed around a single premise: the inexorable increase in the performance of computers can open up new vistas in essentially all fields. We need skilled people to explore and exploit these possibilities, however, and our educational system is behind the times. Current curricula at grade schools and colleges will not educate students to exploit the possibilities opened up by parallel computers and the emergence of the computational methodology. Furthermore, the young but relatively traditional field of computer science will only give us a small fraction of the scientists in the computational wave that will lead the revolution. Computer scientists will develop the wonderful machines—a critical enabling technology. However, what we need most are *computational scientists*—individuals trained to *use* computers. High-performance computing is critical to the nation's needs. The Gulf War illustrated this in our military, but the future battles will increasingly be economic. Thus,

Geoffrey C. Fox is Professor of Computer Science and Physics at Syracuse University.

high-performance computers can assure the industrial competitiveness of the nation, but this can only be true if we educate those who can use parallel computers in new ways for industry.

PARALLEL COMPUTERS IN EDUCATION

Many children now have substantial exposure to computers in elementary and secondary schools, and many more benefit from the VLSI revolution with specialized video games, such as those from Nintendo. Parallel computing will allow us to bring the sophistication of a military flight simulator to the individual's video game. Tomorrow's video games could teach our children more than hand-eye coordination; they will be truly educational. Parallel computing will bring realism to simulations at the low end in hand-held units, and at the high end in tomorrow's theme parks, where exhibits could be controlled by a parallel teraflop supercomputer. This high-performance technology will allow not only realistic simulations, but wonderful graphics experienced perhaps with "virtual reality." One can only hope that this realism will be used to teach about the earth and not just about idealized worlds in galaxies far away in space and time.

I recently read a set of papers about global climate change. Each participant agreed that major undesirable changes in the environment were inevitable unless definitive action is taken soon. But no one could see a way to explain to the public and, in particular, to politicians, the urgency of the situation. They may or may not have agreed that parallel computers will accurately predict the temperature rises coming from global warming, but that is an example where realistic simulations could be used to vividly illustrate these predictions.

Who can produce such simulations? We have seen in other articles how the physical world is naturally parallel, and that simulations can be effectively mapped onto a parallel computer. Producing this simulation, however, requires broad knowledge of many disciplines, including the study of oceans and the atmosphere, computer architectures, and perhaps even the psychophysics needed to effectively present the visualization of the consequences of a rogue climate. Such an interdisciplinary knowledge will not be gained from today's specialized atmospheric science or computer science curricula. It is an example of computational science—a fledgling field that will educate computationalists who will then exploit the opportunities opened up by parallel computers. In the example above, one would need education in both atmospheric science and computer science as well as visualization—a combination that is not typically taught academically in any field.

It is well understood how a theorist in chemistry or physics will use mathematics to express and manipulate ideas, but computation will join theory and experiment as a basic approach to science and engineering. Thus, just as we give scientists a thorough education in mathematics, we should also offer the fundamentals of computation to everybody. You may argue that your university already offers a Fortran programming course, and you have just added the C language and Wordstar. However, mathematics is more than addition and subtraction. In the same way, computation is more than programming and should be taught, not as a technical trade, but as an important, fundamental, and very useful discipline.

Most faculty outside of the computer science department view the computer as a useful but rather tiresome tool which is best regarded as a black box programmed by graduate students and junior researchers. Computer scientists often see the use of computers as grubby numerical work outside of the core of the field, which is centered on the elegant mathematics of idealized machines. The public—and even many students—often think of computer science as scientific computing. These fields are quite distinct; in defining computation as the use of computers, we see that scientific computation is usually taught as a technical skill and not studied as part of the academic mainstream. Computational science—that is, the science of computation—falls into an academic void between computer science and such fields as chemistry and physics that make use of computers. We can understand how this situation developed; the basic design and programming methodology for sequential computers has remained unchanged for thirty years. There have been improvements—such as time sharing, interactive computing, desktop workstations, UNIX, and so on—but the fundamentals of computing have not changed. The supercomputers pioneered by Cray introduced some important new concepts, such as vector processing, but these were not pervasive. If computational science had been a vital academic discipline fifteen years ago when the first Cray-1 was introduced, I believe that vector (super)computing would have advanced much faster. Computational science was smothered by industry standards—the IBM 370 architecture, DEC's VAX, and operating systems such as VM, VMS, and UNIX. These promoted the view of computation as a technical skill and upheld the gap between computers and users.

I believe that the change in computer architectures—and the increased utility that that change creates—implies a change in philosophy. Computation should be taught as part of the academic mainstream, not as training on the job. If we fail to educate computationalists, parallel computing will not realize its potential. This could mean, for instance, that US industry could fail to translate the current US leadership in innovative computer architectures into a global economic edge. If successful, the benefits will be seen throughout society and will feed back into the education process itself.

COMPUTATIONAL SCIENCE AND ENGINEERING

The dramatic performance promised by parallel computers will change the nature of science and engineering in research and in practice. Clearly, an interdisciplinary education in computational science will allow scientists and engineers to perform better. Those who understand the basic principles of computer architecture and modern software techniques will be the leaders in using the first teraflop machines; they will help the computer industry design machines that will be able to attempt the grand challenge problems in physics, chemistry, aeronautics, and so on.

A training in computational science would include the basics of applied computer science, numerical analysis, and simulation. Computationalists need a broader education than the typical physicist or computer scientist. Their training in basic computer science and its applications must be joined with an understanding of one or more application areas, such as physics and the computational approach to physics. Computationalists will need a computer laboratory course so they become facile with the use of computers. These must be modern parallel supercomputers, not the personal computers or workstations now used for students in most universities. This broad education will only be possible if existing fields can teach their material more concisely. In considering a computational physics curriculum, for example, courses in applied computer science could substitute for advanced courses in quantum theory and the parallel computer laboratory for an experimental physics lab. We could train a computational physicist with a reasonable knowledge of both physics and computation. Although the details of parallel computing are changing rapidly, the graduate of such an education would be able to track future changes. Computational science links scientific fields to computer science; specialization in computational science could be an attractive option for computer scientists. An understanding of applications will allow computer scientists to develop better hardware and software. Computational scientists, whether in computer science or in an application field such as physics, will benefit directly from technology that improves the performance of computers by a factor of two each year. Their theoretical colleagues will gain the same level of assistance from technologic improvements; computational science can be expected to be a field of growing rewards and opportunities.

I believe that students educated in computational science will find it a rewarding and exciting experience that should give them excellent job opportunities. Only a few universities offer such a degree, however, and often only at the doctoral level. Fledgling programs exist at Caltech, Cornell, Clemson, Denver, Illinois, Michigan, North Carolina, Princeton, Rice, Stanford, Syracuse, and University of California at Davis. These programs are diverse; no national consensus on the core knowledge of computational science has been developed. The National Science Foundation's supercomputer centers at Cornell, Illinois, Pittsburgh, and San Diego have played an important role in enhancing the visibility and progress of computational science. However, these centers are established outside of the academic framework of universities and do not directly contribute to development of computational science as an academic discipline. These centers, along with industry, the national laboratories, and, indeed, the federal government, with its new high-performance computing and communication initiative, are all advancing the roll of computational science. Academia is lagging behind; not only are there scant computational science education programs, but there are also few faculty who could teach such a curriculum. The poor job opportunities for computationalists in leading universities naturally discourages students entering the field, and that in turn hinders the development of new educational programs. It will not be an easy issue to address, and I expect that only slow progress will be made as computational science gradually gains recognition in universities as a fundamentally exciting field. The inevitable dominance of parallel computing will help, as will the use of parallel computers in the NSF centers that have provided such a critical stimulus for computational science. Industry and the national laboratories already offer computational scientists excellent job opportunities, and the demand for individuals with such training will grow. This market pressure should lead to initiatives from within universities to hire, encourage, and promote new computational faculty, and to educate students in computational science.

There are a number of issues that will inhibit the development of computational science in universities. Because it will be necessary to borrow from and expand upon existing departments—such as computer science, biology, chemistry, and physics—advocates of this new field will face numerous political hurdles on campus; they will be challenging firmly held traditional beliefs of the established faculty. These inevitable difficulties are exacerbated by administrative problems; many universities are facing a no-growth scenario or even a period of declining funding and diminishing faculty size. This means that the creation of a new program will imply reductions in other areas. Computational science has difficulties similar to those faced by other interdisciplinary areas (fields concerned with environmental issues, for example). The peer referee system used in the hiring and promoting of new faculty is perfect for ensuring high standards within the referees' domain of expertise. This tends to lead to very high-quality but isolated departments that find it hard to move into new areas of study. The same effect is seen in the peer review system used for the refereeing of scholarly papers and federal grants. Thus, universities find it hard to change, and new fields like computational science will not grow easily in academia. A key hurdle that must be overcome if the field is to grow will be the development of some consensus within the community that computational science is, as I have asserted, fundamental and existing. A core curriculum must be developed; that body of knowledge will provide a foundation upon which the academic discipline of computational science can be built.

DEVELOPING AND SUPPORTING COMPUTATIONAL SCIENCE EDUCATION

The boldest and simplest way to fill this academic void would be to create an entirely new academic degree in computational science, administered by a new university department. This would give the field great visibility; once created, the independent department would be able to develop its own educational and research programs and hire faculty without direct interference from existing academic departments. Such a department would need strong support from the university administration to flourish, or even to be created. This approach would not be easy to implement, however. There would be opposition from existing academic units for many reasons—some legitimate and some less so. A critic could argue that a free-standing computational science program is premature; there is, as yet, no agreement on a core body of knowledge that could define this field. Students graduating from this program might find it hard to progress up the academic ladder at the vast majority of universities that do not have such a department.

These difficulties could be avoided by using a different approach. Rather than creating a new department, existing fields would be sufficiently broadened to close the educational gap. Students could graduate with traditional degrees and have a natural academic future. This is the approach that has been taken by the existing university programs in computational science and engineering. Consider, for example, the two fields of chemistry and computer science. A computational scientist would graduate with a degree in either chemistry or computer science. Subsequent academic progress would be judged by the scientist's contributions to the corresponding base field. Such an interdisciplinary education would allow the student to be either a better chemist or a better computer scientist. Of course, the chemist who graduates from the computational science program would not have received as complete an education in chemistry as is traditional for theoretical or experimental chemists. Some of the elective chemistry courses would have been replaced by computational science requirements. This change would need to be evaluated and approved by the chemistry faculty, who would also need to identify key chemistry requirements that would have to be satisfied by computational scientists. New courses might include computational chemistry and courses covering the basics of computer science, numerical analysis, and simulation. The latter set would be taught by either computer scientists or interdisciplinary computational science faculty. The education of a computational scientist within a computer science department could be handled in a similar fashion; there would be an emphasis on applied computer science and training in at least one application area.

A degree in computational chemistry would be equivalent to a degree in chemistry within the computational science program. On the computer science side, students could earn a degree in computer science with a minor in chemistry, for example, or a doctorate in computer science with a master's degree in chemistry. At the administrative level, I envision an interdisciplinary program in computational science but no separate department; students would be admitted to existing academic units, and faculty would be appointed by the current departments. This approach to computational science allows us to develop and understand the core knowledge and curriculum in an evolutionary fashion. Implementing even this more modest plan will not easy; well-established degree requirements for existing fields, such as chemistry and computer science, will have to be reevaluated and modified accordingly. These modifications will be easiest at the master's and doctoral levels—this is where most of the new programs have been established so far.

There seem to be very good reasons to establish computational science programs at the undergraduate level in addition to the pioneer programs underway at the graduate level. There also needs to be a greater awareness of the importance of computation in the elementary and high schools. The more visible computational science becomes, the more likely high school students are to choose computational science educational programs and careers.

I believe that, eventually, all college students will learn computational science—it will be part of any general education. When all undergraduates take two years of basic applied computer science—including but not limited to programming—computational science will be a natural extension of these base courses. Computation—just like mathematics, chemistry, physics, and humanities—is essential to the education of tomorrow's scientists and engineers.

N. *Metropolis*

The Age of Computing: A Personal Memoir

I N THE HISTORY OF MODERN TECHNOLOGY, computer science must figure as an extraordinary chapter, and not only because of the remarkable speed of its development. It is unfortunate, however, that the word *science* has been widely used to designate enterprises that more properly belong to the domain of engineering. "Computer science" is a glaring misnomer, as are "information science," "communication science," and other questionable "sciences." The awe and respect which science enjoys and which engineering is denied is inexplicable, at least to one who sees the situation from the other side.

The popular image of science has changed little since it was invented by Jules Verne and H. G. Wells. *Science* represents the search for knowledge, the conquest over nature, the discovery of some very few fundamental laws that will free mankind from worry and toil; this is as true today as it was at the turn of the century.

The word *engineering,* however, carries less exciting connotations. I recall a pleasant evening at the house of the American Academy of Arts and Sciences. In the great hall conversation and gossip flowed freely in anticipation of a brilliant lecture. A distinguished lady, a pillar of Cambridge society, was expressing her admiration for Professor S. She extolled his discoveries and his brilliant insights. "And what department at MIT does he belong to?" she finally asked, by way of indicating that our brief exchange was coming to an end. "Mechanical engineering," I answered. A look of horror crossed the lady's face. "Why, I thought he was a scientist!" she blurted out

N. *Metropolis is Senior Fellow Emeritus at Los Alamos National Laboratory.*

before she could cover up her gaffe. I saw in her eyes the image of a man in a dirty gray frock, a pair of pliers in his greasy hands, bent over some Chaplinesque contraption of gears and pulleys.

But, contrary to the lady's prejudices about the engineering profession, the fact is that quite some time ago the tables were turned between theory and applications in the physical sciences. Since World War II the discoveries that have changed the world were not made so much in lofty halls of theoretical physics as in the less-noticed labs of engineering and experimental physics. The roles of pure and applied science have been reversed; they are no longer what they were in the golden age of physics, in the age of Einstein, Schrödinger, Fermi, and Dirac. Readers of *Scientific American,* nourished on the Wellsian image of science, will recoil from even entertaining the idea that the age of physical "principles" may be over. The laws of Newtonian mechanics, quantum mechanics, and quantum electrodynamics were the last in a long and noble line that appears to have somewhat dried up in the last fifty years. As experimental devices (especially measuring devices) are becoming infinitely more precise and reliable, the wealth and sheer mass of new and baffling raw data collected by experiment greatly exceeds the power of human reason to explain them. Physical theory has failed in recent decades to provide a theoretical underpinning for a world which increasingly appears as the work of some seemingly mischievous demiurge. The failure of reason to explain fact is also apparent in the life sciences, where "theories" (of the kind that physics has led us to expect) do not exist; many are doubtful that this kind of scientific explanation will ever be successful in explaining the secrets of life.

Historians of science have always had a soft spot for the history of theoretical physics. The great theoretical advances of this century—relativity and quantum mechanics—have been documented in fascinating historical accounts that have captivated the mind of the cultivated public. There are no comparable studies of the relations between science and engineering. Breaking with the tradition of the *Fachidiot,* theoretical physicists have bestowed their romantic autobiographies on the world, portraying themselves as the high priests of a reigning cult.

By their less than wholly objective accounts of the development of physics, historians have conspired to propagate the myth of science as being essentially theoretical physics. Though the myth no longer described scientific reality fifty years ago, historians pretended that all was well, that nothing had changed since the old heroic days of Einstein and his generation. There were a few dissenters, such as the late Stanislaw Ulam who used to make himself obnoxious by proclaiming that Enrico Fermi was "the last physicist." He and others who proclaimed such a possibility were prudently ignored. Physicists did what they could to keep the myth alive. With impeccable chutzpah, they went on promulgating new "laws of nature" and carefully imitated their masters of another age. With dismaying inevitability, many of these latter-day "laws" have been exposed as quasi-mathematical embellishments, devoid of great physical or scientific significance.

Historians of science have seen fit to ignore the history of the great discoveries in applied physics, engineering, and computer science, where real scientific progress is nowadays to be found. Computer science in particular has changed and continues to change the face of the world more thoroughly and more drastically than did any of the great discoveries in theoretical physics. The prejudices of the academic world have stood in the way of the historian. One wonders whether a historian of contemporary engineering could get a teaching job at a respectable university. For some reason, histories of long obsolete discoveries, such as the steam engine, are acceptable in academia: dozens of such histories have been written and, undoubtedly, dozens more will be written now that the field has become an established one. However, a history of the transistor is still beyond bounds (no such history has even been attempted, to the best of my knowledge). Thanks to the joint public relations efforts of historians and physicists, the white mane of Albert Einstein remains the unquestioned symbol of genius. It is scandalous, however, that virtually no cultivated person has ever heard of John Bardeen, whose discoveries may have revolutionized the world at least as much as Einstein's. Bardeen's midwestern background and his having taught in Urbana, Illinois, were fatal flaws that prevented his ever being recognized.

It would be tempting to conclude, after an inspection of empty library shelves, that the absence of engineering histories, recounting major discoveries, is due in part to the difficulty of gaining access to essential facts. Practical discoveries are not as easily traceable to research papers as are theoretical discoveries. Such a conclusion, however, would not be warranted. The development of any discovery of even the slightest practical value is generally thoroughly documented in reports, replete with names, careful attribution given to who did what, when, with the funding sources and dollar amounts given. Unfortunately, access to such documents, at present, is severely restricted by bureaucratic barriers deliberately placed in the way of those who have no "need to know." Only the top managers of major business corporations, certain officials of the federal government, and, in times past, selected members of the KGB in the late Soviet Union were privileged to peruse such documents.

In our rapidly changing political and international climate it is possible that such restrictions will soon be lifted. When that happens, it will be inexcusable for a historian of science to neglect the history of the great technological discoveries of our time, including, obviously, the history of computer science.

In offering some random remarks on the possibilities of such a history in the future, I would like to suggest that the history of computer science—if and when it comes to be written—will establish a new and different paradigm for history writing. It may indeed rid us of certain stereotypes common to the history of science, with its overemphasis on the history of theoretical physics.

In contrast to physics, the fundamental ideas that underlie the development and implementation of large-scale computers are almost commonplace. The principles of computer science are now so well known that they are thought to be few and simple. They are unlikely to fire the imagination of a reading public spoiled by science fiction; nor are they revolutionary ideas on which movie scripts can (or will) be written. In fact, they sound pedestrian, predictable, and instrumental, reminding us of the old adage about mathematics, that the ugliest theorems find the best applications, and vice versa. In computer science, simple ideas requiring little or no intellectual or scientific background have often worked out better than the more complex, subtle, and scientifically inspired proposals.

In universities today, students of computer science are the least historically minded group in a student population not known for its historical concerns. They seem to believe that the current concepts in the field have existed from time immemorial, like a patrimony that all have the right to access. Priorities in discovery have been unjustly attributed; individuals who had no part whatever in the development of the field, such as Alan Turing, are now given the status of heroes, while the names of those who did the hard work, like John von Neumann, are scarcely remembered.

The phenomenon of obsolescence is particularly acute in computer science; it works against the historian's task. In the age of the microchip, the history of the vacuum tube has only limited appeal. The discovery of a new computer model surrounds memories of all preceding models with a thick web of irrelevance. In examining a computer of ten or twenty years ago, our first reaction is not one of curiosity mixed with wonder and admiration, as it should be, but of embarrassment, revulsion, almost irritation. The inspection of the creations of our masters elicit smiles, or, more often, giggles. The work of our predecessors has little to teach us, not even in the lessons derived from what we perceive to be their clumsiness. In computer science, obsolescence means a total break with the past, which uniquely distinguishes this field from all others.

The relationship between computer science and mathematics scarcely resembles that which exists between physics and mathematics. The latter may best be described as an unsuccessful marriage, with no possibility of divorce. Physicists internalize whatever mathematics they require, and eventually claim priority for whatever mathematical theory they become acquainted with. Mathematicians see to it that every physical theory, sooner or later, is freed from all shackles of reality and liberated to fly in the thin air of pure reason.

Computer science, in a very different mode, turns to mathematics in much the same way that engineering always has. It freely borrows from already-existing mathematics, developed for altogether different purposes or, more likely, for no purpose at all. Computer scientists raid the coffers of mathematical logic, probability, statistics, the theory of algorithms, and even geometry. Far from resenting the raid, each of these disciplines is buoyed by the incursion. Statistics will never be the same given what the processing of large samples by supercomputers has made possible. The Monte Carlo method, without which computer simulations of neutron diffusion would have been impossible, was developed by Ulam and myself without any knowledge of statistics; to this day the theoretical statistician is unable to give a proper foundation to the method. In a similar way, the theory of algorithms would amount to very little without the needs of computer software. The rebirth of Euclidian geometry in the most classical vein can be traced to the requirements of computer graphics. Like any other engineer, the computer scientist does not stop to work on whatever mathematics he or she may need. Rather, a segment of the mathematical population, relabeling itself "theoretical computer scientists," meets the mathematical needs of the other computer scientists. This shift, if nothing else, has been financially beneficial.

Two branches of mathematics have been wholly revamped, indeed given a new lease on life by being required to meet the needs of computer science. Mathematical logic is one. The other is the once-obscure chapter of probability theory, now called *reliability theory*. The beginning of this transfiguration may be traced to a master's thesis written by Claude Shannon at MIT in 1939. A brief summary of his principal idea will illustrate my point.

Computers are made up of circuits consisting of large numbers of replicas of identically behaving units. Once upon a time the units were vacuum tubes; later, they were transistors; today, they are chips. Every chip processes electric signals which enter at one point and exit at another. Signals going through various chips can be connected in essentially two ways: in series or in parallel. Two chips A and B are said to be connected *in series* when the exit point of A is soldered to the entrance point of B, so that a signal entering through the entrance point of A will automatically be routed through B, and finally exit through the exit point of B. On the other hand, chips A and B are said to be connected *in parallel,* when the entrance points of A and B are soldered together, as well as the exit points of A and B. In this way, a signal entering at the joint entering point of two chips connected in parallel has a choice of whether to go through A or through B before exiting at the common exit point.

Shannon's fundamental insight was that series and parallel connection of chips are analogous to the connectives *and* and *or* of mathematical logic. Indeed, when A and B are connected in series, the resulting circuit will send a signal through if, and only if both A *and* B are processing the signal. When A and B are connected in parallel, the resulting circuit will send a signal through if and only if either A *or* B is processing the signal, not necessarily both.

By this analogy, any logical expression involving *and* and *or* (as well as the third essential logical connective, *not,* covered by a rather ingenious trick) can be replicated by circuits. Simple as Shannon's observation was, it ushered in the age of computing. The design of expert systems in our day further exploits the basic idea that circuits can be made to perform logical operation, for example, by developing circuit-theoretic devices that render the Fregean quantifiers *for all* and *there exists.*

Shannon's idea of relating series and parallel connection with the two basic connectives of logic was to bear fruit in a direction that has proved central to computer engineering. In the logical interpretation of electric circuits, truth and falsehood correspond to whether or not a chip processes a signal. A more realistic assumption, however, is that the chip will work or not with a certain probability, depending on several factors, including the age of the chip. A realistic model for this situation is to assign to each chip in a circuit an exponentially distributed random variable. Random variables corresponding to distinct chips can be assumed to be independent. Thus motivated, probabilists were led to develop a remarkable calculus, which is now known as *reliability theory.*

The principles of reliability theory are simple. If chip A has probability p of failure and chip B has probability q of failure (we disregard the possibility of these probabilities varying with time), then the probability that the series connection of A and B will fail is $1 - (1 - p)(1 - q)$, and the probability that their parallel connection will fail is pq. When p and q are restricted to the extreme values 0 or 1 one finds, as a limiting case, Shannon's interpretation of the logical connectives. Any series-parallel circuit has a certain probability of working, which can be computed by iterating the above two rules. Such a probability is called the reliability of the circuit.

Reliability theory is concerned with the design of circuits of high reliability at a minimum cost. No computer circuit can be designed without allowing for the possibility that one or more components may fail (what von Neumann was the first to call the "synthesis of reliable circuits from unreliable components"). Soldering two or more chips in parallel will increase the reliability, since a signal will still go through even if one the other fails. If chips cost nothing, we could achieve perfect reliability by soldering together chips in multiple parallel connections. In practice, however, the costs of such a design would be prohibitive. Soldering chips in series decreases the cost of the circuit, but it also decreases the reliability. In computer design, the engineer is forced to fall back on his or her own wits (or on those of mathematicians) to design (or "synthesize") circuits of high reliability at a minimum cost.

The design of complex systems of high reliability—whether airplane wings, telephone networks, or computers—is a daunting task. It is unquestionably the central issue of today's computer science. Some of the most ingenious mathematics of our day is being developed in response to the needs of reliability theory.

Although the basic rules for the computation of reliability were long known, it took several years during and immediately after World War II for the importance of the concept of reliability to be explicitly recognized and dealt with. Only then did reliability computation became an essential feature in computer design.

The late Richard Feynman was one of the first to realize the centrality of reliability considerations in all applied scientific work. In the early days of the Manhattan Project in Los Alamos (in 1943 and early 1944), he tested the reliability of his first program in a dramatic fashion, setting up a day-long contest between human operators working with hand-operated calculators and the first electromechanical IBM machines. At first, human operators showed an advantage over the electromechanical computers; as time wore on, however, the women who worked with the calculators became visibly tired and began to make small errors. Feynman's program on the electromechanical machine kept working. The electromechanical computers won out by virtue of their reliability.

Feynman soon came to realize that reliable machines in perfect working order were far more useful than much of what passed for theoretical work in physics, and he loudly stated that conviction. His supervisor, Hans Bethe—the head of T-Division (*T* for *theory*) at the time and a physicist steeped in theory—at first paid no attention to him. At the beginning of the Manhattan Project, only about a dozen or so hand-operated machines were available in Los Alamos; they regularly broke down, thereby slowing scientific work. In order to convince Bethe of the importance of reliable computation, Feynman recruited me to help him improve the performance of the hand-operated desk calculators, avoiding the week-long delays in shipping them to San Diego for repairs. We spent hours fixing the small wheels until they were in perfect order. Bethe, visably concerned when he learned that we had taken time off from our physics research to do these repairs, finally saw that having the desk calculators in good working order was as essential to the Manhattan Project as the fundamental physics.

Throughout his career, Feynman kept returning to the problem of the synthesis of reliable computers. Toward the end of his life, he gave a remarkable address at the fortieth anniversary of the Los Alamos Laboratory where he sketched a reliability theory based on thermodynamical analogies. In contrast to Bethe, John von Neumann very quickly realized the importance of reliability in the design of computers. It is no exaggeration to say that von Neumann had some familiarity (in the 1950s) with all the major ideas that have since proved crucial in the development of supercomputers. Von Neumann realized very early the advantage of parallel computation over series computation. He knew that the day would come when series computations would reach their physical limit, namely, the velocity of light, and that only a computer based on the principles of parallel computation could exceed that limit. Curiously, however, his choice of series computation in preference to parallel computation (now referred to as the "von Neumann computer") was the result of his negative experiences with the first experiments he devised to test the effectiveness of parallel computation. Repeatedly frustrated by his inability to achieve the required synchronicity in a simple parallel computation experiment that he set up (an impossible task in his time), the failure kept him at a distance from all ideas of parallelism for the rest of his life.

The first large-scale electronic computer to be built, the one that may be said to inaugurate the computer age, was the ENIAC. It was built at the Moore School of the University of Pennsylvania by an engineer and a physicist—Presper Eckert and John Mauchly. Their idea, trivial by the standards of our day, was a revolutionary development when completed in 1945. At the time, all electromechanical calculators were built exclusively to perform ordinary arithmetic operations. Any computational scheme involving several operations in series or in parallel had to be planned separately by the user. Mauchly realized that if a computer could count, then it could do finite difference schemes for the approximate solution of differential equations. It occurred to him that such schemes might be implemented directly on an electronic computer, an unheard of idea at the time. They managed to sell their idea to the US Army, which authorized funding of the project, on the condition that the machine be used at the Aberdeen Proving Grounds for ballistic computations. A Captain H. Goldstine was chosen by the Army to supervise the project and was to benefit greatly from the interaction with Eckert and Mauchly.

Alone among the large computers of the time, the ENIAC was designed with paramount concern for reliability. It consisted of eighteen thousand vacuum tubes wired together, with full allowance made for redundancies that would increase reliability. Most of the maintenance work involved the replacement of vacuum tubes that went out of order. To many observers unfamiliar with reliability computations, it seemed a miracle that the ENIAC worked at all. Enrico Fermi, who later was to become one of the first physicists to perform large computer experiments, made only one incorrect prediction so far as I know: he mistakenly computed the reliability of the ENIAC on the basis of the mean free time between vacuum tube failures; he announced that the machine could never work, scarcely realizing that the ENIAC was far more reliable than the counting apparatus in his lab.

In spite of all predictions to the contrary, the computer worked for periods of several hours without error. The designers of the computer resorted to all manner of precautions to keep the vacuum tubes from failing, including keeping "heaters" on at all times. I remember distinctly the time when the ENIAC was dismantled and packed for transportation to the Aberdeen Proving Grounds. Each of the wires was carefully marked and then clipped; I never believed that Mauchly and Eckert would be able to put it back together again. They did, and the ENIAC proved to be a great success.

At the time the ENIAC was installed, von Neumann was a consultant at the Aberdeen Proving Grounds. Realizing that the ENIAC was being underused, he proposed that it be put to work on a computation that would simulate a one-dimensional thermonuclear explosion, following on the notions of Edward Teller's group at Los Alamos. The computation was finally made, and the ENIAC came through with flying colors. The experiment came to be known as the "shakedown cruise" of the ENIAC.

At the end of the war, von Neumann and I began to plan the building of a more powerful computer in Los Alamos, which would benefit from the experience of the ENIAC and the reliability lessons that it had taught us. I spent a year at the Institute of Advanced Study in Princeton to discuss detailed plans with von Neumann. Edward Teller, who was then beginning to do his calculations on thermonuclear reactions, enthusiastically encouraged us to go ahead with the project.

The MANIAC took several years to build. It was finally operational in 1952, and a more realistic computation of a thermonuclear reaction was finally tried on it, with great success. Of all the oddly named computers, the MANIAC's name turned out to be most unfortunate: George Gamow was instrumental in rendering this and other computer names ridiculous when he dubbed the MANIAC "Metropolis And von Neumann Install Awful Computer." Fermi and Teller were the first hackers. They would spend hours at the console of the MANIAC. Teller would spend his weekends at the laboratory playing with the machine. Fermi insisted on doing all the menial work himself, down to the least details, to the awed amazement of the professional programmers. He instinctively knew the right physical problems that the MANIAC could successfully handle.

His greatest success was the discovery of the strange behavior of nonlinear systems arising from coupled nonlinear oscillators. The MANIAC was a large enough machine to allow the programming of potentials with cubic and even quartic terms. Together with John Pasta and Stanislaw Ulam, he programmed the evolution of a mechanical system consisting of a large number of such coupled oscillators. His idea was to investigate the time required for the system to reach a steady state of equidistribution of energy. By accident one day they let the program run long after the steady state had been reached. When they realized their oversight and came back to the computer room, they noticed that the system, after remaining in the steady state for a while, had then departed from it, and reverted to the initial distribution of energy (to within two percent).

The results were published in what was to be the last paper Fermi published before he died. Fermi believed this computer-simulated discovery to be his greatest contribution to science. It is certainly the first major scientific discovery made by computer, and it is not fully understood to this day (though it has spawned some beautiful ideas).

In the same year that the MANIAC was inaugurated, 1952, the first public demonstration of computer reliability was instrumental in convincing the public of the importance of computers. Howard K. Smith employed the UNIVAC on television to predict the outcome of the presidential election. Shortly after the polls closed (within half an hour, actually), the UNIVAC predicted an Eisenhower landslide. The programmers' disbelief that immediately followed this prediction and their subsequent retraction made the computer's prediction all the more astounding. The rise of computer science can be traced to that day.

The history of computer science since 1952 is far more complex. The underlying mathematical and engineering ideas were already known at that time and have since varied only in detail. The gap between these ideas and their implementation, however, was to grow wider as the demand for speed and reliability increased. In fact, the discontinuous leaps forward in computer design went hand in hand with advances in chemistry and material science. The discovery of the transistor, and later the introduction of the miraculous chip, are the two main stages that mark turning points in computer science. It is my hope that a historian of computing will some day tell the fascinating stories of these inventions.

Philip J. Davis

What Should the Public Know about Mathematics?

O N MARCH 21, 1819, THOMAS JEFFERSON, IN RETIREMENT at Monticello, wrote a letter to John Adams, in retirement at Quincy, mentioning certain theories of the stability of the planetary orbits."The calculations," Jefferson admits, "are not for every reader, altho' their results are readily enough understood." No American scientist can scan these lines without experiencing a thrill at the recognition that the founding fathers of the country were men of such training and disposition of mind that they could talk about the ideas of celestial mechanics with some measure of understanding. C. P. Snow—who, a generation ago, warned us against the split between the technological and the humanistic cultures—would equally have been gratified to know that Jefferson, in his very next paragraph, turns to the pronunciation of certain Greek words.

Since the days of Adams and Jefferson, our lives have become increasingly technological and mathematical. The intensity and rapidity with which these developments occurred would have surprised them greatly; it certainly surprises me. Take some very simple examples. If I want to get Amtrak information, I punch a certain 800 number on my phone. I follow this with several further digits corresponding to time and destination. An automated voice then comes on and tells me what my options are. The mathematical underlay of this piece of technology is substantial. Or take an area which will surely strike everyone as nontechnical: sports. Many sports, football for one, have now become the object of statistical and strategic analysis.

Philip J. Davis is Professor of Applied Mathematics at Brown University.

Open the front page of your paper and count how many numbers are on it. Turn to the sports page or the financial page and do likewise. You will find that we are floating—drowning perhaps—in a sea of digits. For the most part, this is mathematics at the level of elementary arithmetic. When it comes to more difficult mathematics, the kind that is taught in college or in graduate school, one finds its application everywhere: economics, the physical and biological sciences, the social sciences.

In view of the increasing mathematization of our civilization, it is paradoxical that the average person knows so little of it, so little of its techniques, its concepts, its history, its aspirations (if the product of our imagination can be said to have aspirations). If asked who the great mathematicians of the past century are, the public very likely would come up only with the name of Einstein, and this would be a misappraisal. Whenever mathematics gets into the headlines it is to alert us to the perennial crises of education and to waggle the finger of guilt: Johnny can't add because . . . . Very occasionally, the newspapers report some new mathematical result just established, and the way it is written up often makes it sound as though the key to the universe had at last fallen into our hands. Less "spectacular" achievements—such as the mathematics that underlies modern oil prospecting techniques or devices that control commercial air traffic or rockets to the moon—are buried at the bottom of a catchall called *computerization.*

Our ignorance of this beautiful subject—a tree of ideas with ancient roots and modern fruit—is profound and beset with fear, superstition, and misinformation. Is the United States, therefore, as some people have claimed, ill prepared to move to a civilization that requires an upgraded level of mathematical expertise? Not necessarily, but one would hope that as it so moves, it at least understands the nature of the movement.

Several months ago one of the top business executives in this county came to me with a confession. He perceived that science and mathematics were increasing in importance and that he, personally, hardly knew a bean about either. In his day-to-day requirements, he made out; he even bought a personal computer and was playing around with it at home. But it was clear to him that he was doing mathematics at a very elementary level indeed. He surmised that—the curriculum of the Harvard Business School notwithstanding—

many of his fellow executives were in the same boat. "How can we make sensible decisions that will affect life ten years down the road, given all this ignorance?" Then he shot out a challenge: "Suppose I were to gather an assembly of twenty or thirty of my colleagues and give them to you for an hour. What would you tell them about mathematics?"

Only one hour? An impossibility. But I accepted the challenge at face value and though the meeting has not yet taken place, I put in a bit of thought as to what I would say in this limited time. In my imagination, I widened the audience so as to include the shades of former chief executives Adams and Jefferson.

The conventional answer to this challenge would be to tell the group something about what is now called *discrete* mathematics. This topic is educationally very hot, and there is considerable effort to move college curricula more strongly in that direction. Discrete mathematics derives from counting, from arrangements of a finite number of objects, from pattern. Discrete mathematics is close to the rules of arithmetic, to computer programs, logic, the mathematics of communication, certain modern theories of physics, problems of optimization, probability, concrete economic modeling, and so on.

Continuous mathematics, which stands as its complement, derives from the study of quantities which are changing continuously in time: the velocity of a car as it accelerates around a curve, the shape of the stream discharged from a running faucet. The Adams-Jefferson correspondence has to do with continuous mathematics, through which celestial mechanics and many other branches of mathematical physics experienced incredible theoretical and practical successes. For this reason, the standard curriculum in high school mathematics has, for many years, read: algebra, geometry, trigonometry, calculus. Calculus is the treatment of continuous variation.

On the other hand, many authorities feel that in the years to come, wide and striking applications will be made using discrete mathematical methods. Its formal study embraces such subjects as Boolean algebra, group theory, matrix theory, automata theory, combinatorics, and many others.

A one hour lecture, then, on discrete mathematics? In spite of its importance, I thought not. Within minutes I would have to get into the nuts and bolts of the subject, and no matter how gently I were to approach it, I would leave my audience behind. Nor would they be left in the position of being then able to echo Jefferson's remark: "Though the details are not for everyone, the implications are fairly clear." And, after all, the business men in my audience are people who, when they sense the need for expertise, are used to going out and hiring it. Mathematics can be hired as one hires any craft skill.

What would be more beneficial would be for me to say something about mathematical thought, about the role that it plays in our technical and commercial life and in the life of the imagination. I would try, also, to talk about the nature of the judgements that were arrived at through mathematics and in this way approach the questions: Why, really, do we want more of it? What would the implications be for daily life if the average level of mathematics required to get along were raised substantially? I would try to put all this across by elaborating five points.

1. Mathematics includes theories of quantity, space, and pattern. It is also the study of the abstract symbolic structures used to deal with these theories.

But it is impossible, really, in several sentences to capture the full scope of mathematics. The world of mathematics is populated by dozens of abstract structures and relationships whose systematic explication and exploitation is at once a science, an art, a language, and a craft. A more accurate statement would require a description of a hundred or so subfields that mathematics embraces. If it has to do with quantity, space, pattern, arrangement, regularities—all interpreted in the widest sense—it is mathematics. If it deals with logical implication, or contingency, with operations that can be symbolized and iteratively manipulated, it is mathematics. These topics are formalized, axiomatized, abstracted, generalized, explored, and applied.

2. All physical sciences and some social sciences have tended toward increased mathematization.

As a creation of the mind, mathematics is part of the world of mental concepts. Its symbolic processes have been found to be able to describe or model certain phenomena of the physical world. Why this should be so is really one of the great mysteries, although philosophers, since antiquity, have attempted explanations.

The uses of a mathematical model are to describe and to predict. In some areas—such as celestial mechanics and navigation, or certain parts of contemporary physics—the success with which this can be done is absolutely spectacular. In areas such as economics, weather prediction, and the theory of war, the successes are yet to be realized. In addition to the descriptive and predictive functions, mathematics also has a prescriptive function. There are, for example, many ways of taxing people; these can be described mathematically. The heavens do not care how we do it; but once having prescribed the mathematical rule, we must deal with its consequences. The consequences may themselves be amenable to further mathematical analysis. Mathematization does not come ready-made. For example, in order to foster good racial relationships, both randomization and quotas have been used. Both are mathematical policies, but of opposite natures.

It follows, then, that successful mathematization brings with it the symbolic and the abstract. It implies the willingness to replace the complexities of the natural world by a simplified (often oversimplified) mathematical imitation of this world. Successful mathematization also implies the willingness to abide by the mathematical consequences of this replacement.

3. New mathematics and applications of old mathematics are constantly being created by the scientific community.

Although the subject is generally presented in schools as a fixed sum of knowledge, mathematics is not a static body of material that can be summarized in, say, fifty volumes. It grows in response to processes from within and without. From within, its very forms and language suggest questions to be answered and these present opportunities for expansion. From without, the desire to solve hard problems of the "real" world leads to the creation of new mathematical concepts, processes, and strategies.

New mathematics may have low public visibility. If mathematical application is very successful, it is often "automated out" and then totally ignored. For example, any landing system for commercial airlines has a heavy mathematical underlay in its computerization. But pilots, air traffic controllers, and the traveling public are called on only to judge its operational quality and not to deal with its mathematical complexities.

The creation of new mathematics has, since World War II, been supported principally by the federal government. While both the emphasis and the levels of future research funding are problematic, the past levels cannot be said to be dangerously low. The eliciting of new mathematics or of applications is not a guaranteed process. The process of discovery or invention cannot be automated. Crash courses in mathematics do not make much sense. A possible recent exception is the recommendation that the country invest heavily in large-scale supercomputers to facilitate the solution of certain very hard problems in science and engineering. In this instance, the goals and methods are both fairly clear, and the national need vis-à-vis competition was substantial.

4. Although the computer is an indispensable tool for the transformation of theory to the bottom line of practical utility, it is not the whole of mathematics.

In the wake of numerous spectacular computational successes, there has been a tendency to identify mathematics completely with computation. While, indeed, it is one of the internal goals of mathematics to routinize its own processes—leading to computerization—such routinization is a matter of discovery and cannot itself be performed automatically in the absence of human interpretation and inspiration.

Some drum beaters for the computer have asserted that the theoretical physics of the near future will undergo a revolution which will make it indistinguishable from computation. The methodologies of Galileo, Newton, Maxwell, Einstein will then be as dead as the celluloid collar.

The future is hidden from us (that's what makes it the future) but it should be pointed out that when technological triumphs are achieved with an indispensable assist from the computer—as, say, with space travel—the computation is based solidly on mathematical knowledge laboriously gained from antiquity to the present and upon the laws of physical motion developed by the scientists just mentioned—as well as many others—beginning in the seventeenth century.

There are few insights gained from the computational experience of the past thirty years that in any way resemble in profundity the fundamental scientific understanding gained through the investigative capacities of the brain in this most fertile period of mathematical physics. It is therefore a mistake to identify computation with mathematics or theoretical physics with computation, or to think that the computer—or the supersupercomputer—is the ultimate transcendent brain and hence the exclusive mechanism of scientific research, development, and teaching.

It is also worthwhile to note that if computation is only a part of mathematics, the newly created subject of computer science has a theoretical aspect that has itself created much new mathematics, but is only partly concerned with real world machines. Vast slices of this new discipline would be found wholly irrelevant to a programmer given the concrete task, say, of working on a new system for stock and bond brokerage.

5. The reasonableness of the goal of wide mathematization cannot be proved or disproved logically. It is a dream, and its pursuit is an act of faith that characterizes our civilization.

Mathematization comes about both consciously and unconsciously, as a result of both the modeling and the prescriptive powers of mathematics. In a certain sense, the pursuit of the mathematized way is our choice. We do not need, in any strictly logical sense, to bring statistics into football. The first Harvard-Yale game in 1883 was not played that way. Computerization of sports leads to new strategies, new stresses—ultimately, to a new game. It is not absurd to think that if the present trend continues, to speak intelligently about football will require an intimate knowledge of standard deviations, optimization theory, and programming techniques.

Architects have a saying that first we build our buildings and then they build us. Mathematics is a structure of the imagination and we simultaneously construct and are constructed by it.

One might imagine a mathematics-free civilization. To understand what this would imply, read descriptions of the Eskimo civilization of fifty years ago. This is not our way. Once accepted, mathematics brings with it certain practical and philosophical consequences. Increased mathematization can change our actions and our deepest beliefs. We hope that the consequences of its pursuit will be agreeable; the pursuit itself is an act of faith.

What starts as an intrusion ends as a necessity. We do not need, in any logical sense, to worry, following Laplace, about the stability of the planetary system. It is, after all, what it is. But to understand the question, as Jefferson did, greatly enriches our perception of the universe and puts the issue—even so slightly—within the range of things about which humans may ultimately be able to take some kind of action.

Jacob T. Schwartz

America's Economic-Technological Agenda for the 1990s

I N JULY 1988 THE UNITED STATES Department of Defense published a report entitled "Bolstering Defense Industrial Competitiveness."[1] Although this document received little notice outside
of the circles typically reached by the defense trade press, it echoed
the growing concerns of a number of important figures in America's
technological community. These administrators are concerned about
the perceived impairment of US technical, industrial, and financial
competitiveness. The trade deficit in particular is identified as having
the potential to undermine the international role, defensibility, democratic stability, and, ultimately, even the independence of the United
States if not actively brought under control. Looking at the national
technical and economic balance sheets of the last decade, they tend to
see a picture of uncontrolled decline in one strategic sector after
another and an unchecked slide from creditor to debtor status, as
well as a loss of banking preeminence and market share in key areas
of technology.

Figure 1 and the following facts lend credence to such concerns. In
1982 the two largest banks in the world (in terms of assets) were
American: Citicorp and Bankamerica; France and Britain boasted the
next five and Japan the eighth. By 1986 Citicorp had sunk to sixth
place, Bankamerica below tenth, and the five largest world banks

*Jacob T. Schwartz is Professor of Mathematics and Computer Science at New York University
and former Director of Information Science and Technology at DARPA.*

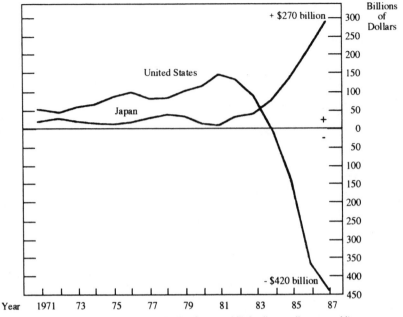

Chart shows America's precipitous decline from world's leading creditor to world's leading debtor, and Japan's astonishing rise. By the end of 1987, estimated net American external assets stood at - $420 billion, while Japan's were + $270 billion.

Figure 1. Net External Assets of the United States and Japan[2]

were all Japanese: Dai-Ichi Kangyo, Fuji, Sumitomo, Mitsubishi, and Sanwa. Between 1982 and 1986 the US share of the overall world semiconductor market dropped from 40 percent to 35 percent while the Japanese share rose from 30 percent to 40 percent. The Japanese advance in the memory chip sector was particularly startling. In 1979 the US share of world computer memory chip production was 75 percent and the Japanese share 25 percent; by 1986 these figures had reversed. The same trends were visible in production of the equipment used to manufacture semiconductors. The US technological position declined with equal rapidity in other key industrial sectors. For example, US machine tool production, which stood at an annual level of $6 billion in 1981, fell to $3 billion by 1987, putting the United States roughly on par with Italy as a machine tool manufacturer. Japanese production, on the other hand, rose from $4 billion to $10 billion, making it the world's leading machine tool manufacturer.

Classically minded economists tend to view such figures with equanimity, seeing in them little more than another temporary and readily reversible, albeit large-scale, movement in a perpetually shifting world trade balance. To many in defense and industrial circles, however, these same figures tell a fearsome tale of abrupt national decline which threatens to become irreversible if not soon checked. Their view reflects an anguished dichotomy. On the one hand they see a self-confident society that possesses great military force as well as political, cultural, and moral influence worldwide. At the same time, they fear that, through a defective sense of national self-interest, perverse surrender to overconsumption, economic-ideological fixations, and unchecked congressional regionalism, this society may loose its preeminence or even allow outsiders to gain control over key sectors of its economy and national destiny.

THEORY

Classical economic theory has shed insufficient light on these strongly felt concerns. This shortcoming has spurred the development of new economic models, which stand in opposition to the neoclassical framework that dominated economic discussion during the Reagan administration. The intellectual issues involved, principally those which surround the General Equilibrium theory of neoclassical economics, are subtle, yet fundamental. Beginning with certain broad economic assumptions, which its further intellectual operations convert into policy-determining certainties, this theory is enormously influential. Its assumptions therefore deserve examination.

In brief, neoclassical theory assumes a stable, linear system—that is, an economy which responds with small fluctuations to changes in its underlying production and consumption schedules but moves smoothly back to its prior condition if these changes are reversed. Its assumption of perfect reversibility and focus on small changes rather than on major trends then come to determine the remaining theoretical and policy views associated with the neoclassical school. For example, attempts to relate the neoclassical equilibrium model to empirical economic fact generally become statistical attempts to estimate "elasticities." This is done by finding constants of proportionality which relate small changes in one or more model parameters to equally small changes in response. The neoclassical focus on small proportional effects implicitly denies the possibility that small persistent effects can have large final consequences; it ignores the ability of a tiny weight thrown into one of the pans of a closely matched balance to move an outcome dramatically to one side or the other. A corollary tendency of the theory is to assume mathematically convenient forms for the curves on which its arguments rest, generally without sufficient (or even any) investigation of the consequences that develop when these curves have shapes other than those uncritically assumed. Related to its implicit assumption of stability is the fact that technological change plays something of a peripheral role in the neoclassical model; technology enters its relatively static world only in muted form, namely as a change in its assumed schedules of unit cost against production volume. However, since the gross form of these schedules rarely becomes the subject of penetrating discussion, this theoretical point often remains without specific consequence.

Given the "linear" predelictions of neoclassical economics, it is only natural that an implicit opposition to its small-differences worldview should develop in military-industrial circles. War is a highly nonlinear environment, full of extreme results following from slight initial imbalances: "For want of a nail the kingdom was lost."

TRADE EQUILIBRIUM IN HIGH-TECHNOLOGY PRODUCTS

The theoretical issues that concern us can be brought into view by considering the supply-demand equilibrium in high-technology products, and by developing a model which is neoclassical in form but shows how entirely nonclassical conclusions can follow from closer consideration of the shapes of the supply and demand curves characteristic of high-technology industry.

Neoclassical economics habitually makes certain assumptions concerning the form that this supply-versus-price schedule will have for "typical" products. These very important though implicit assumptions ultimately derive from eighteenth- and nineteenth-century discussions of agricultural costs and prices, particularly from the observation, by Adam Smith and David Ricardo, that progressively lower-yielding agricultural lands will be brought into production as demand for agricultural products rises. This implies that, given a fixed technology, agricultural production costs and unit prices will be lowest when demand is low, but will rise more and more steeply as

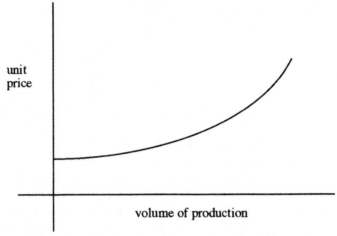

Figure 2. Classical relationship of unit cost to volume of production

demand levels rise, since less and less productive lands will then be brought into use. These considerations, extrapolated to industrial contexts, suggest the neoclassical supply curve invariably seen in introductory economics textbooks.

This figure, familiar to generations of economics students and deeply embedded in the neoclassical worldview, reflects an entirely static view of technology. The forces affecting production costs in high-technology manufacturing are entirely different. In high-technology manufacturing, products and manufacturing methods change continuously and progressively, as a consequence of continually ongoing (and expensive) research and development. This implies, first of all, that the supply curve shown in figure 2 must be regarded as applying, not to a single invariant product, but to whatever is the leading exemplar of a constantly evolving product category, that is, to a whole series of individual products, all having the same general use, even though each product version is improved enough over what has gone before to render all preceding product versions obsolete. A typical example of such a steadily evolving product is a single computer memory chip in its progress though its sixteen thousand bit, sixty-four thousand bit, two hundred fifty-six thousand bit, megabit, and four megabit incarnations. To bring this sort of constantly evolving product into a static framework directly comparable to that assumed in the neoclassical model, one can simply assume that, as long as a sufficient research and development level is sustained, the rate of technological advance will be constant. Such a simplifying assumption allows an unchanging product cost curve to be drawn, albeit for a "current product" that constantly evolves.

Quite different cost considerations are then seen to apply in this new dynamic context than in a technologically static model. For example, in order to produce even one unit of the ever-evolving "current commodity," a firm must maintain a substantial investment in research and development; for complex products this can amount to hundreds of millions of dollars per year or more. Any producer who fails to commit to this level of investment soon loses the ability to produce a technologically competitive product and drops out of the market. Moreover, the required research and development investments allow a fully up-to-date product to be produced, but only in small volumes. To go beyond this—namely to produce a fully up-to-date product in volume and at competitive costs—additional major investments in advanced manufacturing equipment and manufacturing process development are required.

Once these entry costs of research and manufacturing development have been accepted, cost per unit of product can be expected to fall in the course of time as experience allows the weaknesses of complex advanced manufacturing systems to be overcome and as initially experimental processes have time to mature. Manufacturing engineers call such improvements "progress down the learning curve." The reality of this "learning curve" effect, which leads in directions foreign to classical economic reasoning, is apparent in the data shown in figure 3.

These considerations lead to the unit-price-versus-volume curve (figure 5), which differs significantly from the neoclassical variant to which it should be compared (figure 2). Among other things, the new curve slopes in the opposite direction from the neoclassical curve, falling rather than rising with volume of production. This is because cost per unit is extremely *high* (rather than quite *low*) at small product volumes, since high development costs must be amortized even to produce arbitrarily small volumes of product. From this initially high level, the curve diminishes to an initial plateau, at which one encounters the major manufacturing investments needed to bring production costs still lower. Past this plateau, cost per unit *diminishes* rather than *increasing* with rising production volume, since high

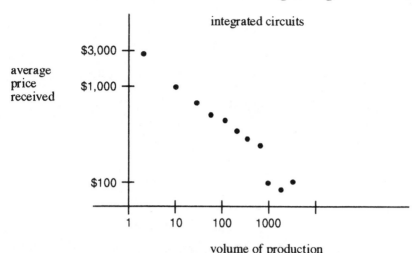

Figure 3. An example of the technological "learning curve"

levels of demand allow firms to progress more rapidly with planned development and manufacturing investments, thereby accelerating their progress down the learning curve.

The high-technology model schematized in figure 5 does not assume a large population of small producers operating along a scale of relatively fixed costs, but rather a relatively small population of fairly large firms, all with roughly equal access to a (steadily advancing) technology, all able to lower costs as sales increase. In this model undersupply *lowers* prices and oversupply *raises* prices (precisely the opposite of the classical conclusion). This is because, in a situation of undersupply, supplying firms will simply increase their production, thereby moving more rapidly down the learning curve; conversely, oversupply will cause firms to cut back on production and thus will slow their average rate of technological progress. Looking at this surprising conclusion in more detail, we can see that, though the initial impact of a condition of undersupply will be to raise prices temporarily (as the classical model would have it), this transient effect will soon be reversed as the supplying firms increase production and come to enjoy lower costs; our model represents the situation that persists after this rapid "bidding-up" period has dissipated.

It should come as no surprise that these two very different mental images inspire entirely different policy conclusions. In the textbook

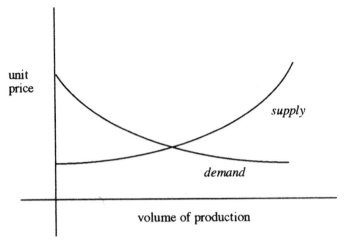

Figure 4. Classical picture of the supply-demand equilibrium

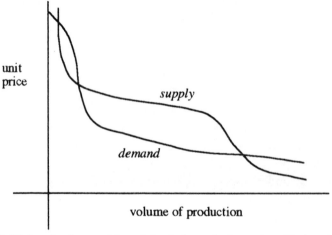

Figure 5. High-technology revision of classical supply-demand equilibrium diagram

neoclassical model shown in figure 4, there will always exist one and only one economic equilibrium—precisely the unique intersection of the rising and falling curves shown. This inherently "placid" equilibrium always responds to small shifts in the underlying supply-demand schedules by moving only slightly. Since the equilibrium point is unique, the influence of past history is continually obliterated by the smooth adjustment of the economic equilibrium to shifts in its determinant supply-demand curves.

The economic equilibria marked by the intersection points in figure 5 behave much more dynamically. Since these intersections are no longer unique, prior history enters as a basic determinant: a society can find itself in one or the other of two possible competitive states, either competitive or entirely overwhelmed, depending on the prior economic history of itself and its competitors. Furthermore, a small shift in either the supply or the demand curve can move crucial parts of one the curves entirely out of contact with the other. This represents the total collapse of an industry overwhelmed by an initially small but persistent price or other advantage accruing to or seized by a competitor.

INDUSTRIAL COLLAPSE

The rightmost equilibrium in figure 5 represents a healthy mass production industry; the intersection point to its left depicts an industry which has lost its mass market but which retains enough priority demand to continue the research and development investments needed for minimal survival as a high-technology enterprise. Analysis of these equilibria reveals the ways in which economic forces can compel transition between these states, and the possibilities for and obstacles to subsequent recovery that then result.

When the right-hand portion of the demand curve in figure 5 drops below the right-hand portion of the supply curve, the high volume supply-demand intersection (the rightmost intersection) disappears, leaving only the low-volume, "high-technology handicraft" equilibria (the two leftmost intersections). This situation can be reached either because demand has fallen (say, because foreign competitors have begun to supply an equivalent or superior product at a lowered price) or because supply prices (for the steadily advancing commodity) have risen. This latter change can, for example, result from the failure of a key supporting industry to advance, thereby making critical but complex manufacturing systems difficult to integrate, or limiting access to advanced tools or materials more easily available to competitors.

Whatever the cause, if and when figure 5 loses its right-hand mass production equilibrium, the firms affected will find that demand has dropped below the level needed to sustain the flow of investment in manufacturing technologies which would allow them to stay competitive in a steadily advancing industry. That will trigger a self-reinforcing negative spiral of investment cutback and accumulating product obsolescence. This decline, inevitable unless checked by policy, will be accompanied by rising effective product price, and hence still lower demand, and will only arrest itself when the second equilibrium is reached. This new equilibrium corresponds to a situation in which all its mass manufacturing capability has decayed, but in which product research can nevertheless be supported, sustaining a much smaller volume of high-cost production oriented to a price-insensitive core of (probably government) demand for advanced technology products.

If even this core of demand is absent, as it may well be in markets serving no government purpose, the declining industry will decay totally, leaving all associated product demand to be satisfied by imports. Much of the infrastructure of supporting services and technical know-how associated with any decaying industry can, of course, be expected to collapse with it. Once this has happened it may be impossible to move back to mass production even if demand subsequently rises. Development would have to start from zero; this would require massive reinvestment, first in product development—involving costs too large, perhaps much too large, to be carried by the few price-insensitive customers originally in sight—followed at once by equally large or larger investments in advanced (and unfamiliar) manufacturing equipment and processes. What this means is that the *zero* product volume case, that is, the situation of complete absence of industry capable of manufacturing a given product, is itself a stable equilibrium of the high-technology model. This implies complete inability to move from the no-industry situation to the other (stable but distant) high-volume, low-price situation.

TEMPORAL FACTORS

The preceding discussion, which views progress down the learning curve as a consequence of production volume only, neglects important temporal issues. This oversimplification is initially convenient since it allows one to use curves without explicit time dependencies to represent supply-demand equilibria. In reality, however, progress toward greater manufacturing efficiency in high-technology industries will occur over the course of time, provided that production continues at a substantial level. For this reason, recurring delay in moving on to new product generations can have an effect equivalent to, hence as fatal as, inherently greater current-product production costs. These delay-dependent effects will often further strengthen a leading competitor's position.

Suppose, for example, that new product generations (say, generations of computer memory chips involving steadily diminishing feature sizes) require steadily more advanced equipment for their production (say, in the same example, more and more refined lithographic equipment). Then, if one of two competitors is able to convert a dominant primary product position (for example, position in memory chip production) into an equally dominant position in regard to related manufacturing equipment items (for example, lithographic equipment), it can cripple outsider attempts to compete—either by outright denial of this equipment or simply by delay.

Such delay can result from any one of many causes. For example, equipment suppliers might be encouraged not to advertise the availability of improved equipment until all of a group of "prime clients" have been equipped, or export approvals or licenses involving lengthy application procedures might be required. If, for example, manufacturing equipment and product both advance steadily at the rate of 50 percent per year, then a competitor whose entry into production is repeatedly subject to six months of delay will remain at a constant 25 percent disadvantage. This is probably enough to cripple all possibility of successful competition on an otherwise level playing field, provided that the commodity in question is as standardized as, for example, memory chips, and as little the focus of countervailing "brand name" preferences.

In such situations a tactic of delay has clear advantages over a tactic of outright denial: denial creates opportunities and incentive for effective objection; delay stifles both. If only delay is involved, all applications for export, duly entered (in the ordinary course of business, this can be expected to involve several weeks of consultation, coordination, and correction as complex forms are filled out and required hearings scheduled on the calendars of busy officials), are approved in due course. Parties awaiting these signatures will generally not wish to complain, since this would only enrage the officials whose approval they are seeking; parties whose cases have just been approved will be in an exultant mood and will not be likely to complain about past delays.

LINKAGES AMONG MANUFACTURING SECTORS

A larger point is implicit in the immediately preceding discussion. Industrial sectors are often linked in a way which makes it possible to convert substantial advantage in one into an expanding circle of advantage in many of the others. These accumulating advantages (or disadvantages) can ultimately have deep effects on the technical infrastructure. It is, for example, commonplace that once manufacturing moves offshore, manufacturing engineering—which can flourish most easily when it is colocated with the manufacturing operations whose problems it must address—will likely follow. Subsidiary engineering services (along with the intricate network of specialized small firms supplying these services) are then likely to spring up at the new location, and shrivel proportionately at the old. Apprenticeships in the skills needed to furnish these subsidiary services are likely to become a concern at the new rather than the old location, since the opposite development would require transnational relocation of medium-level technicians. Falling need for technicians will also reduce demand for the technical skills required to support a declining industry and allow an aging population of technicians to supply all necessary technical services, thus lowering opportunities and motivation for young people to enter apprenticeships. (Note, for example, that the average ages of technicians in American and Japanese machine tool industries are 55 and 31, respectively.) Declining employment opportunities in a shrinking industry will discourage—and eventually eliminate—engineering education in the specialized higher skills that the weakening industry requires, because concentration on the skills it needs will impair a student's employability. Professors of these skills, lacking students, will come to seem old-fashioned. Such accumulated obstacles to industrial participation are precisely what make it so difficult for Nigeria to initiate advanced plastics production or for Saudi Arabia to initiate computer production. In both these cases, the equipment, equipment suppliers, experience, the supporting technical skills, as well as a university system mature and comprehensive enough to support all the needed technical skill are lacking, even though both these nations dispose of ample supplies of the raw materials—oil and sand—needed to produce plastics and silicon chips respectively.

Linkage to key industrial sectors in which a nation is either strong or weak creates national advantages and disadvantages that spill over to other sectors. For example, Japan's very strong position in the high-end consumer camera market strengthens its ability to produce the very advanced optical systems required for submicron lithography. This provides an advantage for production of memory chips, microprocessors, liquid crystal screens (of the type used in miniature portable television sets and laptop computers), large flat panel displays (currently under consideration for HDTV use), and so on. Japan's strong position in consumer electronics strengthens the hand of its computer industry, both by expanding and stabilizing Japanese domestic demand for electronic parts in general and by creating a market for "second vintage" memory chips, good enough for use in some consumer products but not perfect enough for use in computers. Since the United States lacks this market, comparable manufacturers in the United States may simply have to scrap this part of their production. Its strong consumer electronics position gave Japan the demand base it needed to move into related industries such as the production of high-purity crystalline electronic materials and the miniaturized high-precision equipment used in such production.

ECONOMIC STRATEGIES AVAILABLE IN HIGH-TECHNOLOGY COMPETITION

The instabilities and resulting possibilities for sharp, irreversible economic transition which emerge in the preceding discussion encourage certain aggressive economic strategies which could only achieve smaller (or no) advantage in a purely neoclassical setting. In a classical supply-demand scenario, it makes relatively little sense for one of two competing nations to restrict the other's access to its markets, since the fleeting advantage that such action can gain will disappear once these restrictions are lifted, and, while in effect, will burden other industries in the restricting nation by increasing their import costs. In the high-technology area the situation is different. Here, if one of the two competing nations manages, by whatever means, to lower demand for competing products enough to cause the disappearance of competing industries, then, once the game has tipped in favor of the dominant competitor long enough to give it stable technological and capital advantages, releveling of the playing field need be of little concern, because recovery of the weakened opposing industry will anyhow face intimidating obstacles.

An economically adept and ambitious nation can therefore exploit the inherent instabilities of high-technology competition by identifying a succession of industrial sectors in which major development efforts are to be mounted. These efforts can combine: protection of a domestic demand base by import limitation, formal or informal; government subsidy of research and development; organization of major industrial consortia; export subsidy. Once these instruments of advantage have attained success in a particular economic sector, they can be set aside, since the uncoordinated and sporadic challenges of a weakened and disorganized competitor should then be easy to defeat, simply by refocusing the means initially used to gain supremacy in any particular field. Repeated demonstrations of determination not to surrender captured ground, proceeding in this manner from a firm basis in national policy, should in time convince the isolated industrial groups attempting to operate in the less well-organized context of the subdominant trading nation that head-to-head economic slugging matches with the stronger side are hopeless. They may then react as many US corporations have, namely by searching for other, safer opportunities. In this way, demonstrated willingness to fend off challenges can allow many broad markets to be dominated with little actual redirection of resources.

Classical doctrine holds that protection of one industry penalizes others by driving up their input factor prices, since it cuts them off from lower-cost foreign sources of supply. The very different form and underlying assumptions of the high-technology manufacturing model we have been considering lead to a contrary conclusion. First of all, the price rise occasioned by cutoff of foreign supplies is seen as transient. As domestic industry progresses down its own learning curve, which will generally be substantially the same as that of foreign suppliers, this transient disadvantage will vanish. Beyond this, other sectors of domestic industry will benefit as secondary industrial sectors which support them indirectly (but which support the protected industry more directly) are rebuilt. Thus, both consumers and unprotected industries will often be seen to benefit from demand-retention policies.

JAPANESE ECONOMIC DEVELOPMENT POLICY

The economic policies of Japan, preeminent in their recent and still continuing success, deserve careful examination. Perhaps because the Japanese polity has twice been wiped away by foreign technological superiority—once with the fall of the Tokugawa Shogunate following the visit of Admiral Perry's black ships, and again with the atomic bombing of Hiroshima and Nagasaki—Japan has been willing to use a wider range of tools to strengthen itself technologically and economically than the United States has. Indeed, many mechanisms, formal and informal, protect the Japanese domestic market from foreign competition. These include: control of low-cost capital by the Ministry of Finance (MOF) which is able to direct major loan funds to sectors favored for development, typically through prime loans to major banks which are then guided administratively; the many forms of administrative guidance and industrial organization managed by the Ministry of International Trade and Industry (MITI); import restrictions, regulations, and tariffs; restrictive licensing of import trading companies given legal oligopoly power to import particular commodities; special administrative obstacles, for example, in determining the details of applicable regulations or in getting paperwork submissions accepted (which sometimes seem to arise in areas in which foreign competition is not desired); health, safety, and other specific-product rules not infrequently invoked, especially in such cases; tight organization of retailing and wholesaling by indigenous manufacturers, in part by use of the power over credit that they are able to exercise in consequence of the general credit policies of the Ministry of Finance; the dependence of small firms (for example, retailers) or larger corporate patrons encouraged by the relatively informal character of Japanese law and law enforcement, which enhances the importance of powerful patronage as a way of securing rights; the Japanese tradition of conducting business through stable networks of mutual trust; and an exceptional degree of willingness to accept consumer-adverse situations in support of national economic advance and prominence.

Many students of Japanese economic policy have commented at length on the many layers of protection, formal and informal, which surround the Japanese economy. To give just one example, Bela Balassa and Marcus Noland note the protective effect of Japanese product-approval procedures applying to imports:

> Note has been taken of the difficulty encountered in bringing demonstration samples to Japan, in which the restrictive interpretation of customs regulations greatly increases costs and delays the presentation of samples. . . . Products subject to import license receive a permit for a period of three to seven years and the application process has to be started again following a license's expiration. The permits are given to the Japanese importer rather than the foreign exporter. . . . Japanese product approval procedures are import-restrictive in theory as well as in practice. The applicable product approval standards, the methods by which such standards are promulgated, and the procedures established to test and certify imported products for compliance with these standards all provide significant impediments to the importation into Japan of many US goods.[3]

One of many factors impeding foreign penetration of the Japanese market is the exceptional importance of marketing consortia, organized and dominated by manufacturers—the so-called *keiretsu*. The tight control over retail distribution exerted by these organizations poses formidable barriers to would-be foreign entrants into the Japanese market. Among other difficulties, foreign ownership, in excess of 50 percent, of ten or more retail outlets has, in the past, required special approval by the national government, and foreign companies have been prohibited from underwriting installment loans for consumer purchases. The consequences which flow from the lack of corresponding US restrictions is noted by Clyde Prestowitz:

> The high quality and low prices of Japanese automobiles have rightly been praised in the United States. However, distribution is critical to sales. Japanese manufacturers were able to build substantial dealer networks in the United States to a large extent by selling through existing GM, Ford, and Chrysler dealers . . . not because US auto companies welcomed Japanese competition but because American law protected the independence of the dealer. For the same reason, Hyundai of Korea has established a nationwide distribution network in the United States in about two years' time. Hyundai's cars are less expensive than Japanese cars and of good quality. Indeed, the engine and other key parts are imported from Japan. Nevertheless, no Hyundais had been sold in Japan as of January 1988. One reason is

that a Toyota or Nissan dealer who even winked at a Hyundai salesman would find himself in serious trouble with his friendly supplier, who has few antitrust concerns.[4]

Japanese patent and trademark administration creates still another layer of obstacles to foreign penetration of the Japanese market. Balassa and Noland comment on the difficulties in obtaining patent and trademark protection experienced by US firms attempting to operate in Japan:

> Even in the absence of unauthorized copying, the delay experienced in obtaining patents permits Japanese firms to develop products having similar characteristics on their own. This is said to have occurred in the case of fiber optics, where patent protection to US products was delayed by 7 to 10 years. The same fate befell Sohio, which created a process for making high-tech ceramics that was imitated by Japan's Kyocera Corporation following the submission of Sohio's patent application in Japan. Sohio is given little chance to succeed in its patent infringement suit. More generally, it has been suggested that, if foreign companies apply for crucial patents which may give them an important competitive advantage, MITI may delay awarding the patent until Japanese producers have a chance to catch up or apply for patents to cover similar technology.
>
> In the United States the rights to a trademark belong to the firm that first used it commercially, but in Japan foreign trademarks may be registered by Japanese companies with a view toward preempting their subsequent introduction by foreign firms that have used them at home or abroad. A case in point is the cigarette industry. The Japanese tobacco monopoly applied for Japanese trademark rights to 50 foreign brands, including names such as Newport, Tareyton, and Century. In another instance, Nippon Shoe Co. registered the 70-year-old American footwear trademark Allen Edmonds and had to be paid "compensation" to desist from using the trademark. Finally, Japanese companies registered Mickey Mouse as a trademark, and the petitions by Walt Disney Productions to invalidate the trademark were rejected. Popeye has suffered a similar fate.[5]

THE NATIONAL INTEREST

Here we may appropriately note Alexander Hamilton's summary remark on those very similar measures of economic protection which he found to be as important in 1791 as they are to current Japanese economic policy: "Remarks of this kind are not made in a spirit of complaint. It is for the nations whose regulations are alluded to, to judge for themselves, whether, by aiming at too much, they do not lose more than they gain. It is for the United States to consider by what means they can render themselves least dependent on the combinations, right or wrong, of foreign policy."[6] How then is the United States national interest to be conceived?

A first important—but by no means maximally important— national aim must simply be to maintain and improve the national standard of living. In the Hamiltonian view, the only way to do this over the long term is to continually develop the technical-capital infrastructure and the skills on which the US standard of living rests. Although the volume of goods available for consumption or investment can be expanded somewhat through trade with nations having natural endowments and developed capabilities complementary to those of the United States, the potential national benefit of such trade in high-technology areas must be expected to diminish steadily, since the worldwide diffusion of technology gives all developed and developing nations equal long-term ability to produce high-technology goods.

At the next level of importance, the nation must aim, with great vigor, to balance its foreign trade account, even if this means accepting a temporary decrease in the standard of living. Any other policy implies an indefinitely mounting burden of foreign debt, inevitably leading to a progressive loss of national economic independence.

Protecting the national technical infrastructure and community has the highest level of importance. At a minimum, this involves maintaining a well-equipped technical and manufacturing cadre familiar with and actively involved in the advance of all significant technologies, together with technologically first-class, though occasionally small-scale, manufacturing facilities in each such area, used constantly and aggressively to pursue new product development, which must always be capable of rapid scale-up in case of cut-off of foreign supplies or strongly adverse motion in the terms of trade. Absent such capabilities, technical shortfalls, incapable of repair except over years or even decades, will develop to an unknown and potentially uncontrollable degree in sectors dangerous for defense and debilitating economically. In particular, lack of sufficient capability both to manufacture at meaningful scale and to stay abreast of world product innovation exposes the nation to multiple generations of technical disadvantage as competitors develop increasingly sophisticated product designs, uncomprehended by the United States, along with multiple levels of manufacturing technology in support of these designs, and come to hold patent positions able to wall off belated US attempts to reenter lost fields of technology.

The analyses and claims of the advocates of untrammeled world trade must be assessed against this background. Although it is true that, in economic sectors other than the idealized high-technology industrial areas which our high-technology models address, more traditional factors of national advantage can lead to stable patterns of international trade affording all the mutual benefit claimed by ardent antiprotectionists, these factors do not act strongly enough in high-technology industries to prevent the instabilities discussed above from taking hold over the long run. This is especially true if one side tips the balance by protecting its internal markets, or if such cultural-institutional factors as a longer working week, better-sustained diligence, greater tendency to save, or a stronger educational system acts for long to favor one or another side.

Unmanaged trade intimacy in the presence of the inherent tendency of such industrial sectors to concentrate themselves on one side or the other will only be possible if either or both of the trading partners have so great a degree of trust in each other's cultural and political stability and abiding benevolence that they are willing to share industrial sectors in the same confident way that they would be shared among the provinces of a single nation. The technologically secondary nation in such an intimate partnership or multisided relationship might then—by restraining its appetite for high-technology products to what it can persistently earn in the ways open to it—develop a healthy niche economy. Applied to the United States, this is to imagine a situation in which America transforms itself into an enormous Switzerland, which would export aluminum, coal, grain, gourmet wines and cheese, plus services to European and Asian tourists come to seek solace in such unique national resources as the Grand Canyon, Niagara Falls, Rocky Mountain ski resorts, the Oregon coast, and the placid lakes of Minnesota. (Of course, even in such a scenario, administrative steps would have to be taken to prevent sale of these natural assets to foreign multimillionaires, who might otherwise be tempted to put them off-limits except to that servant part of the native population actively involved in their upkeep.)

Arizona might, in this view, develop enormously extensive golf courses which would afford well-to-do residents of Europe and Asia luxurious release from the crowding inevitable in their home environments. By restocking buffalo and deer, parts of the Dakotas might be transformed into game parks rivaling the Serengeti. Through appropriate refurbishment, an urban area such as New York might reverse its present Calcutta-like decay, converting itself instead into a giant Copenhagen or new Vienna, in whose impeccable hotels and immaculate subways, streets, bistros, and opera houses its population would work as multilingual tour guides, hotel chambermaids, chefs, actors, and rock performers of a kind not found elsewhere. Insofar as it was not rendered wholly unnecessary by the rapid moral advance of humanity as a whole, defense would then have to be, indeed could safely be, left to foreign allies, whose abiding and unshakeable fondness for America, developed through consumption of its delightful specialities and many pleasant visits as tourists, would doubtless commit them immovably to this role. Happy America might then come to enjoy the freedom from unproductive international involvements and the political serenity now seen in Canada.

There is, however, another possible outcome of the continuing technological decay occasioned by persistent refusal to either protect the nation's demand base or restrict its consumption of imports to the level that export earnings allow. In this nightmare world, America would sink rapidly to Third World status. The bulk of its population would find itself progressively forced into steadily worse-paying service jobs requiring less and less advanced education, while a better-off but steadily narrowing part of the population would sell assets to sustain access to foreign goods—which could come to be unproducible or simply unproduced in the United States for exactly the same reasons that Ford cars are not produced in Zaire. Even this access to imports would of course narrow year by year as the dollar sank from 275 yen to 125, then to 50, 25, 10, or whatever level brought continuing demand for imported high-technology products into better balance with remaining US exports of logs, grain, coal, blueberries, and tourist services. As imports continued to be financed through accelerating sales of the nation's stock of capital assets (a process already far advanced), the fate of America's remaining industry would come to be determined more and more completely by foreign managers. These managers would then need to determine the extent to which it would be prudent to strengthen their reputation over the long-term by raising their American operations and staffs to full partnership status, versus the extent to which it lay in their interest to prevent any possibility of breakaway competition by neglecting to make key manufacturing technologies and designs available.

As developments of this sort came to collide ever more nakedly with elemental nationalist resentment, the concerns characteristic of such resentment could be expected to rise rapidly into political visibility. Anguished discussion of the level of foreign ownership might then be expected to begin, soon to be followed by accusations of financial dependence on and subservience to foreign interests. As such discussions grew in intensity, they would doubtless come to alarm foreign investors, perhaps thereby diminishing the heavy capital inflows that would remain the dollar's only prop in the face of annual trade deficits exceeding $100 billion. Once this were to happen—especially if one or more foreign central banks were in a mood for retaliation—the dollar's fall could accelerate at any moment, since the volatility of the speculative international markets that operate in this area could easily drop the dollar's value by 10 percent or more within a few catastrophic days.

The shocks that this might transmit to the economy, via wild gyrations of US interest rates, stock and housing prices, and employment levels, might then trigger waves of alarm, convincing the American public that the nation's destiny was adrift in some ill-understood, but nevertheless terrifying sense, while at the same time suggesting to foreign investors that they need to use all the means available to them to assure the safety of their heavy investments in the United States. Aside from direct attempts to influence elections and other American political mechanisms, this would doubtless inspire both open demands for US austerity, of the sort regularly addressed to Third World borrowers, and more direct threats, whispered at first into a few key ears, but certain to become widely and quickly known—and very much resented. Pessimists, swayed by this vision, may well conclude that if new policy measures do not avert this development before it grows to full virulence, the opportunity might arise for some warped genius currently footloose in the nation to rally it behind a slogan like *Wake Up America!,* whose potentially hurricane force is amply suggested by the history of our troubled century.

These grim speculations suggest that unrestricted trade in high-technology sectors, based on an entirely unrestricted national treatment principle, can only stand as a fixed axiom of prudent policy insofar as it concerns nations that share the deepest aspects of history and tradition. National economic merger may be appropriate for nations that are willing to entrust their national fate to each other over the long term—at least to the extent manifest among the European nations about to join in the post-1992 Common Market. But among nations, entirely unguarded trade relations in high technology need to be approached with the same cautious eye for long-term consequence as marriage between individuals. Where sober consideration reveals differences which prevent so intimate and permanent a national relationship, our analysis suggests that it is better for both parties to stabilize their technological relationship by roughly symmetrical control measures, even though this admittedly foregoes a part of the benefit which perfectly unrestricted trade might garner. It is, in particular, useless and even counterproductive in view of this analysis for the more open of two partners to continually hound the other to adopt a like policy of economic openness, perpetually illusory both because of the dangers which deeply rooted national attitudes may suggest and because of the economic instabilities to which such a policy is objectively exposed. It is hard, in this context, to imagine that Japan, having established the record of success visible in figure 1, craves instruction in economics from the US, whose record is as figure 1 shows it to be, or to believe that the perpetually nagging and accusing US voice in trade negotiations achieves much by its endless insistence on rules, fair in the US view, which contravene not only Japan's sense of self-interest but that nation's deeply ingrained cultural preference for conducting business through tight, long-established networks of mutual trust. In this view, to expect that sermons delivered to an insular nation, far more persuaded than even the (pre-EEC) British that "Wogs begin at Calais," will be productive of little more than frustration. Our analysis—like Hamilton's remarks—suggest that the United States accept Japan's present behavior as a clear statement of that nation's immovable policy choice, and that the United States go on to implement policies of its own that can be effective in the world defined by this choice, by other national choices as they are made, and by the fundamental economic forces surveyed in the preceding pages.

THE INTERNATIONAL INTEREST

The antitrust legislation developed in America's nineteenth century "trust-busting" period still forms the bedrock of national economic policy. The theoretical analysis set forth above suggests that corresponding restrictions on economic behavior may be necessary at the international level.

Because prices can fall rather than rise as production volume in a given nation increases, international competitive trade in high-technology products will often be inherently unstable. As soon as one of two initially equal trading nations pulls significantly ahead of another its advantage will become self-reinforcing and will grow unlimitedly.

This fundamental instability encourages economic aggression among nations trading in high-technology goods. If one trading partner unopposedly uses administrative measures to monopolize its internal demand or encourage exports, or is so constituted culturally as to prefer its domestic products with unusual fervor, it can gain the initial advantage needed to ultimately overwhelm any less-determined competitor.

Even though these tendencies would be harmless in an ideal world of international benevolence and trust (after all, the presence of large nuclear weapons facilities in California inspires no fear in Oregon, nor does New York state expect Massachusetts manufacturers to restrict its access to vital technologies) they are far from harmless in the world as it is today. To overcome these tendencies international policies like those represented in United States domestic antitrust legislation may well be necessary. In contrast to the antitrust laws—whose ideological focus is narrowly consumeristic—these internationally oriented policy measures would need to center on retention of technological capability and infrastructure as basic aims. Like the antitrust laws, which make domination of an undue market share a matter of policy concern whether or not the firms involved are of innocent intent, the required policies would have to make such objective current matters as the overall Japanese share of memory chip or VCR production matters of countervailing intervention.

It is clear that in an ideal world such matters might best be settled by an international legislature acting in the interest of general world economic development in all its regional aspects. In the absence not only of such a legislature but of the fundamental social and cultural relationships on which its existence would necessarily rest, the United States needs—now no less than in Hamilton's day—to make the required policies for itself. It must always seek to find truly fair international agreements—whether multinational or bilateral—in the broader international interest, but must also proceed with the understanding that overall stabilization of the otherwise unstable patterns of high-technology production is a valid part of this international interest; one-sided consumeristic arguments may have to give way to this basic concern. If this implies a break with even such treasured shibboleths of US international diplomacy as GATT, then so be it.

MARKET PROTECTION AND RAPID TECHNOLOGICAL ADVANCE AS COMPETING STRATEGIES

The economic models reviewed earlier suggest that to achieve the multibillion dollar flows of research, development, and manufacturing investment required, a national strategy needs to combine some degree of protection of the US domestic high-technology product market with development measures aimed more directly at rapid technological advance. These models also suggest that market protection and the drive for rapid technological advance are complementary alternatives, in the sense that market-protection measures may become unnecessary, at least temporarily, in any sector in which the United States can use the strength of its scientific/engineering community to keep consistently ahead of potential competitors by repeatedly revolutionizing the technical situation.

The fixed aversion to measures of protection that has characterized US policy throughout the postwar period has encouraged technical policy thinking to concentrate on pure let's-advance-technology strategies for restoring the nation's declining competitiveness. Key elements in such a strategy include subsidy of universities and technically progressive industries, encouragement of research consortia such as Sematech, and fast-moving yet sagacious choice of technologically radical projects by the cooperating government, industrial, and management groups responsible for steering the national technical enterprise. This "strategy of nimbleness" has been much favored, since it both sidesteps painful import policy discussions and appeals to a technocowboy self-image with deep roots in the American psyche. Unfortunately, much now acts to undercut this soft alternative. Economic competitors like Japan, having grown immensely rich, are finding it easy to buy as directly as they like into the US innovative machine. Examples include: establishment of long-term technology access arrangements at leading US research universities in return for major endowments and equipment gifts; establishment of US laboratories; and outright purchase of the small and medium-sized firms in which much US leading-edge innovation is concentrated. Foreign support is increasingly being offered to the best US universities and researchers as a pleasant and more lucrative alternative to the tedious process of applying for federal research grants. Ideas travel rapidly across national boundaries; in the absence of wealth, manufacturing processes which demand massive capital setups seem certain to travel orders of magnitude more slowly. America's federal technomanagers can no longer be certain that the ideas being offered to them have not already become known to—and perhaps already been offered to and rejected by—increasingly omnipresent foreign competitors. They cannot be certain that the fruits of their investments, which generally can be no larger than a few million dollars, are not garnered for a few tens of millions by foreign investors—if not right away, then a bit later, perhaps when the startup firms carrying these innovations run into cash-flow difficulties and save themselves by selling themselves.[7]

All of this is not to say that measures accelerating technological advance need not play a role in an overall national technology strategy. The United States obviously needs to strengthen its distinctly inferior elementary and middle school educational system. University research laboratories must be kept up-to-date and well funded as well. A tolerant view needs to be taken of the floundering which is inevitable—even in such relatively large undertakings as Sematech—as formulae for consortia capable of improving the level of effective cooperation between US firms are actively sought. The domestic antitrust law itself needs to be relaxed in ways that realistically reflect the fact that the US economy is no longer an isolated island, and that US firms are forced to operate in an environment containing major foreign competitors who are not subject to comparable restrictions. Policies of targeted subsidy like those advocated by Hamilton need to be thought out. But amidst all these measures direct legislative stabilization of the all-important international trade flows must not be ruled off-limits.

SOME FINAL REFLECTIONS ON THE DANGERS OF SUCCESS

If and when the United States succeeds in getting its own economic-technological house in order, it may need to take steps to repair the damage this adjustment may have caused its allies and trading partners. In such a context, Japan' situation would require special consideration. Once the present competitive decline of the United States is arrested, the economic strengths of the United States and Japan ought to shift to a ratio reflecting the sizes of their respective populations; in addition, some significant advantage should accrue to the United States in view of its much greater land mass and resource endowment. Europe after 1992 should also play an increasingly larger role in international economics. Japan's position may weaken further as East Asian entities—including Korea, Taiwan, and especially China—grow relative to Japan in economic power. Such a scenario could easily inspire alarm in a nation as inherently import-dependent as the ever-pessimistic Japanese. In this scenario, it is easy to see inherent weaknesses in Japan's situation. In American terms, its stock prices are astonishingly inflated in proportion to profits and rest in part on equally inflated land prices. It depends in part on a net of informal interfirm support understandings that may be vulnerable to rupture under sufficient strain, even given the steely tendency of the Japanese to hold together in times of difficulty. It is therefore easy to imagine a scenario in which successful steps on the part of the United States to reverse its present competitive decline could transmit fearsome shocks to the Japanese economy. In such a case the forces of enraged nationalism might mount with substantially greater rapidity in Japan (whose citizens see their nation as having *chosen* the Merchant Way), than is seen as possible in even the grimmest national scenario for the United States (whose citizens believe that their nation *is* democratic). To obviate devastating developments of this kind, a more successful United States might find it appropriate to give Japan binding guarantees against its worst national fears, for example, by committing not only to Japan's defense, but by committing to share resources of food, oil, and minerals in case of major economic difficulty.

ENDNOTES

[1]Department of Defense, *Bolstering Defense Industrial Competitiveness: Report to the Secretary of Defense by the Under Secretary of Defense (Acquisition)*, July 1988.

[2]Burstein, *Yen! Japan's New Financial Empire and its Threat to America* (New York,: Simon and Schuster, 1988), 125.

[3]Bela Balassa and Marcus Noland, *Japan in the World Economy* (Washington: Institute for International Economics, 1988), 217.

[4]Clyde Prestowitz, *Changing Places* (New York: Basic Books, 1988).

[5]Belassa and Noland, 234.

[6]Alexander Hamilton, *Report on Manufactures: Report by the Secretary of the Treasury to the Second Congress of the United States*, 1791.

[7]See the many examples of this trend documented in the brilliant studies of the US microelectronic industry conducted by Professor Charles Ferguson of MIT. See Charles Ferguson, *Sources and Implications of Strategic Decline: The Case of Japanese-American Competition in Microelectronics*, technical report, Center for Technology, Policy, and Industrial Development (Cambridge: Massachusetts Institute of Technology, 1987); see also *From the People Who Brought You Voodoo Economics*, Harvard Business Review (May–June 1988); and Michael Dertouzos, et al., *Made in America: Regaining the Productive Edge*, MIT Commission on Productivity (Cambridge: MIT Press, 1989).

Terrence J. Sejnowski and Patricia S. Churchland

Computation in the Age of Neuroscience

B RAINS ARE MASSIVELY PARALLEL, ANALOG, biological computers. They are far more powerful, flexible, and compact
than any manufactured computer. The computational principles that make brains such effective computers are radically
different from those that are used in conventional digital designs.[1]
Some neurocomputational principles, such as analog processing
in dendritic trees and synaptic plasticity, have already been discovered by biologists, but many more principles have yet to be
identified. Analog VLSI (Very Large Scale Integration) technology
may provide a medium for exploring these principles and creating
new computational architectures. A partnership between neuroscience and computer technology is opening a path toward building
silicon brains that can grapple with the real world. In the next
century, this partnership could provide new insights into the nature of our own brains as well as engender ideas for remarkable
new machines made in our image.

BEES AND AGRIBOTS

Imagine a computing device that would revolutionize the stoop
labor sector of agriculture. In midsummer, the agribot travels up
and down rows of tomato plants, picking those tomatoes red-
dened to maturity while leaving small green tomatoes on the vine.
It sorts the harvest according to size, tossing down for fertilizer

*Terrence J. Sejnowski is an Investigator with the Howard Hughes Medical Institute,
Director of the Computational Neurobiology Laboratory at the Salk Institute in La Jolla,
and a member of the Biology Department at the University of California, San Diego.*

*Patricia S. Churchland is a MacArthur Fellow in the Philosophy Department at the
University of California, San Diego and an adjunct member of the Salk Institute.*

any fruit spoiled by rotten spots. Its sister agribots rove the tomato fields in early spring, some pulling up weeds and some picking off grubs, thereby reducing the farm's dependence on pesticides and herbicides. Other agribots toil in the peach orchards; some prune the trees in early spring, some delicately pick the fruit during the summer.

Although mechanical devices, including tomato-pickers, have been invented for agriculture, typically the machine-product interface requires downgrading the produce so that nondiscerning and inflexible machines can be used. But this compromise is not inevitable. Unafraid of heights and unwearying in their chores, the agribots allow farmers to grow high quality, as opposed to rubbery and tough, fruit and vegetables.

What would it take to make this appealing science fiction real? First, the agribots need computational insides that are *very* small, *very* cheap, and *enormously* powerful. Second, the computational style of the devices must allow for flexibility in sensory categorization and adaptability in motor control. Abandoning the conventional wisdom—"program a universal machine to create a precise virtual machine"— engineers will have to harken to a very different strategy: "create a real-time machine with feedback mechanisms, and let it learn to perform its task." Is this fantasy within the realm of engineering possibility?

Superficially, the bets would appear to be against. Existing digital computers lack the autonomy, flexibility, and adaptability required by the fictional agribots. Nothing remotely close to the desired miniaturization and energy efficiency is available in the electronics marketplace.

A more positive response, however, comes from noting that biological computers replete with the agribot's features do already exist. Brains of insects, birds, fish, and mammals represent an existence proof for powerful, fast, flexible, and self-reliant computers. Nature did it, so it ought to be possible for us to do it. Nevertheless, between the existence proof and the construction kit lies a vast gap.

Consider, for example, the brain of a honeybee, which has about a million neurons compared with the 100 billion neurons in a human brain (figure 1). Consider *energy efficiency*: the bee's brain dissipates less than 10 microwatts (10^{-6}), superior by about

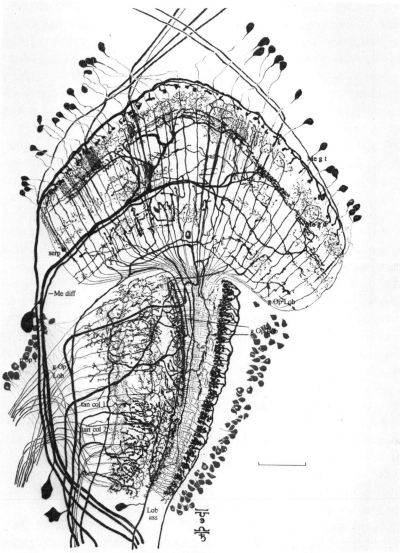

Figure 1. Circuitry in the visual system of the fly (*Musca domesticus*). The organization is very like that in bees, butterflies, and other insects. This drawing shows only about 10% of the actual number of neurons in the region. Even without identifying each pathway and each neuron type, the system's highly organized and regular structure is visible. Note that the large neurons (black, left) differ systematically in the level of their destination, the choice of cells to contact, and the precise location of contact with specific cells. Scale bar is 20 μm. (Drawing by N. J. Strausfeld, *Atlas of an Insect Brain*. New York: Springer-Verlag, 1976)

7 orders of magnitude to the most efficient manufactured computer. Consider *speed*: a bee brain, on a rough and conservative estimate, performs about 10 teraflops (a thousand gigaflops); the most powerful computers approach speeds of only 10 gigaflops (a billion operations per second). Consider *behavioral repertoire*: honeybees harvest nectar from flowers and bring the nectar back to the hive. They maximize foraging benefits and minimize foraging costs, for example, by recognizing high nectar sites and remembering which flowers have been visited. They can see, smell, fly, walk, and maintain balance. They can navigate long distances, and they can predict changes in nectar location by extrapolating from the past regularities. They communicate nectar sources to worker bees in the hive, they recognize intruders and attack, they remove garbage and dead bees from the hive, and when the hive becomes crowded, a subpopulation will swarm in search for a new home. Consider *autonomy and self-reliance*: bees manage all this on their own, without the aid of human intelligence to supervise them, repair them, or nurse them along. A supercomputer, by contrast, needs the constant tender care of a cadre of maintainers and programmers, not to mention financiers. Finally, the entire bee brain takes up only about a few cubic millimeters of space, a marvel of miniaturization.

Research aimed at understanding how brains work will likely be a profitable undertaking, even in the near future. On the one hand are important medical consequences, not to mention the sheer intellectual value of understanding ourselves. Less appreciated, but potentially more significant in economic terms, are technological spin-offs. Knowledge of evolution's computational tricks and architectural ingenuities for speed, power, and flexibility can be applied to a variety of problem domains.

Agriculture may be but one such domain; deep sea mining, defense, pollution clean-ups, and space exploration are others. Current generation neural nets capture some highly general features of brains, such as parallel architecture. Primitive as they are, neural nets of 1990 vintage might be epoched as the "Bronze Age" artifacts of brain-style computer technology. This is not to belittle their very significant beginning, but only to affirm that they are *just a beginning*. Still ahead are epochs advancing the art beyond this first step.

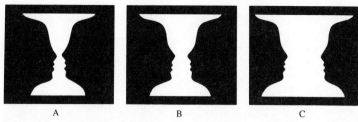

Figure 2. Figure-ground reversal. There are two perceptual interpretations of these images: a pair of black faces, or a white vase. The interpretation can be influenced by conscious attention and biased by features in the image. Thus, the face interpretation is generally favored in A and the vase interpretation in C. (From S. Coren and L. W. Ward, *Sensation and Perception*. San Diego: Harcourt Brace Janovich, 1989)

REVERSE ENGINEERING THE BRAIN

In a very general sense, brains compute. The net result is that they represent the world and manage to survive in it. Computational neuroscience is an emerging field dedicated to figuring out how real brains represent and compute. Computer modeling of neural circuits is essential to the enterprise as a means of addressing how neurons (the cellular components of nervous systems) interact with each other to produce complex effects such as segregating figure from ground, recognizing a banana in many different orientations, or visual tracking of moving targets in 3-D space (figure 2).

Neuroscience contributes three main ingredients to the neuromodeling enterprise: (1) anatomical parameters such as the precise tree structure of various neuron types and the exact connectivity between neurons (who talks to whom) in a particular real network; (2) physiological parameters such as response characteristics of neurons, time constants, synaptic sign, etc., and (3) clues to the network's function and its computational *modus operandi* in executing that function. The main techniques involve intervening in the system, for example by lesioning or by electrical stimulation (figure 3).

Models highly constrained by neurobiological parameters provide a particularly efficient means for exploring the computational wherewithal of nervous systems. Analysis of a highly constrained working model, in turn, can inform neurobiologists about unsus-

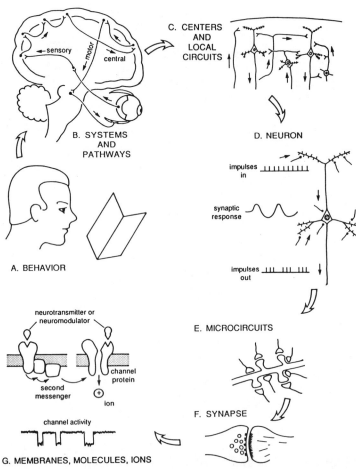

Figure 3. Levels of organization in nervous systems. According to spatial scale, the components of the nervous systems as currently understood include (A) *central nervous system behavior,* including the brain and spinal cord; (B) *systems,* such as the visual system, auditory system, and motor system; in many regions of the brain the topography of neurons corresponds to the topography of its input domain, such as the retina or the skin; (C) *networks* of neurons, which may consist of many thousands of interconnected neurons; (D) the individual *neuron,* which can be either excited or inhibited by inputs from other neurons. (E) On small patches of dendrite of a given cell, the input to synapses interact to constitute a *microcircuit.* (F) At the *synapse,* a signal is passed from the sending cell to the receiving cell, usually by means of a chemical released from the sender that attaches to the receiving cell and changes the cell's voltage a tiny amount. (G) On the *molecular* level, ion channels consist of proteins in the membrane that may reconfigure under restricted conditions to allow specific ions, for example Ca^{2+}, to enter the cell in response to chemical or electrical signals. (From G. Shepherd, Neurobiology, 2nd edition. Oxford: Oxford University Press, 1988)

pected mechanisms and interactions, whose reality can then be tested in actual nervous systems.

By continuously inspiring, correcting, and informing each other, neuroscience and computer modeling can co-evolve to greater accuracy and greater adequacy, respectively. This co-evolution is already producing ideas for innovative computational procedures and architectural design relevant to such problems as real-time interacting, efficient associative memory storage, mixed modality coordination, multiplexing, and attentional selectivity.

SIMULATE OR SYNTHESIZE?

As in simulating a hurricane or a heart on a digital machine, simulating neurons runs afoul of the real time problem. Such machines are not yet powerful enough to both faithfully simulate the system's processes and do it in real time. Either close imitation of neuronal operations or real time has to be sacrificed. The problem is that the simulation strategy consists of compartmentalizing the phenomenon and solving vast numbers of differential equations. It is, therefore, pitifully slow, relative to the real performance-time of the system simulated.

In a neuron, ions pass back and forth across the membrane, signals are integrated, output spikes are produced[2]—all in a matter of a few milliseconds (figure 4). To simulate a millisecond in the life of a neuron, however, thousands of coupled nonlinear differential equations have to be solved. To compound the difficulty, these equation are "stiff," in the sense that they embrace a wide variety of time scales. This means that the simulation's time steps can only be as long as the *shortest* significant interval. Consequently, even a powerful work station will take minutes to simulate a millisecond of real time of a single neuron (figure 5).

Constructing dedicated hardware for synthetic neurons and synthetic nervous systems is the way to circumvent this dead-ending ponderousness of simulation. One obvious strategy, then, is to construct neuron-like chips. To construct chips that compute as wondrously as real neurons, we must first understand how real neurons do it. The production of a spike in the axon of a neuron is indeed an all-or-nothing affair, but the purely digital properties of neurons stop there. Processing in dendrites is analog, including

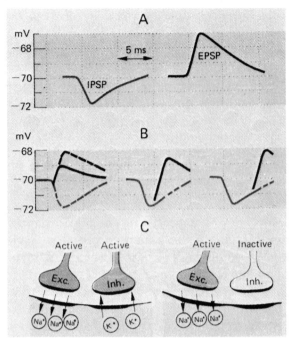

Figure 4. Inhibitory and excitatory synapses on a neuron. (A) The inhibitory postsynaptic potential (IPSP) means that the postsynaptic cell hyperpolarizes (dropping from −70 mv to −72 mv), and the excitatory postsynaptic potential (EPSP) means that the postsynaptic cells depolarizes (from −70 mv to −67 mv). (B) The EPSP was triggered about 1, 3, and 5 sec after the onset of the IPSP. (C) The subsynaptic conductance changes occurring when excitatory and inhibitory synapses are activated simultaneously (left) and when only the excitatory synapse is activated (right). (From R. F. Schmidt, *Fundamentals of Neurophysiology.* Berlin: Springer-Verlag, 1978)

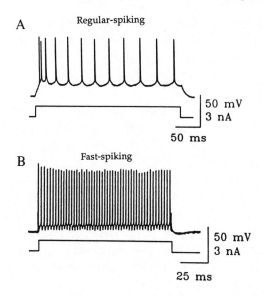

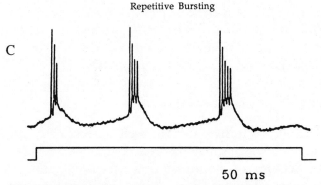

Figure 5. Differences in intrinsic firing patterns of cortical neurons. (A) When stimulated with a suprathreshold step of depolarizing current, regular-spiking neurons respond with an initial high-frequency spike output that rapidly declines to much lower sustained frequencies. Intracellular voltages are displayed in the top trace, injected current steps in the bottom trace. (B) Under similar conditions, fast-spiking cells generate high frequencies that are sustained for the duration of the stimulus. (C) Repetitive intrinsic bursting to a prolonged stimulus. Mean inter-burst frequency was about 9 Hz. (From B. W. Connors and M. J. Gutnick, "Intrinsic firing patterns of diverse neocortical neurons." *Trends in Neurosciences* 13, 1990: 98–99).

both active nonlinear mechanisms that amplify signals as well as passive cable properties. Even axonal spiking is analog in some respects; the time when the spike occurs (it can be any time), the frequency of spikes in a train, the duration of the repolarization period, and so on (figure 6).

Real circuits, of course, have many imperfections. Invariably, they lapse from idealizations and component homogeneity, membranes are typically leaky, components malfunction or drop dead, there can be cross-coupling, and so forth. Contrary to the impulse to shun chip construction in favor of simulation, the farseeing advice is that we find the secret of how to get precision, speed, and power out of imperfect and imprecise components. The point is, somehow neurons operate in real time and cope magnificently, probably *exploiting* "imperfections" to their advantage. Consequently, the coping capacity of real-world neurons is itself computationally interesting.

Neurons are organic. They use lipid molecules to make resistive membranes, complex proteins for ion channels that allow current flow across the membrane, and cytoplasm in which current travels; mitochondria are the micro powerpacks, circulating oxygen is the energy source, and so on. What can the engineer use to construct synthetic neurons, if not these materials?

THE TECHNOLOGY OF CHOICE: ANALOG VLSI

Analog VLSI technology turns out to be well suited to the construction task for two reasons, one theoretical and one practical.[3] (1) The device physics of doped silicon, when operating in subthreshold regions, is comparable to the biophysics of ion channels in neuron membrane; that is, the current passing through a membrane's ion channels follows Boltzmann statistics. This allows one to implement the differential equations directly with analog circuits in CMOS (complementary oxide semiconductor) VLSI. (2) The very same techniques used for creating digital VLSI chips can be adapted to make analog VLSI chips. Carver Mead (at Cal Tech and Synaptics) and Federico Faggin of Synaptics, who played leading roles in digital chip technology, are now spearheading the development of analog chip technology for neural systems (table 1).

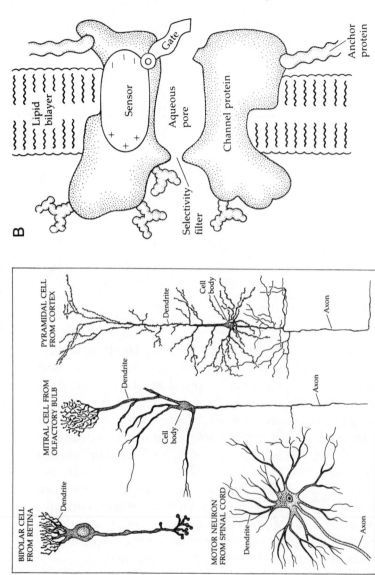

Figure 6. Neurons and neural mechanisms. (A) Examples of neurons illustrating the variety of shapes in different areas of the brain. (From S. W. Kuffler, J. G. Nicholls and A. R. Martin, *From Neuron to Brain: A Cellular Approach to the Function of the Nervous System*, 2nd edition. Sunderland, Mass.: Sinauer, 1984) (B) Working hypothesis for a voltage-gated channel. The transmembrane protein is shown with a pore that allows sodium ions to flow between the extracellular and intracellular sides of the membrane when the gate is open. (From B. Hille, *Ionic Channels of Excitable Membranes*. Sunderland, Mass.: Sinauer, 1984)

TABLE I. VLSI neural nets: figures of merit. Analog VLSI is strikingly superior to digital technology in terms of cost, power and computation density. (From Federico Faggin)

	Cost (MCS[a]/$)		Power (MCS/Watt)		Computation Density (MCS/ft³)	
	1991	2000	1991	2000	1991	2000
Conventional digital	.002	.1	.1	10	.2	10
Special purpose digital	.1	4	10	10K	10	1000
Dedicated digital	5	200	500	50K	40	3K
Dedicated analog	500	20K	50K	5M·	4K	4M
Human brain[b]		10^9		10^{10}		10^{11}

[a] MCS = million connection updates/second
[b] Assumes that the cost of a human brain is $10M

Digital technology is still very much in its heyday. It dominates not only the marketplace but also the imagination-space most people explore in thinking about a problem. The tremendous potential of analog VLSI, especially in addressing messy real-world problems, as opposed to made-exact bench problems, has yet to be fathomed. For example, current algorithms running on a digital machine can perform at about 60% reading written numerals on credit card sales forms. They do this well only because the sales slip "exactifies" the data: numerals must be written in the blue boxes. This serves to segment the several numerals, guarantee an exact location, and very narrowly limit numeral size. The blue boxes mean that the really trenchant problem of segmentation does not have to be solved by the machine.

By contrast, machine reading zip codes on mail is an essentially unsolved problem even in the relatively tidy case where the numerals are machine-printed rather than handwritten. The trouble is, the preprocessing regimentations for numeral entry on the sales slips largely do not exist in the mail-world. Here the computer readers have to face the localization problem (where are the numerals and in what order?) and the segmentation problem (what does a squiggle belong to?) as well as the recognition problem (is it a 0 or a 6?).

The crux of the difficulty is that digital machines typically serialize the problem, so naturally they are programmed first to solve the segmentation problem and after that, to solve the recognition problem by a template procedure. Should the machine missolve or fail to solve the segmentation problem, recognition is doomed. In the absence of strict standardization of location, font, size, relation to other numerals, relation of zip code to other lines, and so forth, digital machines regularly fumble the segmentation problem. The best can not yet read even 50% of real mail presented.

Brains, it appears, do not serialize the segmentation and recognition problems in lockstep fashion. Often as not, recognitional cues are used to solve the segmentation problem. In general the brain's approach looks more like cooperative computation or constraint satisfaction than like theorem-proving. Interactive problem solving appears to be typical in the nervous system, whether the problem is speech recognition, object recognition, or organizing a bodily movement during prey-catching. A major advantage of analog VLSI is that the chip can follow the brain's example, solving the segmentation and recognition problems concurrently.

SILICON NEURONS

The first step in building silicon neurons was reported by Mahowald and Douglas, in *Nature* 1992. Using analog VLSI, they created a chip with selected prominent properties of pyramidal neurons, a type found in cortical structures whose basic properties have been intensively studied by neuroscientists. Their silicon neuron was highly simplified, consisting of only one compartment (an axon) and four types of ion channels in the axon membrane. A real pyramidal neuron, by contrast, might have thousands of dendritic segments as well as an axon, tens of thousands of synapses, and scores of types of ion channels (figure 7).

As a pilot project, however, it rates as successful on several counts. First, it ran in real time. A bonus of achieving the difficult goal of real-timeliness is that Mahowald and Douglas could also

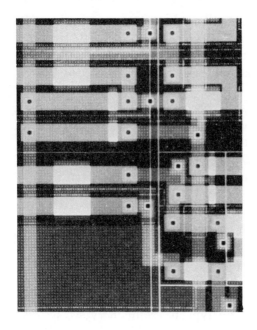

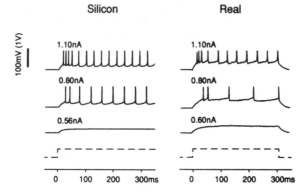

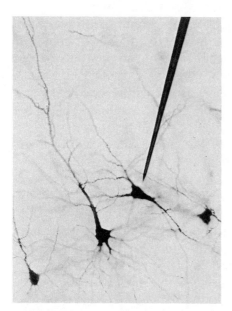

Figure 7. Comparison between the output from a silicon neuron and a biological neuron. (Top left) Magnified view of a part of a VLSI circuit for a silicon neuron. (Top right) Cortical neuron stained with the Goldi technique and a recording microelectrode. (From D. Hubel, "The brain," *Scientific American* Sept. 1979: 44–53). (Bottom left) Response of the silicon neuron to depolarizing current steps. A subthreshold current step (broken lines) injected into the cell body compartment of the silicon neuron evokes a passive charging curve. Larger inputs evoke adapting discharges of action potentials. Response of a cortical pyramidal cell recorded in vitro is provided for comparison. (From M. Mahowald and R. Douglas, "A silicon neuron." *Nature* 354, 1991: 515–518.)

conduct experiments by tweaking many parameters in real time, such as density of channels of a given type, or kinetic rate constants for channel opening. Second, the silicon neuron's output behavior for various injections of current, as displayed by traces on an oscilloscope, closely resembled the output of a real pyramidal cell under various physiological conditions. Third, the Mahowald-Douglas neuron consumes very little power.

With the successful debut of the single, simplified synthetic neuron, a number of developments are on the agenda. One is to upgrade the inaugural realism, for example by adding more compartments (corresponding to dendrites), and a wider range of ion channels. Another step is to build many neurons on a single chip. These synthetic neural circuits can then be explored to learn more about the computational possibilities inherent in the interaction of the various parameters.

A major challenge on this front is the interface between the human creator and the chip. Ideally, the scientist should be able to tweak thousands of parameters in real time, and hence the interface has to be flexible and user-friendly. Using synthetic circuits as experimental preparations means researchers can explore virtual neural-reality rather than sit at a work station watching points appear on a graph.

A further refinement is to make the chip modifiable by "experience" so that hand-setting of neuronal connectivity can be replaced by a training regimen. Mead and his group are currently developing trainable chips, where connectivity is modifiable according to learning rules similar to those believed to underlie plasticity in nervous systems, such as the Hebb rule. Ultimately, one will want to create chips with subpopulations of neurons specialized for different tasks, in the manner that distinct brain regions—visual cortex, auditory cortex, motor cortex, etc.—are specialized. Here again, fruitful ideas may come from seeing how Nature engineers specialization and integration.

Following Nature may require that we model patterns of neuronal connectivity, both long range (on the order of centimeters) and short range (millimeters). Nervous systems are remarkably fault tolerant, in the sense that a circuit and its function can survive quite well the death of individual neurons in the circuit. Comparable fault tolerance might be achievable for artificial systems by imitating the connectivity, modifiability, and processing style of the brain.

NEURAL CIRCUITS IN SILICON

Peripheral sensory organs such as the eye are highly specialized for transduction of external physical signals, such as photons, into electricity activity. The retina is a powerful preprocessor that transforms information about photons into a form suitable for neural representation and computation.[4] In many animals, sensory transducers and preprocessors have evolved to a sensitivity close to the limits of physical possibility. In primates, photoreceptors in the retina will respond to a few photons; the human ear is close to the limits set by the noise from Brownian motion. These transducers do not discretize time as digital computers must do but use powerful analog preprocessors to shape the information to a neural-friendly form. Can these inventions of nature be reverse engineered?

Carver Mead has built a family of silicon retinae. Each is a VLSI chip, merely a square centimeter in area; it weighs about a gram, and it consumes only about a milliwatt of power. Between arrays of phototransistors etched in silicon, dedicated circuits execute smoothing, contrast enhancement, and motion processing. The chip operates in its subthreshold, analog mode. Compared with a typical CCD (charge-coupled device) camera and standard digital image processor, the Mead chip is a paragon of efficiency, power, and compactness. The special-purpose digital equivalent would be about as large as a washing machine. Unlike cameras that must time-sample, typically 60 frames per second, the analog retina works continuously without the need to sample until the information leaves the chip already preprocessed (figure 8).

The operations performed on the current generation of chips capture some of the operations performed by real retinae. For example, resistive grids mimic the function of the layer of horizontal cells that provide lateral interaction between photoreceptors to effect smoothing. There are, however, many more circuits in real retinae that are not included in Mead's synthetic retina, such as amacrine cell circuits. About 30 types of amacrine cells exist in the retina, some are known to perform temporal filtering

A

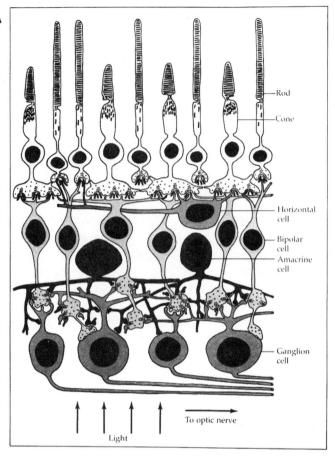

Rod

Cone

Horizontal cell

Bipolar cell

Amacrine cell

Ganglion cell

To optic nerve

Light

Figure 8. Comparison between the organization of biological and silicon retinae. (A) Diagram showing a close-up of a tiny region on the retina that illustrates several prominent cell types. The outer plexiform layer contains synaptic connections between photoreceptors, horizontal cells that provide lateral interactions, and bipolar cells that carry signals to the ganglion cells. (B) Horizontal cells in the white perch retina. (Left) A single horizontal cell injected with a fluoresecent dye. (Right) Horizontal cells have reciprocal connections as revealed here by dye coupling from one cell. (From J. E. Dowling [1987] *The Retina: An Approachable Part of the Brain.* Cambridge: Harvard University Press.) (C) Diagram of the silicon retina showing the resistive network similar in its function to the array of horizontal cells in the retina; a single pixel element is illustrated in the circular window. The silicon model of the triad synapse consists of a follower-connected transconductance amplifier by which the photoreceptor drives the resistive network, and an amplifier that takes the difference between the photoreceptor output and the voltage stored on the capacitance of the resistive network. These pixels are tiled in an hexagonal way. The resistive network results from an hexagonal tiling of pixels. (From C. Mead [1989]. *Analog VLSI and Neural Systems.* Reading, Mass.: Addison-Wesley.)

B

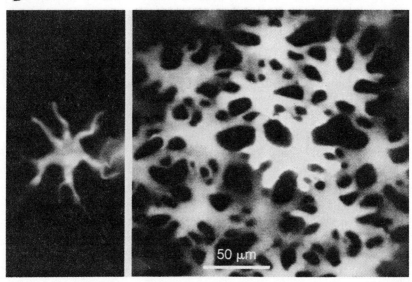

C

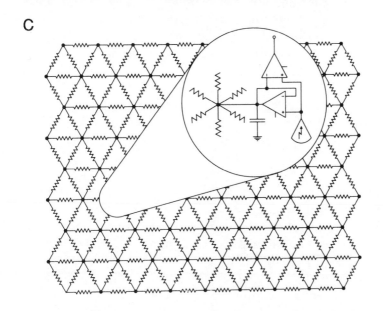

and to provide adaptational mechanisms. So far, however, the precise function of most amacrine cells is not known. The retina is a prime place for the co-evolution of chip design and experimental neurobiology.

To maximize efficiency in the three critical dimensions (power, cost, and density), it makes good sense to build chips. To approximate neural efficiency, however, the technology still has a *very* long way to go. The commercial incentive to push forward with analog VLSI technology will depend on whether the commercial payoff in the long haul looks promising.

SENSORIMOTOR CONTROL

Visual perception in animals, as we all know, is breathtakingly difficult computationally. So far nothing in computer vision has come close even to matching the visual capacity of a bee, let alone that of a rat. In addition to good visual perception, robots will require good coordination between their "eyes" and their "hands." Several observations on the neurobiology of sensorimotor control may provoke new computational insights.

Three features of neurobiological solutions to the problems of sensorimotor control stand out:

1. Control is not assigned to a control center; brains do not have a central executive or planner or dictator. Control is widely distributed in the nervous system, though the secret of how this works has not yet been discovered.

2. In managing control, brains use *both positive and negative* feedback. This is uncommon in engineered control systems, partly because the combination often causes instabilities. The nervous system, however, combines them in a highly successful way. It uses positive feedback signals to predict what happens next in a feedforward control pathway, and negative feedback signals to make small corrections within the movement. This gives the system speed of response with minimum corrective wiggle.

3. Movement of sensory input systems, such as the eyes, appears to make certain computational problems of visual percep-

tion simpler rather than more difficult. For example, head and body movement help in determining depth of objects in a scene by creating motion parallax (near objects have greater relative motion than far, and objects in front of the fixation point move opposite to head direction, those beyond fixation point move isodirectionally). Hence animals often head-bob in order to extract more information through differences in relative motion of objects.

Body Movement Allows Representational Economies

In a surprising way, eye movement reduces the brain's computational load by reducing how much has to be represented in detail at any given saccade (small eye movements we scarcely notice but normally make about every 300 msec). As Dana Ballard, a computer scientist at the University of Rochester, points out, eye movement behavior takes advantage of the general stability of the world to economize on processing.[5] Ballard's idea is that only a small part of the visual field, roughly the central 2% (the foveal region), is processed to a high level.

On each saccade the brain samples a new 2% sector of the visual field. Attentional and motivational mechanisms appear to help guide the scan paths of the eyes. Psychophysical research shows that the eyes systematically scan a scene, returning many times to areas of high interest, relative to animal's current task. Ballard's hypothesis is that the brain does not need to have a richly articulated model of the whole world, because the world is out there to be sampled again and again. The world is largely stable, and relevant changes in the world scene can be picked up quickly.

Nonsmeary Vision During Head Movement

In neurobiology, an especially well-studied and revealing example of active sensorimotor control is the oculomotor system (figure 9). This circuitry is responsible for keeping the visual perception stable and crisp when head or eye (or both) are moving. But for its remarkable speed and tremendous accuracy, our visual image would smear every time we moved our heads. For a basketball player or a cheetah chasing a gazelle, this would be catastrophic.

SENSORY SYSTEMS

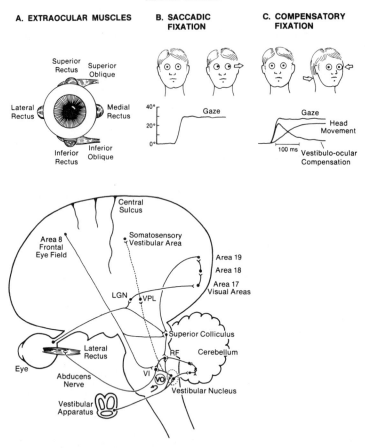

Figure 9. Pathways for visual tracking.[6] (Top) When the head moves, the perception of the object remains crisp as the eyes make compensating movements in the opposite direction. (Bottom) The input comes from the head acceleration-detectors in the semicircular canals. Information is processed in the vestibular nuclei, and the eye muscles are precisely signaled to contract so that the eyeball moves appropriately. (From G. Shepherd, *Neurobiology,* 2nd edition. Oxford: Oxford University Press, 1988)

Enough experimental detail about the anatomy and physiology of the oculomotor system is now known to support the interplay between dry modeling and wet experiments. This research is beginning to reveal how the oculomotor system can be so fast, how it modifies itself to accommodate structural changes in the eyeball, and how it makes efficient use of both feedforward and feedback signals.

Chips for handing the processing of head and eyeball movement are currently in the works at Caltech. Assuming continued progress in neurobiology and chip technology, a Mark I silicon "eye" that tracks slowly moving objects should be ready in a few years. An "oculobot" is still a long way from our fictional, full-fledged agribots, to be sure. Nevertheless, some of the ideas and technology leading in that direction are now in hand.

NEURO-REVOLUTIONS

We are on the brink of two "neuro-revolutions"—one in the science of the brain, and the other in the technology of brain-style computing. Growth of knowledge follows an exponential curve. Often, the more you have, the more you get—and the faster you get it. So it is with knowledge in neuroscience. Almost daily, surprising discoveries about the organization and mechanisms of nervous systems are reported. Setting neurobiological facts in a computational framework raises new questions about how networks of neurons work, which in turn give rise to productive, testable theories about how brains work—about how brains see, learn, and make decisions. In computer science, the VLSI revolution has provided us with unprecedented computational tools to transform what we know about the brain into silicon. Silicon retinae are in production, silicon cochlea are nearing production, and "oculobots" are on the drawing board. Although it is next to impossible to predict precisely other brainwaves in the genre, it is easy to forecast that ever more sophisticated neuro-engineering is in our future.*

Portions of this article were based on our paper "Silicon Brains," Byte. October 1992

ENDNOTES

[1]Patricia S. Churchland and Terrence J. Sejnowski, *The Computational Brain* (Cambridge.: MIT Press, 1992).

[2]See I. B. Levitan and L. K. Kaczmarek, *The Neuron* (Oxford: Oxford University Press, 1992).

[3]Carver Mead, *Analog VLSI and Neural Systems* (Reading, Mass.: Addison Wesley, 1989).

[4]John Dowling, *Neurons and Networks: An Introduction to Neuroscience* (Cambridge: Harvard University Press, 1992).

[5]Dana H. Ballard, "Animate Vision," *Artificial Intelligence Journal* (48, 1991): 57–86.

[6]See also Stephen G. Lisberger and Terrence J. Sejnowski, "A novel mechanism of motor learning in a recurrent network model based on the vestibulo-ocular reflex." *Nature* (in press).

Rob Kling, Isaac Scherson, and Jonathan Allen

Massively Parallel Computing and Information Capitalism

MASSIVELY PARALLEL COMPUTERIZATION IN CONTEXT[1]

Massive Parallelism is an approach to organizing the internal architecture of computers that enables them to rip through large computational problems at previously unobtainable speeds. Parallelism involves the electric image of many processes enacted simultaneously. The intoxicating mixture of high speed and parallelism captures our imaginations. From sports car races to space travel, speed draws crowds. (Many people choose their speeds in a social context, such as preferring the combination of fast cars and slow dancing rather than slow cars and fast dancing.) Parallelism is a robust metaphor, since many human activities, including factories, armies, and jazz bands, illustrate some form of parallelism. It is an engaging intellectual topic, which can stimulate discussions that range from the way neural brains work to engineering strategies for managing multiple activities.

We are interested in characterizing the social repercussions of the use of massively parallel computing. Our analytical strategy differs significantly from that of some of the other contributions

Rob Kling is Professor of Information & Computer Science and Management, Department of Information & Computer Science and Center for Research on Information Technology and Organizations, University of California, Irvine.

Isaac Scherson is Associate Professor, Department of Information & Computer Science, University of California, Irvine.

Jonathan Allen is a member of the Department of Information & Computer Science and Center for Research on Information Technology and Organizations, University of California, Irvine.

to this book. Other authors locate massively parallel computing against a backdrop of the industrial revolution. This reference point provides the advantage of locating the technology in a broad historical context, and discussing applications other than the scientific and engineering computations which dominate the use of massively parallel computing today. However, using the industrial revolution as a primary reference point for understanding the social roles and likely repercussions of the use of this powerful new technology also makes some significant intellectual sacrifices. First, the United States has undergone other substantial industrial transformations since the original industrial revolution. While the first industrial revolution was based on the power of steam engines, later industrial revolutions were based on fossil fuels and transistors. These successive waves of new technological families have had distinctive technological, economic, and social characteristics that differ from the first industrial revolution. In particular, we have much to learn from the large wave of computerization that has swept the United States since World War II. Public agencies and private firms have invested substantially in computerized systems to the point that they are central to key operations of any large organization and many smaller ones. The ways that the use of these computerized systems have reshaped some aspects social life in the recent decades while leaving others unaltered can help us better understand the likely roles of applications based on massively parallel computing in the foreseeable future. This chapter examines the likely uses of massively parallel computing in light of this recent and rich social history.

A key part of this social history is the body of contemporary writings about the social meanings and repercussions of computerized systems. The collection of nonfiction books and articles that examine the social meanings and likely repercussions of various forms of computerization is as old the earliest digital computers. When there were few computers and applications, this literature was composed of a few books and articles which were necessarily speculative. As the technology spread in applications and importance, scholars and other careful observers began to produce richer and more empirically grounded studies. The body of theorizing about forms of computerization and social change grew in theoretical sophistication. Before we embark on our specific inquiry into the social roles and repercussions of massively parallel computing, we will examine some highlights of these analyses of numerous other forms of computerization.

BEYOND THE UTOPIAN AND ANTI-UTOPIAN IMPULSES

The computer science community invents powerful technologies, and some of them can play important roles in facilitating social change. But there is rarely a simple and direct link between changes in computer technology and changes in social life. Even the link between using a faster computer and comparably productive work is often indirect. If a task is repetitive, like printing large batches of fund-raising form letters for a political campaign, a doublespeed printer should print about twice as many in a day, decreasing the turnaround time. However, it is much less likely that a professor with a quadruplespeed computer and a quadruplespeed printer could produce four times as many research papers in a year. The faster computer does not do much of the research and thinking that would be required for most scholarly papers. This simple example indicates that there can be substantial slip between advances in technology and corresponding improvements in social life.

The computer science community usually writes about new technologies as they may be used in narrowly drawn task-specific social contexts. But periodically, it produces collections of essays about the major social implications of emerging technologies.[2] These books usually take the form of celebrations, which primarily highlight the possible virtues of new technologies. Celebrations are not places to ask hard questions. When a Fourth of July speaker refers to the United States as "the greatest country on earth," it's time to cheer, not to ask for explicit criteria and systematic evidence. It's a time to be inspired, not a time to inquire about the scale and growth of systematic social and environmental problems. One who raises serious and systemic questions in the midst of a celebration often spoils the fun. And there can be resulting polarization between the cheerful party goers and the distraught skeptics.

Unfortunately, the many of the essays about the social implications of emerging technologies produced by the computer science community are so permeated with technological utopianism, that they invite a countervailing technological anti-utopianism.[3] The renowned debates between the artificial intelligence community and Joseph Weizenbaum illustrate this process, as well as how these debates can polarize without producing deeper bodies of research and commentary.[4]

Some recent discussions of massive parallelism and social change have displayed some similar technologically utopian elements by fixating on benign social changes that can be stimulated or facilitated by massively parallel computing.[5] But other more complex, and more likely, trajectories of social change have been ignored in these discussions. It is possible, for example, that massively parallel computing plays no special role in fostering substantial societal change. This line of thought is not very interesting; but it encourages those who see massively parallel computing as an important technological shift to be careful in linking this technology to specific social changes. It is important to critically explore the potential social changes that powerful new technologies can facilitate for many reasons, above and beyond the intrinsic interest of the topic to scientists, technologists, and people interested in social change or public policy. Most arguments about technology policy, public funding of research in advanced technologies, and regulatory policies pertinent to various technological applications hinge on projections of alternative possible social futures and the quality of life for people who live with them. However, one needs complex logics to link powerful new technologies with specific social consequences to move beyond technological determinism.

A large part of the literature about the social consequences of emerging computer technologies is written by enthusiasts and is a junkyard of broken dreams. For example, computer specialists have speculated that computerization would necessarily improve the productivity of organizations,[6] that management information systems would reduce the number of middle managers in large organizations,[7] that certain forms of computer-assisted instruction could readily revolutionize K–12 education,[8] that PCs would democratize large corporations,[9] and that expert systems could democratize access to important analytical skills.[10] None of these predictions has been very accurate, despite strong arguments by their advocates.

Each of these computer technologies has fascinating technical features and novel uses. But these deterministic analyses had some common features that undermined their predictive value. Often they stripped the focal technology and key social relations out of the social contexts in which they are most frequently used. For example, most analyses of computers and schooling treat schools as learning places, rather than as institutions for socializing children and keeping many of them off the streets during the day. Schoolteachers spend much of their time keeping order, and unfortunately, many teachers would find numerous curious kids too troublesome to manage. Many analyses of computerization in schools jump directly from some special information processing feature of a computerized technology to the way that classroom life could be reorganized. Further, they usually undervalue the kinds of social forces that facilitate or inhibit changes in the ways that schools and classrooms function as social systems.

This recent history of failed analyses about the social roles of computerization sensitizes us to the kinds of arguments that mislead. One common kind of error results from emphasizing revolutionary but benign social possibilities without examining the social conditions that enable them. Another kind of error results from ignoring other social changes, or the possibility of negligible change, when key conditions do not alter in ways to facilitate the desired change.

Analysts who want to argue that a new technology is revolutionary in its consequences need to show that the argument is not subject to similar weaknesses. In the following sections we try to carefully link our arguments about the use of massively parallel computing and resulting social changes to plausible social processes that transform information processing into altered social relationships. This paper advances the discussions about the social changes that might result from the diffusion of massively parallel computer systems by focusing on the next twenty years, and by linking this form of new technology to the social conditions that it may alter most directly.

The best analyses of the adoption and use of computing in the last 40 years of computing often carefully link the use of technologies to broader social patterns.[11] Organizations selectively adopt technologies which serve the interests of coalitions that can afford them. When computers are inexpensive, as in the case of

PCs, poorer groups can afford them. When they are much more expensive, as in the case of the largest central machines, then richer and more powerful coalitions try to shape their uses. The next section illustrates the usefulness of paying careful attention to the social as well as to the technological. In subsequent sections we discuss important technological trends in the case of massive parallelism, and link these to the selective enhancement of a set of social trends we refer to as "information capitalism" in the commercial world. We then describe how the marriage of more widely diffused massively parallel computing and information capitalism could alter important aspects of social life in the United States. Of several possible topics, we have chosen two for careful examination: the structure of national labor markets and changes in relationships between organizations and their clients.

CONCEPTUALIZING COMPUTERIZATION AND SOCIAL CHANGE

While we can imagine exciting social possibilities for many powerful technologies, only a few seem to play important catalyzing roles in transforming key parts of the social order. The automobile serves as a common example in many discussions of technology and social change because most readers are likely to be familiar with some of its social roles. Some business have changed their approaches to service to cater to car drivers (as in the case of fast-food restaurants and drive-through banking), and the spread of cars may have hastened the development of suburbs and fostered postsuburbia.[12] But cars alone did not transform industrial organizations into fundamentally new forms and force people to create modern urban gridlock.

The roles of instructional technologies in changing schooling practices is another common example of the ways in which technologies interplay with preexisting social practices. While many writers predicted that educational television could enrich schooling, instructional TV has had little systematic impact on education in K–12 schools. Instructional television can be educationally effective under special conditions: when the potentials of the medium are exploited, when the content is vividly visualized, and when it is used by a skilled teacher.[13] Unfortunately these conditions seem to be rare.[14] Commercial network television has played a much larger role in the reshaping of mass culture, and even of presidential political campaigns, than instructional television has had on K–12 education. Some forms of television have had significant social effects. But the accuracy of claims about what television does or does not do depends on the nature of the programming, the audiences, and the social contexts in which the videos are viewed. Examples like these suggest that technologies have complex roles in altering social life and the magnitude of their effects can be substantially different in different institutional settings.

Sometimes computerization helps restructure the way that people conduct some aspect of social life, such as in making airline reservations. More frequently, computing is integrated into a preexisting set of social relations and social practices.[15] For example, giving students word processors does not cause them to be better writers. However, teachers who want their students to write more or to improve their writing through successive revisions can find that word processing is helpful *if they require their students to revise their papers*. In this example, a teacher selects a technology and adapts it to facilitate a particular pedagogical strategy. The use of technology rarely forces people who have discretion in the way they integrate it into their work to adopt a specific strategy or paradigm. This family of examples generalizes well beyond teachers and schooling to the causal relationship between all sorts of technologies and social practices.

It is common for technologists to list marvelous applications of new kinds of computer systems, and then to suggest that these technologies will be likely to change the world in line with the most exiting possibilities. For example, some authors speculate that high-speed computer networks will enable school students to explore new bodies of knowledge.[16] But it takes significant changes in curricula and classroom practices, above and beyond the use of new technologies, to realize these possibilities. It helps, for example, to have classroom teachers who are truly interested and capable of stimulating children's curiosity. Schools work with their existing teaching staff; they do not hire a cadre of enthusiastic teachers when they install computer networks (although some enthusiastic teachers eagerly foster such experiments). When a new technology is implemented on a school-wide basis, it is used, adapted (or ignored) by teachers with varying commitments to high levels of teaching.[17]

Technological utopianism refers to a mode of analysis that places technologies in a pivotal role as enabling uniformly benign social changes. Technological anti-utopianism is similar, except that the changes that result from new technologies are primarily dismal. Technological utopianism suggests possibilities and gives hope to technological enthusiasts, their followers, and their audiences; but it has a dark side in overestimating the ease and pace of systematic social change. It can lead people to develop overly high expectations, and to invest scarce resources in expensive technologies that have relatively limited value. It can lead to complacency in ignoring problems that are exacerbated by new technologies by encouraging hope that still newer technologies will resolve any serious problems. Technologically utopian analyses understate the relevance of history by portraying the future world as one which will be readily and happily transformed when new technologies are put in place. Technologically utopian analyses can mystify and make it harder for people to understand the conditions under which they live and work, their actual interests, and the ways that they might improve their lives.

For example, in his introduction to *The Age of Intelligent Computers,* Raymond Kurzweil[18] argues that the last century of industrial development in the United States raised living standards. He cites a sevenfold increase in the GNP per capita in the United States between 1870 and 1970, and claims that there has been "a similar change in the actual earning power of the available jobs." He argues that these economic trends will continue, despite "some ebbs and flows in economic development." This argument sets the stage for a book which provides a rich and buoyant assessment of the researchers' promises about artificial intelligence, with little attention paid to possible problems. A key limitation of Kurzweil's cornucopic approach to economic and social change is rapidly glossing over deep social and economic problems that show up in the distribution of jobs and wealth across social groups, rather than in aggregate analyses. Later in this chapter we will examine changes in the mix of better and worse information handling jobs in the U.S. economy.

Two kinds of examples illustrate the inappropriate simplicity of Kurzweil's genteel complacency. In the 1980s there was a substantial increase in the number of homeless people living in major U.S. cities. Further, the rate of unemployment in many urban black ghettos was in the double digits throughout the 1970s and 1980s. We do not see a close causal relationship between computerization and homelessness. But computerization seems to play an important role in leading employers to want more edu-cated workers at all levels. The decrease in the availability of unskilled jobs most hurts those who have the least formal edu-cation. Deep structural employment problems are not visible in selective broad glances at the economy. Kurzweil's analysis illus-trates the rhetorical ploys that make it harder for us to understand the nature of our present conditions and social choices. It obfus-cates rather than clarifies what may be done to help improve the lives of people throughout society.

It is seductive to link the use of powerful new technologies to epochal social changes. The conventional wisdom in our culture focuses on the role of new technologies in fostering the various industrial revolutions. But it takes careful analysis to make a compelling argument about technology and social transformation. For example, Eric Hobsbawm[19] devotes one chapter of *Industry and Empire* to examining the multiple conditions that fostered the first industrial revolution in England. He carefully examined the way in which the industrial revolution spread sequentially through England, France, the Netherlands, and Germany during a period of over 70 years. He explored the possibility that the industrial revolution might actually have started sooner in En-gland, before 1790, closer to the time that Watt invented the steam engine and that other cotton spinning and weaving ma-chines were invented. In the course of these analyses, he found that the industrial revolution depended not just on new technol-ogies, but also on developing new ways of organizing work in factories and the availability of captive colonial markets for British goods. Hobsbawm argues that the German states did not expe-rience much of an industrial revolution until after their unification under Bismarck and the simplification of a complex tariff system. The "technology was available," but the social relationships be-tween the German states impeded industrialization.

Other historians have linked later technological advances, particularly those of coal, steel, and railroads to a distinct second wave of industrial development.[20] Mass manufacturing, the Fordist system of assembly lines, and a fine division of labor, was part of this second industrial revolution.[21] Like the first, the second industrial revolution depended on an interesting and subtle marriage of technologies and social arrangements both to stimulate and to exploit them.

Every few decades there are new families of technology that excite someone's imagination about revolutionary social potential. Railroads, electricity, airflight, rockets, automobiles, telephones, nuclear energy, radio, television, designer drugs, and genetic engineering have all been the subject of such discussions. Each of these technologies is socially transformative in some ways, but none is quite the unique catalyst of major social changes like the rise of multinational corporations, the development of postsuburban regions[22] the prevalence of the two career professional family, and the recent rise of homelessness in major U.S. cities. Also, significant advances within these technological families can be exciting and important without ushering in yet another social transformation. For example, jet planes are an important technological advance over propeller-driven aircraft. But the social role of commercial jet planes has been to elaborate travel patterns and forms of social mobility that were established in the several previous decades when commercial propeller aircraft ruled the skies. In addition, the recent radical restructuring of the airline industry has more to do with the deregulation of rates and perhaps the institutionalization of computerized reservation systems rather than with the shift from propellers to jet engines. We argue that the social changes that can be attributed to massively parallel computing in the next 20 years extend important preexisting social patterns, in a manner similar to the shift from propeller-driven planes to jets.

The first step in a social analysis of the significant spread of massively parallel computing is a description of important technological trends. Because we seek to describe not just what could happen with the widespread adoption of massive parallelism, but how it would likely spread and selectively enable social change over a 20-year period, we pay as much attention to commercial application and cost as leading-edge architectural features.

MASSIVE PARALLELISM AND TRAJECTORIES OF TECHNOLOGICAL CHANGE

Massive parallelism is, in principle, a powerful but not unlimited approach to speeding up computers. The microprocessor, a tiny square centimeter piece of silicon, is nowadays composed of millions of transistors and packages a tremendous computing power. Single semiconductor processor chips are limited in their computational capabilities. Levels of miniaturization are limited by the physics of the semiconductor device.[23] A more stringent limitation is the maximum velocity of electrons, which limits the processor's switching speeds. Speed is one of the major concerns of digital computer designers. Some members of the scientific and engineering communities have always demanded faster computing engines to solve problems that are currently intractable due to their computational complexity.

Because of the technological limitations in fabricating faster processors, technology-independent approaches were sought. Parallel processing emerged as a paradigm that promised speedup of several orders of magnitude. Its fundamental idea is strikingly simple. By analogy to team work, parallel processing exploits the concurrent execution of different tasks that integrate into a single solution. Parallel processing is actually so intuitive and simple a concept that analogies can be found in diverse workplaces. When a job is too big for one person to handle, management (similar to a computer's control unit) breaks the job into smaller tasks and assigns one to each worker. When all smaller tasks are completed, their results are integrated to complete the bigger job.

Not all jobs can be broken down into smaller pieces. The size of the problem at hand determines the resources necessary for its completion and, in many cases, the size of the work team. A larger team can multiply the efforts of any individual. But a larger team may also be inefficient, because people need to communicate and delays in some people's work can leave the whole group waiting for a key item. Hence small teams are sometimes faster than large ones. This observation also applies to massively parallel computers, and suggests that quadrupling the number of processors may not always quadruple the speed of the resulting computations. The effective speedups depend on the communications architectures and capacities as much as on processor speeds.[24] Further, some problems differ substantially in the extent to which they can be easily sped up with a particular parallel computer architecture.

The value of parallel processing depends on the problem being solved. Higher levels of speedup are easiest to achieve by specializing the computer architecture to the structure of the particular problem. How big is good parallel processing? Some computer scientists advocate the use of a small number of powerful microprocessors, generally in the order of hundreds. The idea is to break large problems at a coarse level of granularity and solve them as independently as possible in each processor. This approach is useful in projects where the bigger job can be decomposed into smaller, very independent, processes.

A finer level of granularity leads to massively parallel processing. This approach is suitable for problems where large amounts of data are processed with repetitive operations on very small data subsets. Because massively parallel machines are generally used to process very large independent data sets, the approach is also known as data parallel processing. Computers of this kind could consist of tens of thousands of processors, although today they are usually much smaller.

Through the mid-1980s, massive parallelism was primarily envisioned for designing supercomputers, which have been used primarily for large-scale numerical computations for scientific, engineering, and military applications. The massively parallel marketplace was stimulated with massive federal research funding. The Grand Challenge computing applications, such as weather modeling,[25] are a class of complex computational problems whose solution could effectively utilize supercomputers and whose importance laymen can readily comprehend. One possible line of inquiry would have been to examine the social repercussions of widely available massively parallel computers which could rapidly simulate some of these systems. One can imagine a weather service that could more accurately forecast severe storms weeks before they happen. Since most readers sometimes care about the weather, they could imagine tight links between computation, prediction, and the actions they could take. But the links would be much weaker between having high-quality simulations of air pollution patterns and actually improving the quality of air in highly industrialized and urbanized regions, since one would have to mobilize a political system, numerous organizations, and hundreds of thousands of people to restructure their activities.

We decided not to explore the social repercussions of simulating Grand Challenge applications because we see other important uses and repercussions of massively parallel computing that are less frequently discussed. If the discussion of massively parallel computing focuses on the exciting frontier of comptutationally demanding scientific and engineering applications, it can skew our understanding away from important social effects.

Two important trends in massively parallel computing in the next two decades are likely to be socially significant: (1) the application of massive parallelism to commercial computing, such as transaction processing and document searching; and (2) the trickling down of massively parallel architectures from multimillion dollar computers to much less expensive machines.[26]

First, the applications of massively parallel computing are expanding to new sectors of the society. Today, a handful of organizations are experimenting with parallel supercomputers for large commercial problems, such as selling information retrieval services or updating records on millions of customers in real time. A number of vendors, including the NCR subsidiary of AT&T, Kendall Square Research, and MasPar are now offering massively parallel computers for huge volumes of on-line transaction processing. Oracle, a supplier of relational database systems, has developed a parallel version which works on massively parallel computers like these. These vendors aim at industries such as banking, airlines, and finance, as well as public agencies with huge clienteles, like the U.S. Internal Revenue Service. These expanding markets are attracting both traditional vendors of massively parallel computers such as Thinking Machines Inc and Ncube, as well as firms with established commercial clients, like NCR.

Second, in the next decades massively parallel architectures will "trickle down" to workstation priced computers. Today, the prices for massively parallel computers start in the low hundreds of thousands of dollars and top off in the tens of millions, with the typical computer costing over several million dollars. It is difficult for an outside observer to estimate the costs of any large-scale computer model because vendors sometimes offer steep discounts to special customers. On the other hand, adjunct equipment, such as disk memory, high-speed printers, computer networks, displays, and a rich set of software, can significantly increase the overall costs of acquiring any large-scale computer system. We do not expect the prices for adjunct equipment to fall as rapidly as prices for central processors and memory chips. Even so, the floor prices for massively parallel computers should drop steadily, similar to the declines in computer prices during the last two decades. Part of the reason for our economic optimism is that vendors of massively parallel computers use commonly available "merchant" processor chips rather than much more expensive custom chips. Thus they benefit the competitive pressures in huge markets for commodity processors fabricated in huge numbers by firms such as Intel, Motorola, and Hewlett Packard.

In this coming period, the tacit definition of "massive" will scale up to denote computers with even more processors. Today, the Paragon XP/S, which is advertised to operate with up to 4,000 processors, and both the MasPar MP-1 the CM-5 Connection machine, which accommodate 16,000 processors, fit everybody's conception of massive. But the CM-5 is also advertised in a 32-processor configuration. And even a Cray Y/MP-C90 supercomputer with only 16 processors is sometimes referred to as a massively parallel computer. The term *massively parallel* does not refer to a specific number of processors, and probably the meaning will not stabilize for some time. The question of which computers will deserve the appellation "massively parallel" is a combination of advertising, the contexts in which people cluster or differentiate various computers, and also inevitably rising standards of hardware performance.

In the computing world, the conventional standards of size and speed change rapidly. In the early 1980s, the typical Apple IIs had 16K or 32K bytes of random access memory. The microcomputers that ran CP/M microcomputers were usually configured with 64K RAM. In 1981, the IBM Personal Computer seemed very generous with 256K RAM, which could at first be most easily expanded to 512K, rather than 640K of RAM on PCs. Today, 640K of RAM seems limited for many applications, especially with newer windowing environments. In a similar way the social definition of massive may rapidly rise so that a parallel computer with 128 processors may seem merely "large" in 10 years and very standard in 20 years. In a decade, many people who acquire scalable multiprocessor workstations may be unsure exactly how many processors are in the box under their desks. Nor should they need to care, unless they are concerned about upgrading for more speed.

Two other developmental streams about parallel computing hardware are important to bear in mind. First, the lowest end of the parallel marketplace, where computers exploit 2–16 general processors in parallel, is beginning to take off and should be an established niche for faster "affordable" computation in the next decade. This move is coextensive with general hardware speedups in computing in the $10,000 1992 dollar price range. Little of the excitement for fundamentally new capabilities that scientists and technologists exude for massive parallelism is likely to be focused on applications in this segment of the computing market. These speedups can be useful in providing organizations with faster file servers, and in giving people with computationally intensive uses another dollop of computing power.[27] These advances are generally good news, but they do not constitute a "new era in computation." However, advertising copywriters will often celebrate even modest technological advances as revolutionary triumphs, and unfortunately, many journalists will echo their serenades.

Second, there will be continuing development of ever higher performance computers in the multimillion dollar price range. Today, the most public face for this developmental stream focuses on the construction of computers that can compute at today's computational "sound barrier": computing at teraflop[28] speeds. Computers with top speeds of a teraflop on some specific algorithms seem within reach in a few years, and computers that can reliably compute a larger variety of problems at teraflop speeds will then steadily trundle out of the labs and into the marketplace. Then a new performance target, such as pentaflop speeds, will be set, and new engineering energies will again be mobilized.[29] We cannot readily characterize the limits that would impede some organizations in seeking highest-performance highest-cost computing machinery.

It is easy to be positively jubilant about the trends in price and performance of computing hardware. Smiles dampen a bit when one tries to turn more powerful computers into devices that will speed up work and organizational performance proportional to their gains in technological prowess.

MASSIVELY PARALLEL COMPUTERS AND SOCIAL TRANSFORMATION

The improvements in actual human activity from faster computation are contingent, context sensitive, and discontinuous. For example, many professional writers turned from typewriters to wimpy microcomputers in the early 1980s. They felt that electronic cutting and pasting and rapid reformatting gave them substantial advantages over writing and revising with typewriters and paper. Newer word processing software was often easier to use, and provided nicer control over formatting, spell checking, and so on. Today's conventional microcomputers run from six to ten times faster than their precursors of 1982, and are less expensive as well. But professional writers are not producing six to ten times as many books, articles, reports, and memos than they did a decade earlier.

There is often significant *slip* between the speedups in the technological performance of a machine and the pace of actual human work which uses that machine. The least slip occurs when the tasks are repetitive and are accomplished primarily with the focal technology. A doublespeed printer could print twice as many form letters in an hour. But it might print many fewer if there are numerous print jobs to be set up. There is more slip when the activity requires a lot of adjunct work off of the computer. Some of this work involves working with diverse and sometimes not entirely well integrated equipment ensembles. Other time can be spent in filling supplies, repairing malfunctioning equipment, and numerous support tasks.

Further slips in speed between the benchmarked performance of a technology and the resulting gains in human performance occur when the technology only enhances a portion of the actual work. For example, few writers compose the same article over and over again, despite some occasional jibes from their colleagues. Consequently the thinking time for a new article is not reduced tenfold when a writer obtains a tenfold speedups in computing power. Rapid data computations do not automatically translate into comparable speedups in interpretation; and analysts will not write their new analysis with tenfold reductions in keyboard time.

These slips between the potentials of computer speeds and the actualities of human and organizational performance are even more vexing with massively parallel computers since only some problems take well to parallelization. For example, graphical display, image processing, certain kinds of database searches and certain kinds of numerical computations can benefit immensely from parallelization. But many database searches and numerical computations do not benefit much, if at all, when they are run on parallel computers. Today, specialists spend considerable time adjusting the computational form of specific problems to the particular parallel computer architecture on which they will be executed.

Like Deng, Glimm, and Sharp,[30] we see massively parallel computing being used for a wide variety of purposes. But one cannot simply add up the applications of a new technology and effectively understand its social roles. For example, one cannot add up the uses of cars and deduce the expansion of suburbia. One has to understand the roles of technologies in fine-grained social relationships in diverse contexts. Further, we have to be alert for the ways in which other social forces help drive some of the resulting changes. One then induces the ways in which technologies enable people and groups to fundamentally transform key social relationships or whether the technologies are simply absorbed into ongoing social patterns.

When we examine the possible social changes that may be come from the significant spread of massively parallel computing, we have two major choices in causal argument. One form of analysis makes massively parallel computing the key catalyst of epochal changes in some aspects of social life, such as industrial organization, commercial practice, or culture.[31] The other form of analysis examines major industrial, social, or cultural changes in which society might absorb massively parallel computing and be somewhat reshaped without being fundamentally transformed. The revolutionary argument is more interesting, but it requires bold speculative leaps that have often proven unreliable in other accounts of computerization and social change.[32] Consequently, we will examine the ways organizations effectively restructure or reinforce different aspects of the social order by adopting and applying massively parallel computing.

Which Applications Merit Our Attention?

One interesting strategy would be to examine the kinds of new computer applications which the much less expensive massively parallel computers that we expect after the year 2010 might make technically and economically feasible. We could focus on advances in speech recognition, neural nets, and other forms of artificial intelligence. We could also examine advances in the various kinds of simulations and multimedia experiments which undergird virtual worlds (so-called virtual reality). This strategy offers the possibility of seeing the potentials for inexpensive massively parallel computing to make new devices and services possible. This approach would be most attractive if some of these new products and services become common in 20 years.

A crude cost analysis, however, leads us to not expect massively parallel computers to become widespread within the next 20 years. Today's massively parallel computer typically sells for several million dollars, and the price of a comparable computer could drop by a factor of 10 to several hundred thousand 1992 dollars in 10 years. In 20 years the cost of a comparably powerful computer with hundreds of massively parallel processors should drop again to cost in the tens of thousands of 1992 dollars. There might be some additional price reductions by factors of 2 to 5 since these cheaper massively parallel computers of the future could be mass-produced in huge volumes with all the resulting economies of scale. These crudely projected prices (which ignore the costs of software, networking, and technical support) should make the computational equivalent of today's massively parallel computers commonplace in the sorts of places where equipment in this price range is most plausible, such as engineering and science labs, graphics studios, and the workgroups of high roller financial and market analysts.

One important wild card in projecting the future role of massively parallel computing is in estimating the pace at which important software that readily exploits advanced hardware speedups becomes available. In the past decade there have been interesting new families of software, such as expert systems and hypertext, which have not had much influence in most workplaces. A few simple families of applications, such as database systems, spreadsheets, engineering computation, and word processing, account for the primary uses of computing in most organizations. It would be interesting to frame an analysis around certain kinds of computer applications that can lead in new directions, such as networking, speech recognition, and graphical simulations, which are likely to become increasingly important in the forthcoming decades. But we have adopted a less speculative emphasis to help anchor the discussions of massively parallel computing in more "solid" realities.

Some of these applications, like speech processing and rich graphical simulations, require several orders of magnitude in computer speedups to become much more effective. We do not expect the equipment that supports these speedups to be affordable for many white collar workers in the next 10–15 years, if not somewhat longer. An analysis based on the importance of new families of software like these also requires plausible 20-year social forecasts about the ways people work and live, and the social forms into which they may integrate these new technologies. Such forecasts rest on judgments about the nature of the economy and common patterns of community life. Will the U.S. economy rapidly rebound or are we beginning a long-term decline similar to Britain's? Will families continue to break up, or will there be new sustained family forms? This would be a plausible kind of study, but it is fraught with the traditional risks of long-range social and technological forecasting.

We have taken a different, and relatively conservative but sound, approach by focusing on one important set of developments in the next 20 years. Massively parallel computers are beginning to be used for commercial record processing applications. And these kinds of applications are likely to dominate their usage and social roles in the next few decades. This kind of analysis is anchored in an understanding of information technologies and social relationships we can observe today. It also has repercussions which technologists, professionals, and policy makers could act on today.

The Engine of Information Capitalism

Different forms of computers and applications are most attractive and affordable to different kinds of people and organizations. Many journalists find notebook computers to be attractive and adequate for their work while few meteorologists and materials engineers could carry out key calculations on them. Conversely, even the largest newspapers are unlikely to be willing or able to send $20 million 1992 dollars on a supercomputer for text processing while some large oil firms find those costs affordable to enhance their ability to explore and exploit new energy sources. These adoptions are not simply predicted by some conception of "need." They are the result of complex interplays of managerial and professional preferences, perceptions of competitive advantage, wealth, and conventional ways of doing business in a specific institutional matrix.

If we were focusing on portable and miniature computers, we would want a way to characterize the people and organizations that would most readily buy and use them. This is a different and probably much more heterogeneous group than those who would be likely to adopt massively parallel computing. Similarly, the sheer costs of massively parallel computers mean that they will be selectively acquired by wealthier organizations with huge databases and turned to certain kinds of high-performance applications.

In the next 20 years, we expect massively parallel computing to be absorbed into and then accelerate an interesting social trend—the expansion of information capitalism. *Information capitalism* refers to forms of organization in which data-intensive techniques and computerization are key strategic resources for corporate production.[33] The owners and managers of agricultural, manufacturing, and service firms increasingly rely on imaginative strategies to "informationalize" production. Computerized information systems have joined factory smokestacks as major symbols of economic power.

As an organization shifts its managerial style to be more information capitalist, analysts organize, implement, and utilize information systems to improve marketing, production, and operations. Information systems multiply, as cost accounting, production monitoring, and market surveys becomes a key resource in advancing the organizations' competitive edge. Capitalism is a dynamic system, and the information capitalism metaphor joins both information and the traditional dynamism of capitalist enterprise. The information capitalist metaphor is expansive because this style of management and organization is also used by non-profit organizations such as public agencies, special interest groups, and political campaigns.

Information capitalism is a useful metaphor because it marries information with capitalism's dynamic and aggressive edge. Capitalism as an institutional system depends on structures that facilitate reinvesting profit into a developing organization. Capitalism is nourished by the hunger of entrepreneurs, their agents, and their customers. Capitalism is stimulated when consumers lust after lifestyles of the rich and famous rather than when they rest content by emulating the lifestyles of the happy and innocent poor. Capitalism can reward the kind of entrepreneurial angst that stimulates some players to develop a new product, or a more effective way to market it or sell an older one. While there are numerous complacent managers and professionals in capitalist economies, there are often the prospects of good rewards for their competitors who can develop a more clever angle on making a business work. This underlying edge to capitalism comes from the possibility of good rewards for innovation and the risk of destruction or displacement when the complacent are blindsided by their competitors. A by-product of the way that capitalism civilizes and rewards greed is a system in which some participants opportunistically innovate in the "search for more."

The concrete forms of capitalist enterprises have changed dramatically in industrialized countries in the last 200 years. Until the late 1840s, capitalist enterprises were usually managed by their owners. While some firms, such as plantations, hired salaried supervisors, managerial hierarchies in businesses were small and numbered in the dozens at most. In contrast, some of the largest U.S. firms today can have over a dozen levels separating the salaried Chief Executive Officer from the lowest level employee, and they can be managed by tens of thousands of specialized managers. Alfred D. Chandler, the business historian, characterizes this newer form of capitalism as "managerial capitalism," in contrast with the older and simpler "personal capitalism."[34] Managerial capitalist enterprises were large enough producers to give countries such as the United States, Germany, and Japan strong presence on world markets. A more recent shift in the organization of U.S. industrial firms to manufacture most or all of their products overseas, often in Asia and Mexico. Robert Reich refers to this emerging shift in capitalist organization as "global capitalism."[35] Information capitalism refers to a different, but contemporary, shift in the ways that managers exploit information systematically.

Firms that are organized by these various forms of capitalism coexist in the same economy. Numerous small businesses are managed only by their owners at the same time that the U.S. industrial economy is increasingly characterized by global capitalism. Similarly, the shift to information capitalism is most pronounced in certain organizations, especially those who have thousands of customers or clients. But the larger organizations that employ an information capitalist managerial approach are most likely to effectively exploit the use of massively parallel computers as database systems. Their opportunism will play a key role in the development and use of massively parallel computing in commercial, rather than scientific and engineering, applications.

Computerization promises to facilitate the "search for more" by helping inventive entrepreneurs, managers, and professionals to reach out in new ways, to offer new products and service, to improve their marketing, and to tighten their control over relations with their customers.[36] But the key link between information capitalism and massively parallel computing is the possibilities for enhanced information processing provided to analysts whose managerial strategies profit from significant advances in computational speed and or in managing huge databases. Massively parallel computing, like many "high end" technologies, offers unequal advantage to those who can afford it and best exploit it. A fast, but expensive, computer is a much more profitable investment for the financial firm whose analysts model a complete stock market by the hour than it is to the retiree who tracks two stocks a month for his personal portfolio. A parallel computer offers more special advantages to the chemist who is trying to model a complex biochemical process than it does to the team that writes an application to a regulatory agency to approve the resulting drug. Large massively parallel computers organized for transaction processing offer more relative advantage to the retail chain with a million customers than to the leather craftsman who sells his wares in a small shop with a local clientele. Any of these parties may benefit from computing in some form, but the second party in each of these pairs would be most likely to find lower end microcomputers to be adequate for their tasks.

Point-of-sale terminals, automated teller machines, credit cards, and the widespread appearance of "desktop computing" are some of the visible by-products of information capitalism. Platoons of specialized information workers—from clerks to professionals — are hidden behind these information technologies which have become critical elements for many businesses and public agencies. A chain of fast-food restaurants provides one good kind of example of information capitalism in action. Viewed as a service, fast-food restaurants simply sell rapidly prepared food for relatively low prices, and stimulate a high rate of customer turnover. They are simply furnished, provide no table service, and are staffed by low-paid workers (often teenagers) to keep costs down. It is a traditional service managed in traditional ways to act as a low-cost service provider. Fast-food chain restaurants differ from other low-cost restaurants by buying in immense volume, advertising with standard menus, serving food through drive-up windows and walk-up counters, and franchising their outlets in special ways.

From the vantage point of information capitalism, fast-food restaurant chains are especially competitive and successful when they have an infrastructure of skilled information professionals and technologies. The information component helps them to select restaurant sites, to alter their menus to match the changing tastes of their clienteles, to audit the services of each establishment, and carefully to monitor costs, cash-flows, inventory, and sales. Their operational efficiencies hinge on information technologies as much as on economies of scale—from the microphones and audio systems that make it easier for drive-through customers to order food to the simplified electronic cash registers that automatically calculate costs and change so that less skilled teenage workers can be relied on as labor. The skills of back-stage professional analysts consuming bytes of data expedite the large-scale sale of bites of food. Fast-food restaurant chains have not shifted from selling bites of food to selling bytes of information, but their operations have become intensively informationalized. Information capitalism gives certain organizations greater leverage than their less technologically sophisticated precursors.

An interesting concrete example is the Mrs. Fields' Cookies chain. It utilizes an expert system to guide store managers in several areas of business.[37] Its database of historical sales for each store helps tailor advice about the quantities of different kinds of cookies to bake at specific times during the day. Other modules guide managers in sales strategies when sales are slow, and prompts them with questions to ask prospective employees in employment interviews. Mrs. Fields' Cookies employs young managers who usually have no previous experience in bakeries or in managing fast-food outlets. While they could send their novice managers to a special school, similar to McDonald's Hamburger U, the firm profited handily in the first few years of its growth by substituting their expert system for longer-term managerial training. The way that Mrs. Fields organizes work illustrates one trend which we believe massively parallel computing may extend. Behind their expert systems is a group of diverse and highly skilled symbolic analysts at corporate headquarters who design, refine, and maintain them. The stores are operated by a much less sophisticated and less well-paid cadre of workers who are very unlikely to join the symbolic analysts at the corporate headquarters in Utah. Before examining information capitalism in more detail, we will examine some twentieth century social transformations that make information capitalism efficacious.

INDIRECT SOCIAL RELATIONSHIPS, THE RISE OF NATIONAL ORGANIZATIONS, AND THE GROWTH OF LARGE-SCALE PERSONAL DATA SYSTEMS

One of the major social transformations of the last 100 years in industrial societies is the growth of a mobile population, and the commensurate growth of organizations with hordes of customers and clients. The difference between a person's dealing with the small-town store and a store in a huge retail chain like Sears is not in the logic of retail store-based sales, but in the way in which customers rarely deal with people who know them outside of these specific narrow business transactions. The small-town shopkeeper also knew his clients from their going to school with his children, from going to church together, and so on. Yet even in small-town societies, people sometimes find it necessary to deal with large and distant organizations such as tax collectors and the military.

New means of transportation—trains, buses, cars, and airplanes—have transformed the way that life in industrial societies is organized. In the early nineteenth century, most people who were born in the United States lived and died within 50 miles of their birthplaces. Today, in a highly mobile society, a huge fraction of the urban population moves from city to city, following better jobs and better places to live. Adolescents often leave their home towns to attend college, and may move even farther away for jobs. Further, more than 130 metropolitan areas in the United States number over 250,000 in population. Even moving "across town" in one of these cities can bring a person into a new network of friends, employers, and service providers. This combination of mobility and urban development means that many people seek jobs, goods, and services from businesses whose proprietors and staff do not have much firsthand knowledge about them.

In the last 100 years the scale of businesses and the number of government agencies with huge clienteles have also increased. In the nineteenth century few businesses had thousands of clients; and a smaller fraction of the public interacted frequently with the larger businesses of the day. Similarly, government agencies were also smaller. Overall, most business was conducted through face-to-face (direct) relations. Only very specific government activities, such as taxing and drafting, was carried out between people who did not know each other at all. Craig Calhoun[38] characterizes contemporary industrial societies as ones in which a significant fraction of people's important activities are carried out with the mediation of people whom they do not see and may not even know exist. Today, banks can readily extend credit to people who come from anywhere in the country. They can do so with relative safety because of large-scale credit record systems that track the credit history of more than 100,000,000 people. The credit check brings together a credit-seeker and employees of the credit bureau who are related *indirectly*.

Other private firms, such as insurance companies and mail order companies, also extend services to tens of thousands of people whom local agents do not—and could not—personally know. In these transactions, judgments about insurability and credit worthiness are made via indirect social relationships, and are often mediated with computerized information systems. Furthermore, many new government agencies, responsible for accounting for the activities of millions of people, have been created in the twentieth century: the Federal Bureau of Investigation (1908), the Internal Revenue Service (1913), the Social Security Administration (1935), along with various state departments of motor vehicles, and so on. The sheer scale of these services requires that indirect social relationships be routinized effectively, and massive record systems support these efforts.

In any era, organizations use the available technologies for keeping records; papyrus and paper were used for centuries. But in modern societies, where computers and telecommunications are a common medium for storing and accessing organizational records, the opportunities for operating a enterprise that has millions of customers or clients, the ability to tighten social control over a dispersed and mobile population, and the nature of potential problems, have changed a great deal.

There is significant payoff to organizations that can effectively exploit the informational resources that this systematic record keeping entails for identifying potential customers, for assessing credit risks, and so forth. Further, third-party data brokers, like TRW Information Services, Trans Union, and Equifax, have developed lively businesses by catering to these markets—through custom search services, passing information to client firms, and also devising new information products to facilitate precision electronic marketing.

MASSIVELY PARALLEL COMPUTING AND THE EXPANSION OF INFORMATION CAPITALISM

Parallel computing and interlocking technologies, like computer networks, database management systems, and graphics can play key roles in increasing the scale of data that firms can manage and analyze. The know-how involved is not primarily computer expertise. Rather it is deep expertise in some domain, such as finance or marketing, and sufficient computer expertise to bring computational power to bear on the problem framed by the analyst. Massively parallel computing helps organizations manage and analyze data in three major domains:

1. Changes in production, with greater emphasis on managing data as a strategic resource resulting changes in the structure of (information) labor markets.
2. Improving control over relationships with customers and clients, especially the elaboration of indirect social relationships.
3. The development of more information products.

None of the social changes which we examine require massively parallel computing. But the more computationally intensive forms of these patterns are likely to be enhanced and elaborated by the use of massively parallel computing for record-keeping and the analysis of databases.

Five years ago, massively parallel computing was primarily a computer architecture to support supercomputing, which was used almost exclusively for large-scale engineering and scientific computations. But the applications of massive parallelism are broadening toward commercial applications. Computer industry analysts and spokesmen foresee commercial firms as major purchasers of massively parallel computers in the next decades. This shifting market parallels the original shift in the mainframe computer business in the 1950s and 1960s as early information capitalists pioneered commercial computation for computers that had previously been the province of scientists and engineers.

Today, a handful of commercial firms have purchased parallel supercomputers; they illustrate the kinds of markets and applications where information capitalists are likely to find massively parallel computing attractive in the next two decades. In 1989 Prudential Securities bought a 32-processor Intel iPSC/2 to replace a rented Cray supercomputer, which in turn had replaced their set of DEC VAX minicomputers. Prudential has been a commercial showcase site for Intel, and by 1991 had upgraded to an IPSC/860.[39] This purchase is part of a trend among Wall Street securities firms to utilize advanced computation to track and model global financial markets. A different kind of commercial application of massive parallelism was pioneered by Dow-Jones News Retrieval when they had complaints about response times from some of their 300,000 customers in the late 1980s. They acquired two Connection Machines from Thinking Machines Inc. to help improve the performance of their commercial document retrieval systems.[40] Firms that are releasing newer models of massively parallel computers are explicitly targeting commercial markets with their configurations, their product announcements, and in the way that they organize their marketing efforts. NCR is aiming its new model 3600 at large-scale transaction processing in banks and public agencies, such as the U.S. Internal Revenue Service. Early in 1992 Kendall Square Research was reported to have some problems in effectively engineering their massively parallel computer and have withheld its release because of problems in configurations that would be attractive for commercial applications. Not only are individual vendors seeking commercial applications, but some vendors have banded together in consortia to pool their talents in finding new applications for parallel computing.

We believe that these kinds of activities signal an important trend in restructuring the high end of the commercial computing markets. But we are also cautious in estimating the speed at which massively parallel computer systems will be effectively used in a wide array of commercial applications. First, many computing applications may not gain anywhere near the maximum possible increase in speed because they have few parallelizable computations. Computer specialists and information capitalists are in a relatively early stage of experimenting with the match between massively parallel computing and diverse commercial application mixes that run on a particular computer. Second, computer applications are not driven by hardware alone. Software is critical, and there are currently no standard operating systems, database languages, and support tools for commercial applications for massively parallel computers. However, software vendors are developing new systems and tools, or reconfiguring existing ones, for massively parallel computers.[41] Recently Oracle, an established database management system vendor, announced a parallel version of its relational database management system and it is being ported to parallel computers by several vendors. It may take well over a decade for the array of systems and database software for massively parallel computers to be as rich as those currently available for the major conventional mainframes.

The growth of these applications of massively parallel computing have some key ramifications for ways that organizations function, the kinds of services that business sell, the kinds of jobs the economy generates, and changes in the relationships between organizations and their clients. We will examine two of these topics, work structure and client relations, in our next two sections.

INFORMATION CAPITALISM AND THE STRUCTURE OF INFORMATION LABOR MARKETS

The commercial application of massively parallel computing promises to generate numerous jobs for technical specialists in the computer industry and also in organizations that utilize these powerful systems to enhance information capitalist management strategies. It is easiest to focus on the interesting work that it takes to design massively parallel computers, their systems software, and their networks, and to conceptualize applications that make information capitalist management strategies really work as organizational innovations. It is tempting to use simplified slogans, such as claiming that the use of massive parallelism to support information capitalism is a high-cost, high-value activity. Consequently, commercial firms and public agencies that adopt massive parallelism will hire many highly skilled analysts who have the special expertise to exploit these technologies effectively. These will be relatively interesting and well-paid jobs.

But the impact of the commercial use of massively parallel computing on jobs is unlikely to be limited to the most visible and interesting professional jobs. The organization of work and labor markets are more complex. Computers are built by production workers with relatively routine jobs. The securities firms that develop rich, computationally demanding models of international financial markets are likely to employ hundreds of clerks to help sell their services and provide information about the performance of the products that dozens of skilled analysts develop.

The ways that the diffusion of massively parallel computing can help shift the occupational structure is not easily inferred by simply listing applications and their designers or users. The work structure in organizations that employ information capitalist strategies can be reconfigured in various ways, not just in ways that necessarily improve or degrade all of the work simultaneously.

It would be helpful to have data about the changing mix of jobs in organizations that utilize very large-scale computing. This data could best give us some direct insights about the likely mix of occupations to expect in information capitalist organizations that adopt massively parallel computing. Unfortunately, data of this kind are not available.

Our best alternative is to examine long-term shifts in the mix of occupations that are most directly influenced by information capitalism—the information sector.[42] We may be able to make some inferences about the mix of jobs brought about by the use of massively parallel computing by examining occupational trends in the recent decades, since this has been a period of intensive computerization. For example, if computerization has increased the relative availability of professional jobs, they should be much more common in the information labor sector today than in the 1960s.

The information labor sector is a relatively new concept. It is composed of those jobs in which people record, process, or communicate information as a large fraction of their work.[43] These diverse occupations include managers, lawyers, accountants, realtors, stock brokers, and clerks of all kinds. People process information in important ways as part of any job—including truck

TABLE I. The U.S. Information Work Force (in thousands): Five-Strata Breakdown, 1900–1990[60]

Year	Full Prof.	Semiprof.	Sales & Superv.	Clerks	Blue Collar	Total Work Force
1900	280	1288	1557	1604	209	29030
1910	338	2125	2126	2933	288	37291
1920	437	2602	2586	4438	344	42206
1930	595	3738	3469	5952	469	48686
1940	687	3994	3773	6992	506	51742
1950	1065	5257	4900	9508	786	59230
1960	1338	7371	5803	12286	913	67990
1970	2152	8539	6796	16600	1192	80603
1980	3328	16997	8047	20487	1249	99303
1990	4227	19428	5367	23499	3307	117914

drivers, trapeze artists, and machinists. The label "information work" is a concise way to characterize jobs where information is a key product of the job, or where the person is likely to spend a large fraction of each workweek communicating, reading, search for information, or handling paperwork in its various forms, including electronic transactions. The information occupations mushroomed in size from 17% of the United States work force in 1900 to 55% in 1990 (tables 1 and 2). Information sector jobs vary widely in quality. One succinct way to characterize the quality of jobs is by their location in the status hierarchy of occupations. No single criterion captures the rich meanings of specific jobs for specific people in an economy with well over 100 million workers. But this simplified conception captures important aspects of pay, status, autonomy and other working conditions.[44] We can divide the information labor sector into five broad occupational groups which differ in the overall quality of their jobs.

1. *Professional occupations* include the eight most highly professionalized occupations in the United States in the information work force, including accountants, architects, lawyers, and physicians. The most highly developed professions have legal monopolies over legitimate practice and credentialing requirements. These are usually the most prestigious occupations, and many of these occupations pay relatively well—on average. Jobs within

TABLE 2. Occupational Strata as Percentage of U.S. Information Work Force

Year	Full Prof.	Semiprof.	Sales & Superv.	Clerks	Blue Collar	% of Total Work Force
1900	5.7%	26.1%	31.5%	32.5%	4.2%	17.0%
1910	4.3%	27.2%	27.2%	37.6%	3.7%	20.9%
1920	4.2%	25.0%	24.8%	42.6%	3.3%	24.7%
1930	4.2%	26.3%	24.4%	41.8%	3.3%	29.2%
1940	4.3%	25.0%	23.7%	43.8%	3.2%	30.8%
1950	4.9%	24.4%	22.8%	44.2%	3.7%	36.3%
1960	4.8%	26.6%	20.9%	44.3%	3.3%	40.8%
1970	6.1%	24.2%	19.3%	47.1%	3.4%	43.8%
1980	6.6%	33.9%	16.1%	40.9%	2.5%	50.5%
1990	7.6%	34.8%	9.6%	42.1%	5.9%	47.3%

these occupations vary considerably along other criteria, such as stress.

2. *Semiprofessional occupations* include 19 occupations that have some professional standing and are not fully fledged professions, such as computer specialists, engineers, managers, school administrators, social workers, and teachers. Semiprofessional occupations are usually less prestigious and less well-paid, on average, than the full-fledged professionals. But they are usually much more autonomous and prestigious than the occupations in the next lower stratum.

3. *Supervisory and upper-level sales occupations* constitute a category whose status lies between that of semiprofessionals and that of clerks. It includes advertising agents, health technologists, insurance agents, office managers, purchasing agents, real estate agents, and stock brokers. This is a complex stratum that lies between the moderately prestigious semiprofessional occupations and the less prestigious, less autonomous, and lower paid clerical occupations.

4. *Clerical occupations* include clerical jobs of all kinds (including cashiers and sales clerks). We view clerical jobs as prob-

lematic because they usually pay poorly compared with other information jobs. Clerical jobs vary considerably in autonomy—from telephone operators to executive secretaries. But they are often fairly regimented.

5. *Blue collar occupations* include technicians who install or repair communications, printing, and other information processing equipment.

Relatively few information sector jobs are fully professional, and clerical jobs form a large occupational stratum (tables 1 and 2). Clerical jobs grew in relative numbers between 1900 and 1970. Professional and semiprofessional workers, taken together, formed a stable *minority of the information work force,* about 30% through 1970.

Since 1900, clerks have been the largest strata of information workers. They rose from 32% of the information work force in 1900 to about 42% in 1920 and remained relatively stable through 1970. Simultaneously, the higher-level sales and supervisory stratum shrank from about 30% to 20% of the information work force. These two lower white collar strata formed the *majority* of information workers. One key observation is that the relative number of mid-level jobs has declined significantly since 1900, while clerical jobs have risen in relative number.

There are signs of a different pattern of occupational growth and decline between 1970 and 1990, which has been a period of intensive computerization in the United States. The proportion of highly professionalized and semiprofessional workers rose to about 42% of the information work force. Clerks have dropped a bit from their 1970 peak, but are comparable in number to the professionals and semiprofessionals (table 2). The occupational stratum between clerks and semiprofessionals—the supervisory and upper level sales workers—has steadily declined in relative size. In 1900 it was about three times as large, in relative size, as it was in 1990.

The information work force contains a relatively impermeable barrier that prevents both clerical and supervisory and upper level sales workers from easily moving into semiprofessional and professional occupations. Our arguments that the information

TABLE 3. Occupational Strata as Percentage of Total U.S. Work Force

Year	Full Prof.	Semiprof.	Sales & Superv.	Clerks	Blue Collar
1900	1.0%	4.4%	5.4%	5.5%	0.7%
1910	0.9%	5.7%	5.7%	7.9%	0.8%
1920	1.0%	6.2%	6.1%	10.5%	0.8%
1930	1.2%	7.7%	7.1%	12.2%	1.0%
1940	1.3%	7.7%	7.3%	13.5%	1.0%
1950	1.8%	8.9%	8.3%	16.1%	1.3%
1960	2.0%	10.8%	8.5%	18.1%	1.3%
1970	2.7%	10.6%	8.4%	20.6%	1.5%
1980	3.4%	17.1%	8.1%	20.6%	1.3%
1990	3.6%	16.5%	4.6%	19.9%	2.8%

labor markets are segmented are very simple. Access to most occupations in the professional and semiprofessional strata is limited by special education and licensing requirements. The full professions usually require specialized college or postgraduate degrees. Some professions, such as law and medicine, also impose stringent professional licensing requirements. Many of the semi-professions have similar barriers that inhibit people from "moving up" into them, although some of them do not require formal training or licensing.[45]

Clerks are predominantly female, and there are important structural barriers that seal off many women from professional and semiprofessional careers. Women who wish to rise from clerical jobs to "something better" often lack the special education and credentials required for fully professional and semiprofessional jobs.[46] The supervisory and higher-level sales jobs are within reach for a larger number of clerks since they do not have significant educational and credentialing barriers. Some of these pay more than semiprofessional jobs, but they have steadily declined in relative proportion (table 3). There are relatively few slots for clerks in the next stratum: clerks who want to "move up" in the information sector find a significantly smaller number of jobs they can qualify for without significant formal education.

While the information work force became more segmented, access to many information jobs has become more difficult. The educational and credentialing requirements for jobs at all strata in the information sector have generally tightened during this century. College degrees were once the prerequisites for only the most specialized and technical or most professionalized occupations. Since World War II there has been a form of credential inflation; bachelors (and sometimes graduate) degrees have become commonplace requirements for many semiprofessional jobs. Some employers are beginning to hire people with college degrees into clerical jobs. Clerical work is probably the primary occupational opportunity for the majority of college-educated women with degrees in the liberal arts who do not acquire professional or graduate degrees.

This analysis gives us some clues about the role of computerization in changing work and also some suggestions about the possible repercussions of massive parallelism for the structure of the work force. Information capitalism will be fueled by the imagination and work of engineers, computer specialists, marketing analysts, and financial analysts. Organizations that utilize more complex computerized systems to support information capitalism will require a cadre of technical specialists. Most of these jobs are semiprofessional, an occupational stratum that has grown steadily since 1970. However, clerical employment has also remained strong. While it is conceivable that clerical work will disappear, we think that such scenarios are unlikely in the next few decades. There is a significant role for routinized office and sales support which constitutes clerical work, even in highly computerized settings. Further, clerical work is becoming more of an occupational trap for someone who wants to move onto more professionalized work. Last, for a technology like massive parallelism to make a substantial difference in the distribution of jobs, organizations would have to computerize with significantly new strategies of organizing work than those common since the 1970s.

We do not see the widespread adoption of massive parallelism having only one kind of impact in the structure of the information work force. There are significant choices in organizational design which would lead to two different kinds of occupational mixes in firms that push information capitalist strategies. Today, many organizations have opted in the direction taken by Mrs. Fields' Cookies, which expands by deploying platoons of low-skilled workers whose work is guided and monitored by increasingly sophisticated computer systems. Another strategy is being adopted by some firms that have found that a low-skilled work force does not help them deal adequately and flexibly with sophisticated customers and with a diverse array of complex products that fit different market niches. These organizations, relatively few in number today, are utilizing advanced computer systems to provide diverse products, such as numerous and more complex forms of insurance or investments, and also recruiting more sophisticated staff to sell and support them. A third, mixed strategy is also common today. Some organizations develop and sell more complex or diverse products, but try to sell and support them with relatively unsophisticated staff. Organizations that opt for this mixed strategy often find that computerization does not provide the benefits their managers anticipate, but they can be sufficiently profitable that they do not alter their strategies.

These patterns of employment could be influenced by the policies and practices of commercial firms and public agencies. They are not foregone social facts. Organizations might invest more in educating their lower-level staff, and the public might support a stronger K–12 educational system. Improved K–12 education could shift the occupational mix.[47]

MASSIVE PARALLELISM AND CHANGING PATTERNS OF SOCIAL CONTROL

In an earlier section we discussed the rise of organizations with huge clienteles and the growing prominence of indirect social relations when people interact with organizations. A society where social relationships are often indirect can give people a greater sense of freedom. One can move from job to job, from house to house, and from loan to loan and selectively leave some of one's past behind. Managers in organizations that provide long-term services, such as banks, insurance companies, and apartment houses, often want to reduce their business risks by reconstructing what they believe are relevant parts of a person's history.

Consequently, larger organizations, such as some of the biggest banks, insurance companies, and public agencies, took an early lead in adapting mainframe computing to support their huge personal record systems in the 1950s and 1960s. In the 1970s and 1980s these organizations enhanced their computer systems and developed networks to communicate data regionally, nationally, and internationally more effectively. Many of those organizations have massive appetites for "affordable" high-speed transaction processing and tools to help them manage gigabytes and even terabytes[48] of data. Some have been experimenting with supercomputing, and they have cadres of professionals who are eager to exploit new technologies to better track and manage their customers and clients. Massively parallel computing supports finer grained analyses of indirect social relationships, such as precision marketing to improve the abilities to target customers for a new product, or the ability of a taxing agency to search multiple large databases prowling for tax cheaters.

Managers and professional in business organizations and public agencies characterize their searches for information about people in limited and pragmatic terms that improve their rationality in making specific decisions about whom to hire, to whom to extend a loan, to whom to rent an apartment, and whom to arrest.[49] From the viewpoint of individuals, these searches for personal information are sometimes fair and sometimes invasive of their privacy.[50] Information capitalists, like other entrepreneurs in a capitalist economy, are sensitive to the costs of their services. When there is no price on goods like clean air or personal privacy, they are usually ignored, except when there are protective regulations to compensate for market failures.

Some of the key policy debates about computerization and privacy reveal conflicting values, not just conflicting interests. At least five major value orientations influence the terms of key debates.[51] These values can also help us understand the social repercussions of personal data systems which run on massively parallel computers:

Private enterprise model: The preeminent consideration is profitability of financial systems, with the highest social good being the profitability of both the firms providing and the firms utilizing the systems. Other social goods such as consumers' privacy or the desires of government agencies for data are secondary concerns.

Statist model: The strength and efficiency of government institutions is the highest goal—government needs for access to personal data on citizens. The need for mechanisms to enforce citizens' obligations to the state will always prevail over other considerations.

Libertarian model: Civil liberties, such as those specified by the U.S. Bill of Rights, are to be maximized in any social choice. Other social purposes such as profitability or welfare of the state would be secondary when they conflict with the prerogatives of the individual.

Neo-populist model: The practices of public agencies and private enterprises should be easily intelligible to ordinary citizens and be responsive to their needs. Societal institutions should emphasize serving the "ordinary person."

Systems model: Financial systems must be technically well organized, efficient, reliable, and aesthetically pleasing.

In different instances, policies and developments may support, conflict with, or be independent of these five value models. Each of them, except the systems model, has a large number of supporters and a long tradition of support within the United States. Thus, computing developments that are congruent with any of these positions might be argued to be in "the public interest." Information capitalism is most directly aligned with the private enterprise value model for guiding social action. But the information capitalist approach can also support statist values in cases where public agencies use computerized information systems to model and explore alternative revenue-generating programs, to assess the effectiveness of social programs, or to track scofflaws through networks of records systems. It is conceivable that information capitalism could support neo-populist consumer control, by constructing databases that report on the quality of commercial products and services, or by enhancing access to government records systems. However, such uses are extremely rare and are not accessible to the majority of people, who are not computer savvy. It is difficult to imagine that many new computerized systems would, on balance, support libertarian values. However, enhanced privacy regulations reduce the extent to which computerized systems that support statist or private enterprise values further erode personal privacy in the United States.

Computer-based information systems can be used in a myriad of ways that help organizations with huge clienteles better manage these relationships. For example, in 1991 American Express announced the purchase of two CM-5 massively parallel computers from Thinking Machines, Inc., which it will probably use to analyze cardholders' purchasing patterns.[52] American Express' purchase of these two multimillion dollar computers illustrates how the conjunction of massive parallelism and information capitalism tilts the social system to emphasizing private enterprise values over libertarian values. While American Express is an innovator in experimenting with massively parallel computing for market research, other firms that manage huge numbers of indirect social relationships with their customers will follow suit as the price and performance of these computers, the quality of the systems software, and the technical know-how for using them all improve in the next decades. These styles of computer use systematically advance private enterprise values at the expense of libertarian values.

In order to help organizations manage their relationships with a large population of clients with whom they often have indirect social relationships, organizations increasingly rely on formal records systems. Today's computerized systems provide much finer grained information about people's lifestyles and whereabouts than was readily available in earlier record systems. While these data system primarily serve the specific transaction for which the customer provides information, it is increasingly common for computerized systems with personal data to serve multiple secondary uses, such as marketing and policing.

During the last two decades, direct mail marketing and precision marketing have gotten big boosts through new techniques for identifying potential customers.[53] In the early 1990s Lotus Development Corporation was planning to sell a CD-based database, Marketplace:Household, which contained household marketing data provided by an Equifax Marketing Decision Systems Inc., which is affiliated with a large credit agency, Equifax Inc. The database would have given anyone with a Macintosh access to data on more than 120 million Americans obtained from Equifax. Lotus MarketPlace:Household provided marketers with detailed portraits of households so it would be easier to ascertain where to send direct mail and what places were the best for telemarketing. All names came encrypted on the disk, and users were required to purchase an access code and use a "metering" system to pay for new groups of addresses to search.[54] Lotus attempted to reduce privacy problems by omitting phone numbers and credit ratings from MarketPlace:Household and by selling the data only to those who could prove they ran legitimate businesses. The street address could be printed only on paper and not on a computer screen. These measures did not adequately assure many people.

Lotus withdrew Marketplace:Household in 1991 after it received over 30,000 complaints from consumers. Some industry observers speculated that Lotus withdrew Marketplace:Household because its upper managers feared that bad publicity and consumer backlash could harm its sales of other software. Lotus did, however, release a companion product, Marketplace:Business, which characterizes business purchasing patterns, through a licensing arrangement.

Lotus MarketPlace is an interesting kind of information product that illustrates another face of information capitalism, since it would be sold to small business which could more readily afford microcomputing. These users of Lotus MarketPlace:Household would have a new resource to help expand their own use of information capitalist marketing strategies. The particular computer platform for a product like Lotus MarketPlace:Household has some consequences for personal privacy. For example, it would be much easier to rapidly and consistently remove records of objecting consumers from a centralized database than from hundreds of thousands of CDs of various vintages scattered throughout thousands of offices around the country. Consequently, another firm that provides a mainframe-based version of Marketplace:Household might face less resistance. Further, if the firm did not risk loss of business from consumer complaints, they might tough out a wave of initial complaints. Thus, a credit reporting firm like Equifax or TRW might offer a variant mainframe-based version of Marketplace:Household.

In 1991 the U.S. Bureau of the Census proposed developing a unified government database by connecting data from government agencies and private firms. The sources included Internal Revenue Service records and county assessors' records. The Census Bureau would also employ the large databases owned by large credit companies such as Equifax and TRW.[55] A massive data system of this scale is likely to tax the largest and fastest of today's supercomputers, and also make significant demands on high-speed computer networks. Historically, the Bureau of the Census has had a good record in protecting the privacy of individual data. But networked systems of the sort they now propose could lead to looser controls through quid-pro-quo arrangements with other organizations and "data leakage."

Debates about whether certain computerized systems should be implemented typically reveal major conflicts between civil libertarians on the one hand, and those who value the preeminence of private enterprise or statist values on the other. Any particular computerized system is likely to advance some of these values at the expense of the others. Many socially complex information systems are enmeshed in a matrix of competing social values, and none is value free.

Problems for the people about whom records are kept arise under a variety of circumstances, for instance, when the records are inaccurate and people are unfairly denied a loan, a job, or housing. Large-scale record systems (with millions of records) there are bound to be inaccuracies. But people have few rights to inspect or correct records about them—except for credit records. During the last 30 years, people have consistently lost significant control over records about them. Increasingly, courts have ruled that records about a person belong to the organization that collects the data, and the person to whom they apply cannot restrict their use. Consequently, inaccurate police records, medical records, and employment histories can harm people without their explicit knowledge about why they are having trouble getting a job, a loan, or medical insurance.

New ways of doing business—taken together with computer systems—have reduced people's control over their personal affairs. On the other hand, representatives of those private firms and government agencies that have an interest in expanding their computerized information systems frequently argue hard against legal limits or substantial accountability to people about whom records are kept. They deny that problems exist, or they argue that the reported problems are exaggerated in importance. They also argue that proposed regulations are either too vague or too burdensome, and that new regulations about information systems would do more harm than good. The proponents of unregulated computerization have been wealthy, organized, and aligned with the antiregulatory sentiments that have dominated U.S. federal politics during the last 15 years. Consequently, they have effectively blocked many attempts to preserve personal privacy through regulation.

In this way, many representatives of the computer industry and of firms with massive personal record systems behave similarly to the representatives of automobile firms when they first were asked to face questions about smog. As smog became more visible in major U.S. cities in the 1940s and 1950s, the automobile industry worked hard to argue that there was no link between cars and smog.[56] First their spokesmen argued that smog was not a systematic phenomenon, then they argued that it was primarily caused by other sources, such as factories. After increases in smog were unequivocally linked to the use of cars, they spent a good deal of energy fighting any regulations which would reduce the pollution emitted by cars. Overall, the automobile industry slowly conceded to reducing smog in a foot-dragging pattern which Krier and Ursin[57] characterize as "regulation by least steps." Similarly, the organizations that develop or use personal record keeping systems behave like the automobile industry in systematically fighting enhanced pubic protections.

The increasing importance of indirect social relationships, which we described earlier, gives many organizations a legitimate interest in using computerized personal records systems to learn about potential or actual clients. These organizations usually act in ways to maintain the largest possible zone of free action for themselves, while downplaying their clients' interests. The spread of larger and more interlinked personal data systems will not automatically provide people with corresponding protections to reduce the risks of these systems in cases of error, inappropriate disclosure, or other problems.[58]

The history of federal privacy protections in the United States is likely to be continued without a new level of political mobilization which supports new protections. The Privacy Act of 1974 established a Privacy Protection Study Commission, which in 1977 issued a substantial report on its findings and made 155 recommendations to develop "fair information practices." Many of these recommendations gave people the right to know what records are kept about them, to inspect records for accuracy, to correct (or contest) inaccuracies, to be informed when records were transferred from one organization to another, and so on. Less than a handful of these proposals were subsequently enacted into federal law.

Leaders of the massive parallel computing movement and its associated industry could help reduce the possible reductions of privacy that their applications foster by helping to initiate relevant and responsible privacy protections. However, expecting them to take such initiatives would be futile, since they work within social arrangements that do not reward their reducing their own market opportunities. The commercial firms and public agencies that will utilize massively parallel computing systems in the next decades face their own contests with their clients and data subjects, and they fight for legal and technological help, rather than hindrance. As a consequence, we expect privacy regulation in the next two decades to be similarly lax to the previous two decades. While the public is becoming sensitized to privacy as a mobilizing issue, it does not have the salience and energizing quality of recent issues such as tax reduction, abortion, or even environmental pollution.

CONCLUSIONS

Massively parallel computing systems promise to expand the frontiers of computational speed over the next few decades. The applications that this technology enables are likely to be of substantial social consequence. Unfortunately, most of the discourse about massively parallel computing focuses on technological innovation and applications in narrow social contexts.

There are numerous niches within the computer science community and the computer industries where professionals identify with some specific family of technologies; artificial intelligence, expert systems, computer-assisted design, computer networks, hypermedia, computer-assisted instruction, computer-supported cooperative work, databases, medical informatics, factory automation, and massively parallel computing are but a few. One remarkable feature of these scientific and professional communities is the way in which they develop somewhat insular literatures. This insularity is particularly apparent when participants in these diverse communities examine the social dimensions of their specialized technological niche de novo—as if none of the similar investigations by participants in other computerized niches is relevant. The computing world is cosmopolitan in many ways, but is peculiarly provincial in this way. The efforts by participants to differentiate themselves from other communities, and to create an exciting aura of specialness, also limits the depth of their social investigations.

Technological utopianism is one of the first lines of social analysis which participants in new technological movements advance.[59] Technological utopianism offers excitement, a sense of direction, and hope by tightly linking specific technological advances to an improved social order. Early in this chapter we discussed the character and analytical limits of technologically utopian arguments. It takes a careful argument to show how a specific technology is socially transformative. The arguments advanced in the case of special forms of computing are often oversimplified.

The key pieces of evidence about the social consequences of a specific kind of technology are highly empirical. Numerous careful empirical studies of computerization in practice have found that technological utopianism and anti-utopianism are poor predictors. Yet it is useful to understand the possibilities of emerging technologies before their use is widespread. For new technologies whose use is just beginning, like massively parallel computing, systematic empirical observation is insufficient and often impossible.

We have examined some likely social repercussions of massively parallel computing in a way that is congruent with key insights from 20 years of systematic empirical research about the social repercussions of various kinds of computerized technologies. We have focused on emerging commercial applications, such as large-scale transaction processing, since that is the backbone of many large organizations. The diffusion of massive parallel computing systems into these applications may take 10–20 years. The social logic of these uses is likely to selectively amplify and reinforce specific recent social trends rather than to create a rapid revolution around fundamentally new social patterns.

Information capitalism is one dynamic that can drive larger organizations to adopt multimillion dollar massively parallel computing systems. The use of massively parallel computing systems can influence the distribution of jobs and also alter relationships between organizations and their clients.

In the case of labor markets, we have examined the information labor work force from 1900 to 1990 and observed a significant rise in the number and importance of both professional and clerical jobs. However, the divide between these labor strata has increased, and there is nothing in the most likely pattern of massively parallel computing systems to reduce this gap. While the use of massively parallel computing systems will increase the demand for certain kinds of computer specialists and savvy professionals who can exploit the technology for applications such as precision marketing and financial modeling, there is likely to be a corresponding increase in clerical employment to support their systems they implement.

We also examined the use of massively parallel computing systems to extend the scope of personal record-keeping systems. The growing importance of indirect social relationships in North American society leads many organizations to seek data about potential and actual clients. Some organizations collect their own data, and some rely on specialized data brokers to help them construct specialized personal histories pertinent to their specific concern, such as credit worthiness, insurability, employability, criminal culpability, etc. The positive side of these informational strategies is improved organizational efficiencies, novel products, and interesting analytical jobs. However, as a collectivity, these strategies reduce the privacy of many citizens and can result in excruciating foul-ups when record-keeping errors are propagated from one computer system to another, with little accountability to the person being investigated.

These social changes could be influenced by the policies and practices of commercial firms and public agencies. They are not inevitable social trends. Organizations might invest more in educating their lower level staff, and the public might support a stronger K–12 educational system. Improved K–12 education could shift the occupational mix. Further, the public might insist on stronger fair information practices to reduce the risks of expanding records systems.

We are not sanguine about any substantial shifts of these kinds in the next two decades. Without changes like these, which are exogenous to the direct use of specific computer applications, the trends we have discussed are likely to continue. However, these trends are also very much subject to systematic empirical inquiry. One can, for example, study organizations that adopt massively parallel computing to better understand the applications which they automate, their changing employment of clerks and professionals, and changes in their relationships with their clients.

Massively parallel computing is an important family of innovations in computer architectures with significant repercussions for organizations that exploit and manage huge data systems. This is a superb time to carefully observe the social dynamics that generate these uses, and the ways that they, in turn, influence organizations, jobs, and social life.

ENDNOTES

[1] Acknowledgments: Werner Beuschel and Roberta Lamb were invaluable discussants at various stages of this project. John King, Mitzi Lewison, and Mark Poster gave us the kind of close critical readings of the complete manuscript which make them very cherished friends and colleagues. Carolyn Cheung helped analyze data about the information work force in 1990.

[2] M. Dertouzos, and J. Moses, eds., *The Computer Age: A Twenty Year View* (Cambridge: MIT Press, 1979). R. Kurzweil, *The Age of Intelligent Machines* (Cambridge: MIT Press, 1990).

[3] See "The Dreams of Technological Utopianism" by C. Dunlop and R. Kling in C. Dunlop, and R. Kling, (Eds.), *Computerization and Controversy: Value Conflicts and Social Choices* (Boston: Academic Press, 1991). Also see R. Kling, "Reading 'All About' Computerization: Five Common Genres of Social Analy-

sis" in D. Schuler, ed., *Directions in Advanced Computer Systems, 1990* (Norwood: Ablex Publishing, in press).

⁴Weizenbaum's book, *Computer Power and Human Reason* (San Francisco: Freeman, 1976) mixed the intriguing idea that some computer systems were too complex to be comprehended with a moral critique of developing technology for its own sake. Weizenbaum aimed much of his critique at artificial intelligence researchers, who often responded harshly. These debates often polarized into positions "pro" or "anti" AI developments. Unfortunately, Weizenbaum's ideas have not stimulated any substantial body of research and commentary about the practice of building highly complex computerized systems. Some of the recent examinations of the human risks of complex computer systems, for example, could have built upon these ideas. See *Part VI, Security and Reliability* in C. Dunlop and R. Kling in C. Dunlop, and R. Kling, (Eds.), *Computerization and Controversy: Value Conflicts and Social Choices* (Boston: Academic Press, 1991).

⁵See, for example, W. D. Hillis, "What is Massively Parallel Computing and Why is it Important?" *Dædalus* 121(1)(Winter 1992): 1–16 and Y. Deng, J. Glimm, and D. Sharp, "Perspectives on Parallel Computing," *Dædalus* 121(1) (Winter 1992): 31–52.

⁶H. A. Simon, *The New Science of Management Decision* (Englewood Cliffs: Prentice-Hall, 1977).

⁷H. Leavitt, and T. Whisler. "Management in the 1990's," *Harvard Business Review* 1958.

⁸See S. Papert, *Mindstorms: Children, Computers, and Powerful Ideas* (New York: Basic Books, 1980). Also, Kurzweil's analysis of computing in education, which focuses on the character and availability of technologies while virtually ignoring teacher orientations and classroom organization: Kurzweil, R., *The Age of Intelligent Machines* (Cambridge: MIT Press, 1990), especially pp. 429–432.

⁹B. Pfaffenberger, "The Social Meaning of the Personal Computer: Or, Why the Personal Computer Revolution Was No Revolution" *Anthropological Quarterly* (January 1989):39–41.

¹⁰E. Feigenbaum, and P. McCorduck, *Fifth Generation: Artificial Intelligence and Japan's Computer Challenge to the World* (New York: New American Library, 1985).

¹¹See, for example, K. Laudon, *Computers and Bureaucratic Reform.* (New York: John Wiley, 1974); J. Danziger, W. Dutton, R. Kling, and K. Kraemer, *Computers and Politics: High Technology in American Local Government.* (New York: Columbia University Press, 1982) and K. L. Kraemer, S. Dickhoven, S. F. Tierney, and J. L. King, *Datawars:The Politics of Modelling in Federal Policymaking* (New York: Columbia University Press, 1987).

¹²See Bottles, S. *Los Angeles and the Automobile, The Making of the Modern City.* (Berkeley: University of California Press, 1987) and R. Kling, S. Olin, and M. Poster, "Emergence of Postsuburbia" in R. Kling, M. Poster and S. Olin (Ed.) eds., *Postsuburban California: The Transformation of Postwar Orange County* (Berkeley: University of California Press, 1991).

[13]See M. Cambre, "A Reappraisal of Instructional Television." Syracuse, N.Y.: ERIC Clearinghouse on Information Resources, Syracuse University. (ISBN: 0–937597–14–7).

[14]It is hard to find systematic evidence about the role of television in typical classrooms. But diverse evidence suggests that it is rarely used as a powerful instructional medium. Harry Wollcott, for example, reported an intensive field study of a class which viewed an instructional TV program twice weekly. He found that the program was viewed in the afternoon when the instructor was short of things to do, in contrast with the structured morning activities which focused on "basic" subjects such as math and language. See "Ethnographers Sans Ethnography: The Evaluation Compromise" in David Fetterman (ed.), *Ethnography in Educational Evaluation* (Beverly Hills, Ca.: Sage Publications, 1984). According to one of our informants, who has worked as an administrator in a Southern California middle school, the poorest teachers often used television the most. It served as an "electronic baby sitter" and allowed them to do less preparation for class.

[15]See, for example, the references mentioned in endnote 11 and J. Yates, *Control through Communication: The Rise of System in American Management* (Baltimore: Johns Hopkins University Press, 1989); H. Shaiken, *Work Transformed: Automation and Labor in the Computer Age* (Lexington, MA: Lexington Books, 1986). For recent reviews of key studies, see K. Kraemer, and J. King, "Computing and Public Organizations," *Public Administration Review* (1986), R. Kling, "Computerization and Social Transformations," *Science, Technology and Human Values.* 16 (3)(Summer 1991):342–367; and R. Kling, and C. Dunlop, "Key Social Controversies About Computerization and Worklife" in R. Baeker, J. Buxton, and J. Grudin, (eds.), *Human Computer Interaction.* (Morgan-Kaufman, to appear.)

[16]See, for example, R. Kurzweil, *The Age of Intelligent Machines* (Cambridge: MIT Press, 1990), especially pp. 431–432.

[17]For example, Ronni Rosenberg argues that computer literacy classes are often ineffective in K–12 classes, in part because most teachers focus on relatively mechanical aspects of computing (and especially programming) rather than teaching key concepts. See "Debunking Computer Literacy," *The Journal of Computing and Society* 1(2)(1990): 165–191.

[18]R. Kurzweil, *The Age of Intelligent Machines* (Cambridge: MIT Press, 1990).

[19]E. Hobsbawm, *Industry and Empire: An Economic History of Britain since 1750* (London: Weidenfeld and Nicolson, 1968).

[20]E. Hobsbawm, *Industry and Empire: An Economic History of Britain since 1750* (London: Weidenfeld and Nicolson, 1968). S. Cohen, and J. Zysman, *Manufacturing Matters: The Myth of the Post-Industrial Economy* (New York: Basic Books, 1987).

[21]S. Cohen, and J. Zysman, *Manufacturing Matters: The Myth of the Post-Industrial Economy* (New York: Basic Books, 1987). D. Hounshell, *From the American System to Mass Production 1800–1932* (Baltimore: The John Hopkins University Press, 1984).

[22]R. Kling, S. Olin, and M. Poster, "Emergence of Postsuburbia," in M. Poster, S. Olin, and R. Kling, eds., ... *PostSuburban California: The Transformation of Postwar Orange County* (Berkeley: University of California Press, 1991).

[23]The smallest transistor will fit in a square area of less than 0.1 micrometers on the side.

[24]For example, Dewitt and Gray claim that the performance of most computer designs would degrade significantly if they relied on parallel devices. They claim that if each processor slowed down the others by 1%, then a 1000 processor system would have about 4% of the computational capacity of a single processor system! See D. DeWitt, and J. Gray, "Parallel Database Systems: The Future of High Performance Database Systems," *Communications of the ACM* 35(6)(June 1992): 85–98.

[25]See Y. Deng, J. Glimm, and D. Sharp, "Perspectives on Parallel Computing," *Dædalus* 121 (1) (Winter 1992): 31–52.

[26]See D. Pountain, and J. Bryan, "All Systems Go: Parallel Processing is Showing Unparalleled Performance and Computing will Never be the Same," *Byte* 17(8)(August 1992):112–116, 125–126, 130, 132, 134–136.

[27]See D. Pountain, and J. Bryan, "All Systems Go: Parallel Processing is Showing Unparalleled Performance and Computing will Never be the Same," *Byte* 17(8)(August 1992):112–116, 125–126, 130, 132, 134–136.

[28]A teraflop is the equivalent of 10^{12} floating point operations per second.

[29]For an insightful discussion of the costs of massively parallel computers to reach teraflop and pentaflop computing speeds, and the times scales for these developments see, G. Bell, "Ultracomputers: A Teraflop Before its Time," *Communications of the ACM* 35 (8)(August 1992): 27–47.

[30]Y. Deng, J. Glimm, and D. Sharp, "Perspectives on Parallel Computing," *Dædalus* 121 (1) (Winter 1992): 31–52.

[31]W. D. Hillis, "What is Massively Parallel Computing and Why is it Important?" *Dædalus* 121(1)(Winter 1992): 1–16.

[32]A different direction of possible inquiry would be to examine changes in culture which are being facilitated by various media, including simulation. See, for example, D. Harvey, *The Condition of Postmodernity: An Enquiry into the Origins of Cultural Change* (Oxford: Basil Blackwell, 1989) and Mark Poster's essay on Baudrillard in M. Poster, *The Mode of Information: Poststructuralism and Social Context* (Chicago: University of Chicago Press, 1990).

[33]T. Luke, and S. White, "Critical Theory, and Informational Revolution, and an Ecological Path to Modernity," in J. Forester (ed.), *Critical Theory and Public Life* (Cambridge: MIT Press, 1985), 22–53. R. Kling, S. Olin, and M. Poster, "Emergence of Postsuburbia," in R. Kling, S. Olin and M. Poster (eds.), *Postsuburban California: The Transformation of Postwar Orange County* (Berkeley: University of California, Press, 1991).

[34]A. D. Chandler, "The Emergence of Managerial Capitalism," *Business History Review* 58(Winter 1984): 473–503.

[35]R. Reich, *The Work of Nations: Preparing Ourselves for 21st Century Capitalism* (New York: Vintage Books, 1992).

[36]The growing importance of information capitalism as a managerial strategy can be seen in the literature on the strategic use of information systems. For example, see F. W. McFarland, "Information Technology Changes the Way You Compete," *Harvard Business Review* 61 (4) (1984): 91–99, or S. Ives and G. P. Learmouth, "The Information System as a Competitive Weapon," *Communications of the ACM* 27 (12) (1984): 1193–1201.

[37]K. Ostrofsky, and J. Cash, "Mrs. Fields' Cookies," in J. Cash, Jr., F. McFarland, J. McKenney, and L. Applegate (eds.), *Corporate Information Systems Management: Text and Cases* (Boston: Irwin, 1992).

[38]C. Calhoun, "The Infrastructure of Modernity: Indirect Social Relationships, Information Technology, and Social Integration," in H. Haferkamp, and N. Smelser (eds.), *Social Change and Modernity* (Berkeley: University of California Press, 1992).

[39]D. Davis, "Intel Woos Business Users: Intel Marketing Supercomputers to Business," *Datamation* (May 1, 1991): 34–38.

[40]See C. Roberts, "Dow Jones Makes a Friendlier Database: But Is It Too Little, Too Late?" *Lotus* (May 1989): 18–22.

[41]For a description of commercial computers optimized for processing massive parallel databases, See D. DeWitt and J. Gray, "Parallel Database Systems: The Future of High Performance Database Systems," *Communications of the ACM* 35(6)(June 1992): 85–98.

[42]This section draws heavily on data and analysis from R. Kling, "More Information, Better Jobs?: Occupational Stratification and Labor Market Segmentation in the United States' Information Labor Force," *The Information Society* 7(2) (1990): 77–107.

[43]See D. Bell, "The Social Framework of the Information Society," in T. Forester (ed.), *The Microelectronics Revolution: The Complete Guide to the New Technology and Its Impact on Society* (Cambridge: MIT Press, 1981), 500–550.

[44]For a more detailed discussion of this criterion and its limitations, see R. Kling, "More Information, Better Jobs?: Occupational Stratification and Labor Market Segmentation in the United States' Information Labor Force," *The Information Society* 7(2) (1990): 77–107.

[45]"Writers, artists, and entertainers" are perhaps the most intriguing occupations since in principle anyone can write, paint, or play. But managers and administrators account for the majority of semiprofessional jobs in the United States' economy.

[46]Management is the primary semiprofessional occupation that does not require college credentialing. Historically managerial jobs have been male dominated, while many clerical specialties became female dominated by 1900. While managerial jobs have become more open to women in the last decade, they have remained male dominated.

[47]R. Reich, *The Work of Nations: Preparing Ourselves for 21st Century Capitalism* (New York: Vintage Books, 1992).

[48]A terabyte is equivalent of 10^{12} bytes of data.

[49]See, for example, R. P. Kusserow, "The Government Needs Computer Matching to Root Out Waste and Fraud," in C. Dunlop, and R. Kling, (eds.), *Computerization and Controversy: Value Conflicts and Social Choices* (Boston: Academic Press, 1991).

[50]See, for example, J. Shattuck, "Computer Matching is a Serious Threat to Individual Rights" in C. Dunlop, and R. Kling, (eds.), *Computerization and Controversy: Value Conflicts and Social Choices* (Boston: Academic Press, 1991) and K. Laudon, *Dossier Society: Value Choices in the Design of National Information Systems* (Columbia University Press: New York, 1986).

[51]See R. Kling, "Value Conflicts and Social Choice in Electronic Funds Transfer Systems Developments," *Communications of the ACM* (August 1978): 642–657 and R. Kling, "Value Conflicts in New Computing Developments," in C. Dunlop, and R. Kling (eds.), *Computerization and Controversy: Value Conflicts and Social Choices* (Boston: Academic Press, 1991).

[52]John Markoff, "American Express to buy 2 top supercomputers: massively parallel supercomputers from Thinking Machines Corp." *New York Times* (141) (Wed, Oct. 30, 1991):C7(N), D9(L).

[53]See, for example, M. Culnan, "How Did They Get My Name? An Exploratory Investigation of Consumer Attitudes Toward Secondary Information Use." Unpublished ms. (School of Business Administration, Georgetown University, Washington, DC, 1992).

[54]Steven Levy, "How the Good Guys Finally Won: Keeping Lotus MarketPlace Off the Market," *Macworld* 8(b) (June, 1991): 69–74.

[55]Rory J. O'Connor, "Our Privacy Threatened: US Bureau of the Census Proposes Creation of National Data Base." *San Jose Mercury News* (April 14, 1991):1F.

[56]James Krier, and Edmund Ursin. *Pollution & Policy: A Case Essay on California and Federal Experience with Motor Vehicle Air Pollution, 1940–1975* (Berkeley: University of California Press, 1977).

[57]James Krier, and Edmund Ursin. *Pollution & Policy: A Case Essay on California and Federal Experience with Motor Vehicle Air Pollution, 1940–1975* (Berkeley: University of California Press, 1977).

[58]See Part V of C. Dunlop, and R. Kling (eds.), *Computerization and Controversy: Value Conflicts and Social Choices* (Boston: Academic Press, 1991).

[59]See R. Kling, and S. Iacono, "The Mobilization of Support for Computerization: The Role of Computerization Movements," *Social Problems,* 35(3)(June 1988): 226–243.

[60]For the methods used in constructing these tables, see R. Kling, "More Information, Better Jobs?: Occupational Stratification and Labor Market Segmentation in the United States' Information Labor Force," *The Information Society* 7(2) (1990): 77–107.

BCA. A.C